# A HISTORY OF ECUMENISM IN WALES

1956–1990

# A HISTORY OF ECUMENISM IN WALES

## 1956–1990

Noel A. Davies

UNIVERSITY OF WALES PRESS
CARDIFF
2008

© Noel A. Davies, 2008

All rights reserved. No part of this book may be reproduced, stored in a retrieval system, or transmitted, in any form or by any means, electronic, mechanical, photocopying, recording or otherwise, without clearance from the University of Wales Press, 10 Columbus Walk, Brigantine Place, Cardiff, CF10 4UP.
*www.uwp.co.uk*

**British Library Cataloguing-in-Publication Data**

A catalogue record for this book is available from the British Library.

ISBN 978-0-7083-2150-8

The right of Noel A. Davies to be identified as author of this work has been asserted by him in accordance with sections 77 and 78 of the Copyright, Designs and Patents Act 1988.

Printed in Great Britain by CPI Antony Rowe, Chippenham, Wiltshire

Dedicated with deep thankfulness to the memory of
Philip Morgan (1930–2005),
a good friend,
a minister in the Disciples and Reformed traditions,
whose roots were in Wales and whose ecumenical
commitment never wavered.

# Contents

| | |
|---|---|
| General Editor's Foreword | ix |
| Foreword | xi |
| Preface | xv |
| Introduction | 1 |
| 1 The search for Christian unity in Wales: the beginnings | 9 |
| 2 The beginnings of the Covenant in Wales | 21 |
| 3 Fostering local ecumenism in Wales | 31 |
| 4 Relationships with the Roman Catholic Church | 47 |
| 5 The churches and society: beginnings and foundations | 67 |
| 6 The churches and self-government in Wales | 83 |
| 7 The Christian witness in industrial society | 101 |
| 8 The churches and the dispute in the coal-mining industry | 121 |
| 9 Wales and racism in southern Africa | 137 |
| 10 War and peace: nuclear disarmament | 159 |
| 11 War and peace: the Malvinas war | 177 |
| Concluding reflections | 194 |

## CONTENTS

| | | |
|---|---|---|
| Appendix I | Officers of the Council of Churches for Wales, 1956–90 | 210 |
| Appendix II | Summary of the work of the Liturgical Study Group | 214 |

Notes 216

Selected bibliography 232

Index 239

# General Editor's Foreword

Since its inception in January 1998, the Centre for the Advanced Study of Religion in Wales, located within the School of Theology and Religious Studies, Bangor University, has encouraged scholarly research on Welsh religious history and ensured its publication. The Bangor History of Religion series has already contributed towards a stronger and wider understanding of religious expression among the Welsh people.

Much of Christian history is plagued by schism and division, the identification of those who belong to the elect community of the faithful and those who, through deviant doctrine or questionable practice, can be identified as heretics and consequently excommunicated from that community. Yet, building on the missionary movement of the previous hundred years or so, the twentieth century became the ecumenical century with different ecclesiastical communions entering into unprecedented cooperation aimed at mutual edification and more effective mission. This occurred on both a local and global scale, primarily through formal commitment to live and work alongside each other through ecumenical councils but occasionally also through formal ecclesiastical union.

In this book, the ecumenical adventure is analysed as it pertained to Wales. The story is told of the development of ecumenical bodies, the move towards the signing of a Covenant for Union, and the fostering and coordinating of social action through the Council of Churches for Wales which impacted upon local issues such as industrial relations and the debate about self-government as well as matters of international significance such as the Anti-Apartheid Movement, the Campaign for Nuclear Disarmament and the war in the Malvinas. The result is a fascinating account of inter-Church activity whose focus is Wales, but whose relevance is international. It will prove to be of interest to historians of Welsh society and religion as well as ecumenists.

# Foreword
by the late R. Tudur Jones

One of the most interesting topics in the history of Christianity is the relationship between the various churches, denominations and sects. It is also one of the saddest. In different periods they would revile each other, persecute each other and go to war against each other. One could understand someone who reached the conclusion that quarrelling was part of the essence of Christianity. However eloquently and poetically religious leaders talked about love and mercy, they had little trouble convincing themselves that persecuting other Christians was a loving means of saving their souls. Of course, those who suffered this treatment saw the value of forbearance but very often as the sufferers became more numerous and more powerful than their tormentors, they were soon tempted to become persecutors also.

As we look back over the history of Wales we find very little evidence of murder and killing in the name of Christianity. But in the modern period there is evidence of considerable less effective persecution and oppression of people on religious grounds. It was not without reason that Jeremi Owen wrote in his *Y Ddyletswydd Fawr Efengylaidd* (The Great Evangelical Duty) (1733), referring to the period after the Restoration in 1660, that:

> Our fathers have drunk deeply from the cup of suffering, that has been placed in their hands. They had to gather by night to worship God, and their enemies transformed this into their shame, as the persecutors did with the Chief Christians: Many were cast into prison; many were robbed of their possessions; which they suffered joyfully; yes, many suffered death.

Even after legislation brought an end to such oppression, disagreement often poisoned the relationships between the factions within Christianity, one faction rejoicing in the difficulties the other suffered. From time to time leaders would deplore this, calling for a more gentle spirit. For example, John Roberts, Llanbrynmair (1767–1834), the most gentle of men, pleaded for reconciliation between Congregationalists and Calvinistic Methodists and rejoiced when the Catholic Emancipation Act was passed in 1829, saying, 'I look upon this as one of the most glorious Victories that freedom has won for more than one hundred years'. Step by step during the nineteenth century, civic conditions were achieved by legislation which placed the members of different churches on a par with each other. But achieving legal equality is one thing, fostering a conciliatory spirit is another. Denominational loyalty could still create some quite ugly feelings.

It is against this historical background that the development of the Ecumenical Movement in the twentieth century is significant. It is true that its roots go far back into the past. We find Walter Cradoc (who died in 1659) condemning those Independents and Presbyterians 'who were bitter against others if they crossed them or disagreed with them over the slightest matters.' Stephen Hughes (who died in 1688), who was invited during the age of persecution to preach in the parish church, condemned the works of the Anglican Rhys Pritchard and cooperated with Bishop William Thomas in publishing Welsh books, with the sponsorship of Archbishop John Tillotson among others. And the truth is that this golden thread was not broken throughout the generations.

The formation of the Evangelical Congress (for England and Wales) in 1846 was an important step in the history of the development of interdenominational organizations. There were enthusiastic meetings here and there throughout Wales to mark its formation and its suggestion that the first week of the year should be set aside to pray for unity among Christians was adopted. The bond of unity within the Congress was agreement over doctrine. But it was not within the intention of the Congress to aim at the unity of the denominations with one another. Indeed, the prospects of broadening the range of interrelationships were poor. For one thing, the struggle to disestablish the Church of England from the state led to a souring of the relationship between Nonconformists and

Anglicans. Furthermore, the setting up of international denominational bodies led to a deepening of denominational pride. While it is true that the Lambeth Conference of 1888 had encouraged ecumenical dialogue, the other similar organizations did not. In 1875 the first conference of the World Congress of Reformed and Presbyterian Churches was held and in 1881 the Methodist Ecumenical Conference was held. The International Congregational Council was held in 1891 and the Baptist World Congress in 1905. The keen interest of the Welsh denominations in these developments did lead to a widening of horizons but it did not engender a closer relationship between them.

And yet, in all the denominations there were people who felt the need for greater mutual understanding and collaboration. Welsh representatives such as Principal Thomas Charles Edwards and T. Edwin Jones, the Vicar of St Mary's, Bangor, were present at conferences in Grindelwald, Switzerland, between 1892 and 1895. No one was more committed to fostering cooperation between the denominations than Owen Owen (1850–1920). He succeeded in gathering representatives of all the denominations to Shrewsbury, on 22 and 23 April 1890, and consequently the Welsh Nonconformists Council was founded. It survived for a short period only, because it was deployed almost immediately in support of the Disestablishment of the Church of England. It was replaced by the National Council of the Free Churches set up in Manchester in 1892 (and covering England and Wales). Its membership consisted of individuals rather than denominational representatives and in March 1896 another body was formed, namely the National Council of Evangelical Free Churches which consisted of representatives appointed by the denominations (in England and Wales). In 1907 a National Council of Wales was formed under its wing. By 1908 it had 167 local branches in Wales. These various movements were able to create considerable local interdenominational activity but there was a strong conviction at the beginning of the twentieth century that it could do no more than foster cooperation within a federal framework and that there was little point in raising the issue of seeking union between the denominations.

## FOREWORD

The beginning of the twentieth century brought rapid developments within the Ecumenical Movement. In 1910 the large missionary conference was held in Edinburgh and in its wake structures were set in place for discussing the faith and order of the churches, on the one hand, and Christian life and work, on the other. This is where Dr Noel Davies begins.

The focus of his study is the history and contribution of the Council of Churches for Wales, which was established in May 1956. This topic is important for a number of reasons. It will be seen that a large number of church leaders in Wales contributed to the Council's activity. The breadth of its interests will also become clear. Naturally, it was very enthusiastic in its support for anything that could unite the churches. The Council did not have the authority, of course, to unite churches, because that is a task for the churches themselves. But it would be a mistake to think that church unity was the Council's only interest. It becomes clear in reading this work that the Council had been very involved in seeking to offer leadership in those matters that appertained to the future of Wales, economically, socially and culturally. It also gave considerable attention to youth work and did its best to face the crises that arose in relation to war and peace. The Council had considerable influence on the Christian and secular life of Wales in the second half of the twentieth century. It had its critics, of course, and Dr Davies does not seek to silence them. But whether people commended the Council or were critical of it, they were forced to reconsider carefully their assumptions and principles.

This is a pioneering work. This is the first academic review of the place of the ecumenical movement in the life of Wales. Readers will discover much that will be new to them or will be reminded of people and events that they had forgotten. Since he has spent many years in the service of the Council, Dr Noel Davies is in a particularly advantageous position to undertake this task. His detailed scholarship is clear on every page and he analyses the evidence fairly and objectively. In a word, we are given a scholarly treatment of a particularly important aspect of our contemporary history.

Bangor
Easter 1998

# Preface

The basis for this book is a doctoral thesis submitted at the University of Wales, Bangor, in 1997 on the history of the Council of Churches for Wales, 1956–90 (the period of its life-span). It is the product of more than thirty years' close involvement with the ecumenical movement, in Wales and worldwide, as well as academic research. A number of significant aspects of the ecumenical story have had to be omitted, as those who are familiar with that story will recognize, in order to keep this volume within reasonable limits. Two aspects, namely, the churches' responses to the WCC report, *Baptism, Eucharist and Ministry*[1] and an account of the Council's engagement with youth work, may be found in the doctoral thesis upon which this book is based. A shorter Welsh version of this work was published by Cytûn: Churches Together in Wales in 1998, under the title *Un er mwyn y byd* ('One for the world's sake'). In presenting this present volume, I recognize my debt to many people.

First, I am indebted to early ecumenical and worldwide influences through the United Missionary Council for Wales and the Student Christian Movement, which opened up windows on the ecumenical vision that those bodies had such a key role in forming and fostering. I am indebted to the late Principal John Marsh, the late Dr George Caird and Dr Donald Sykes at Mansfield College, Oxford, who were committed and active ecumenists. I am indebted to those in Wales who gave me, very early on in my ministry, the opportunity to become involved in the Council through the Liturgical Study Group and the Department for Ecumenical Action. The turning point for me, of course, was my appointment in 1977 as the first full-time General Secretary of the Council of Churches for Wales and the Commission of the Covenant Churches. I deeply appreciate the confidence they had in me and the support I received throughout the years. During subsequent years doors

## PREFACE

have been opened to me in very unexpected ways and to very unexpected places. I have been granted the enormous privilege of sharing in the fervour, challenge and frustration of the ecumenical movement in Wales and worldwide. To all those colleagues who became friends, in Wales and in countries around the world, in the British Council of Churches, and its successor body, Churches Together in Britain and Ireland, and in the World Council of Churches, I extend my warmest thanks.

Secondly, I cannot measure my debt to, sadly, the late Dr R. Tudur Jones.[2] He supervised my research work and was keen from the beginning to see the publication of its results. Even though he had thought that he had supervised his last research student, he willingly and enthusiastically agreed to supervise my work. His enthusiasm throughout the period was a great encouragement. His comprehensive knowledge of Christian history throughout the centuries in Wales and worldwide, enlightened me on many matters raised by my work. And the fact that he was not always an ecumenical enthusiast gave added objectivity to the work of someone who had been so intimately involved in so much of the activities being studied! I express my deep gratitude to him. He willingly agreed to write a Foreword to the shorter Welsh version of this work, which most helpfully sets my contemporary account in its historical context. I am most grateful to Dr Jones's family for their permission to include a translation of the original Foreword, written very shortly before his very sudden and sad death in 1998, as a foreword to the present volume.

Thirdly, I wish to record my thanks for those that have made the publication of this work possible: to the Centre for the Advanced Study of Religion in Wales, at Bangor University, and its first Director, Dr Geraint Tudur and the Secretary, Dr Robert Pope, later its Director; to Cytûn: Churches Together in Wales, for their encouragement in undertaking the original research for this work, when I was serving as General Secretary of Cytûn between 1990 and 1998, and most especially for the support and encouragement (and the long-suffering 'waiting with patience' – of Pauline dimensions!) of my successor as General Secretary, Gethin Abraham-Williams; I am grateful to Cytûn also for a very generous grant of £2,000 towards the translation of Chapters 6 to 13 and to Mr Marcus Wells, of Ystalyfera, for

## PREFACE

undertaking the translation with meticulous care; and to my recent employers, the Welsh National Centre for Ecumenical Studies, Trinity College, Carmarthen, the College of the Welsh Independents and the Union of Welsh Independents, for giving me space to finalize the detailed preparation of this text for publication.

Finally, I wish to express my thanks to my family: to my father, the late Revd Ronald Anthony Davies, a Welsh Congregational minister in Dowlais (in Glamorgan), Cellan and Llanfair (in Cardiganshire) and Pontycymer (also in Glamorgan) for an ecumenical upbringing, directing me without any pressure of any kind, towards the Christian ministry; to my mother, Anne Davies, who remains one of the most enthusiastic supporters of the ecumenical movement and is healthily impatient (at 95 years of age) with the churches' slowness in their search for unity; and to both of them for sacrificing everything to ensure that I had the best that was available, even though they lived throughout my father's ministry on a pitifully small salary; and to my wife, Pat – it was the Student Christian Movement that brought us together, we have shared the ecumenical vision ever since and she has been constant in her love, encouragement and support.

At a time when many are talking about 'an ecumenical winter' and when the nature of the ecumenical commitment in Wales and worldwide is being reviewed and challenged, my hope is that this book will assist individuals and churches to understand and learn from the history of creativity, faithfulness and commitment (as well as failure and disobedience) represented by the story that is told here and that through such learning we can discover fresh ways of being faithful, at the beginning of the twenty first century, to the New Testament calling to 'spare no effort to make fast with bonds of peace the unity which the Spirit gives' (Ephesians 4:3, REV).

Noel A. Davies

# Introduction

The Council of Churches for Wales was inaugurated in Swansea on 24 May 1956, following detailed discussions by the churches and denominations in Wales over a period of two years or so. The Council was brought to an end on the last day of August 1990 when its successor, Cytûn: Churches Together in Wales, was established in a special service in Aberystwyth on 1 September 1990. This volume explores some of the most central aspects of the history of the Council, and as such it records the history of a movement – the ecumenical movement – which was at the heart of the life and relationships of churches and denominations in Wales and worldwide during the twentieth century. It could be argued that it is impossible to understand the history of the churches during the century without a consideration of the fundamental influence of this movement on the life and witness of the churches.

It was the influence of the ecumenical movement that led William Temple, the Archbishop of Canterbury and the first President of the British Council of Churches, to declare in his sermon at Canterbury when he was enthroned as Archbishop in 1942: 'The great new fact of our era (is that there is now) a Christian fellowship which extends into almost every nation.'

The origins of the Council of Churches for Wales – and the contemporary ecumenical movement as a whole – may be traced back to the world conference on mission and evangelism in Edinburgh in 1910.[1] According to Adrian Hastings,[2] 'Edinburgh 1910 marks with confident optimism the first great step forward in what was to be in truth an ecumenical century.' The Faith and Order and the Life and Work movements which came together to form the World Council of Churches in 1948, were the direct result of this conference, as was the International Missionary Council which became part of the World Council of Churches in 1961.

## INTRODUCTION

Within Wales, a number of organizations contributed to the commitment among the churches and denominations that enabled the Council to be formed. Chief among these was the Joint Committee for the Promotion of Mutual Understanding and Co-operation between the Christian Communions in Wales, which was established in Shrewsbury in February 1929 and ceased to exist when the Council of Churches for Wales was formed in Wales in 1956. The disestablishment of the Church of England in Wales to form the Church in Wales in 1920 and the restated call of the Lambeth Conference of Anglican Bishops, also in 1920, for Christian union, were very influential factors in the formation of the Joint Committee. During the years of its existence, the response to the committee was mixed, with many being critical of it and labelling it no more than a talking shop for denominational leaders. Nevertheless, there is no doubt that the Council of Churches for Wales was one of the fruits of these discussions and friendships.

Similarly, the Welsh Ecumenical Society, which was formed in 1954 as a successor to *Urdd y Deyrnas* (The League of the Kingdom, established in the early years of the contemporary ecumenical movement), had significant influence, especially locally. The aim of the society was 'to promote an understanding of the Ecumenical Movement . . . to offer fellowship to those who saw in this Movement the work of the Holy Spirit . . . and fostering ecumenical contacts with other groups within and outside Wales'.

All these organizations were deeply indebted to the Student Christian Movement in Wales (which was affiliated to the World Student Christian Federation, established in 1895), which had been the means of nurturing generations of young people to be leaders of the ecumenical movement.

As will become clear, the inauguration of the British Council of Churches (in 1942) and the World Council of Churches (in 1948) were central not only to the beginnings of the Council of Churches for Wales but also to its activities throughout the years.

In tracing aspects of the history of the Council of Churches for Wales in the chapters which follow, it has been necessary to omit detailed consideration of some developments which have considerable ecumenical significance and which demand

## INTRODUCTION

further study. Amongst these are the Inter-church Aid and Refugee Service (established in 1945 and later renamed Christian Aid) and Wales for Christ, (established in 1971 with the assistance of the Council and which developed into the evangelism movement of the churches in Wales, more or less independent of the Council). Nor will the story of the New Welsh Bible be told. This project was initiated by the Council, which invited the churches and denominations to form a Joint Committee in 1961, which in its turn translated the Bible, publishing the New Testament in 1975, the Psalms in 1979, the whole Bible in 1988 and a revised edition in 2004. Nor is there space to tell the story of Christians against Torture, the human rights campaign of the Council of Churches for Wales, established in 1981, largely at the initiative of Roy Jenkins, minister of Ararat Baptist Church, Whitchurch, Cardiff and later Senior Producer at BBC Wales. This campaign has been extremely successful in enabling individual Christians, as well as local groups, to focus on people around the world who are being tortured, and to campaign on their behalf through prayer, letter-writing and education. The Council also had a number of other committees, the history of which it has not been possible to record here, such as the Liturgical Study Group,[3] the Communications Committee, the World Development Committee, the Theological Education Forum and the Community of Women and Men Working Group.

The main sources for this study have been the archives of the Council of Churches for Wales, which are now lodged in the National Library of Wales in Aberystwyth. This is the first time that they have been researched in such a detailed way. Space and time did not permit a similar study of denominational minutes, reports and periodicals. There is material for a further extensive study in these sources. The main purpose of this study has been the research of the Council's own archive. This is an attempt to trace the main developments of the modern ecumenical movement in Wales and its contribution to the life, partnership and witness of the churches and denominations during the period under consideration. An attempt has also been made to trace Welsh and worldwide influences on the priorities and activities of the Council.

## INTRODUCTION

In one sense, the period of the Council's existence has been a time of disillusionment in the experience of the majority in Wales, with the losses and horrors of the Second World War resulting in the destruction of communities and families, and of faith and hope for many. According to R. Tudur Jones, 'realizing the incredible barbarism of the holocaust' had led many to feel 'that the sun had gone down on Western civilization'.[4]

This period also saw the end of the British Empire, and the self-confidence that accompanied it, when more and more nations gained their independence. The Welsh sense of nationhood also gained strength and became a cause for considerable political and social campaigning. Indeed, Kenneth O. Morgan claims that this may be the main characteristic of Welsh history during this period, although national self-confidence was not always a mark of this sense of nationhood.[5]

Campaigning for the rights and future of the Welsh language also happened during this period, with Saunders Lewis's radio lecture in 1962 becoming the inspiration for forming the Welsh Language Society and the campaigning for the language that followed.

The coal and steel industries were nationalized during these years, and they were transformed as a result. In many ways these industries flourished and there was a marked increase in wages. In the early 1950s – the formative years of the Council – steel plants were opened in Margam (Port Talbot), Trostre (Llanelli) and Felindre (outside Swansea). By the end of the period, the situation had been changed dramatically. The large majority of the coal mines were closed following the 1984–5 strike. There have been dramatic reductions in the steel industry in south Wales (with the Felindre plant having been closed) and in Shotton in Clwyd. The agricultural industry saw a similar development, with farmers depending increasingly on government subsidies and, by the end of the period, becoming increasingly dependent on payments from and the regulations of the European Union. The Welsh economy had been completely transformed. Although the depression of the 1920s and 1930s did not return, many communities had to face deep crises, while other areas showed signs of economic and social recovery.

INTRODUCTION

According to Kenneth Morgan, the century to 1980 (with the latter half of that century being a formative period in the history of the ecumenical movement in Wales) had been characterized by confusing changes:

> The land underwent successively an upsurge of political and economic advance, and of patriotic consciousness; a shattering collapse in its economic fabric with social despair and new cultural tension; and finally, a period of economic rehabilitation and renewal in which the awareness of nationhood flourished anew . . . The characteristic features of Welsh society . . . were surviving with difficulty in a world which was rapidly leaving old landmarks behind.[6]

Morgan believes that the growing awareness of nationhood amongst the Welsh people during this period has been a means of renewal and of liberation from old captivities, which were 'more relevant to the dissolving certainties of later twentieth century Britain':

> . . . the attachment to local communities, to local or native traditions; the revolt against centralization and bureaucracy; the emergence of modes of social organisation other than those prescribed by distant, once unchallengable, now increasingly vulnerable authority in London.[7]

These social developments had enormous influence on the life and work of the churches and the Council of Churches for Wales. During the period which is surveyed in this volume, there has been a diminution in church membership, a reduction in the churches' influence (typical of the secularized societies of Western Europe during this period) and an increasing difficulty with maintaining a church machinery inherited from the nineteenth and the beginning of the twentieth century. But the ecumenical movement and the struggle to root the ecumenical vision in the soil of Wales has been an attempt to renew the churches by ensuring that Wales has its own self-supporting and independent inter-church structure, which would enable the churches to face the challenge of the times.

The inaugural meeting of the Council of Churches for Wales was held in St James's Church, Swansea on 24 May 1956. The founding members of the Council were the Church in Wales, the Presbyterian Church of Wales, the Union of Welsh

## INTRODUCTION

Independents, the Methodist Church, the Baptist Union of Wales, the Congregational Union of England and Wales, (the United Reformed Church from 1972 onwards, following the Congregational Union's union with the Presbyterian Church of England, and subsequently with the Churches of Christ in 1982), the Baptist Union of Great Britain and Ireland and the Salvation Army. The Religious Society of Friends was an observer from the beginning and the Roman Catholic Church became a consultant observer in 1968. In addition, many inter-church organizations in Wales were bodies in association with the Council. The Council was formed as a fellowship of churches and denominations that acknowledged the Lord Jesus Christ as 'God and Saviour' but in 1969 a fuller basis was approved which was based on that of the World Council of Churches agreed a few years earlier in the New Delhi Assembly:

> The Council of Churches for Wales is a fellowship of churches which confess the Lord Jesus Christ as God and Saviour according to the Scriptures and which seek to fulfil together their common calling to the glory of the one God, Father, Son and Holy Spirit.

Throughout the Council's existence there were discussions about reviewing and restructuring, discussions which would include almost without exception a consideration of the need for a full-time General Secretary to foster the Council's growing workload. There were reviews in 1960, 1963, 1969 and 1974. On each occasion there was a recommendation that a full-time General Secretary should be appointed. On each occasion it was resolved that financial resources did not permit such an appointment. But throughout the years, incredible work was undertaken by general secretaries who had other very demanding ministries and who had to accomplish their work for the Council in their 'spare' time. They all made an enormous contribution to the effectiveness of the Council and the success of the ecumenical movement in Wales.

Then in 1976, following the decision by five of the Council's member churches to enter into a Covenant towards Union, it was agreed to appoint a full-time General Secretary, jointly between the Council and the Commission of the Covenanted Churches formed in 1976 to foster the Covenant. The Covenanted Churches agreed to contribute *pro rata* twice as much as the other denominations and it was this that made the appointment possible. This arrangement continued until 1990, when the Council gave way to Cytûn.

The present author held this post from July 1977. He was appointed initially for a seven-year period at a salary of £2,700, but continued in the post until August 1990. At first he worked from home, in Glanaman, where he was a Union of Welsh Independents minister, and then from offices in Swansea. From the beginning, Mrs Wendy Richards worked as his assistant, in due course becoming the full-time Administrative Officer of the Council and subsequently of Cytûn.

The appointment of a full-time General Secretary was a turning point in the ecumenical movement in Wales. For the first time, the denominations had a salaried ecumenical officer and appropriate priority could be given to the ecumenical enterprise. Many of the leaders of the ecumenical movement believed that the joint appointment between the Council and the Commission was significant in itself as a contribution to fostering the denominations' united witness. The willingness of the covenanted churches to contribute twice as much as the other denominations was an indication that the covenant commitment to union among these churches was more than mere words; they were willing to share resources also!

There was further restructuring in 1981 following a review initiated by the General Secretary, which was intended to ensure better relationships and cooperation between different aspects of the Council's work. But in 1984 there began a far-reaching process that would lead in 1990 to the establishment of Cytûn: Churches Together in Wales as a successor to the Council of Churches for Wales. The Roman Catholic Church would be a full member of Cytûn in Wales, as it would also be of the other new bodies, ACTS in Scotland, Churches Together in England and the Council of Churches for Britain and Ireland. These bodies would denote a new ecumenical commitment and were intended to express a fundamental change in the nature of the ecumenical commitment from being an addition to the churches' normal programme locally and nationally to being a central element of all that they would do.

The regular reviews and the constant search for effective patterns showed that the Council was not a static, unchanging

## INTRODUCTION

structure but a dynamic instrument which sought to adapt its patterns and priorities in order to respond more effectively to the demands of God's call to the churches it sought to serve. There was continual growth in its work and it had growing resources at its disposal.

The chapters that follow tell the story of this instrument – and the pioneers and officers who were so crucial to its work and effectiveness – as it fostered the ecumenical movement amongst its member churches in Wales.

## ~ 1 ~
# The search for Christian unity in Wales: the beginnings[1]

The search for Christian union and unity was a central aspect of the work and contribution of the First Assembly of the World Council of Churches in Amsterdam in 1948:

> The World Council of Churches came into existence because we acknowledged a responsibility towards each others' churches in our Lord Jesus Christ. There is only one Lord and one Body. Therefore, we cannot be at peace with our present divisions. Before God we are responsible for one another.[2]

Since the Amsterdam Assembly was one of the main impulses for the formation of the Council of Churches for Wales, it was natural that the search for Christian unity was a central element in the influences that shaped the Council. For example, Huw Wynne Griffith,[3] editor of *Yr Efrydydd* (the periodical of the Student Christian Movement in Wales), believed that the formation of the Council could 'begin a new chapter in the religious history of our country, when the churches cease from looking suspiciously at each other but rather look together to their one Lord and, with their Lord, towards the world'.[4] In the same way, Alun W. Francis,[5] believed that the conviction had grown over the years 'that there was a real need in contemporary Wales for religious reunion'.[6] J. Alwyn Charles[7] argued that the search for Christian unity in Wales should give priority to 'wrestling with the different views among us on (the responsibility of the church for the pagan society)' and suggested that the nationalist awakening in Wales 'could be a starting point for ensuring a measure of church unity . . . [since] ecumenism means far more that an attempt to bring institutions as such together'.[8]

In the February 1954 issue of *Y Dysgedydd*, there is a debate between Erastus Jones[9] and Leornard Hugh[10] on the ecumenical movement. Both were very supportive of its aims, welcome enthusiastically the formation of the World Council of Churches and saw in it an important contribution to the churches' witness in 'the world of the H-Bomb'. But there was a difference of opinion between them on the future of denominations as such and on the nature of Christian unity. Erastus Jones urged that every denomination should face its own demise so that it can become 'an organic part of a new and broader ecclesial unit'. On the other hand, Leornard Hugh did not support the eradication of denominations as such because 'as channels of the truth, they are of priceless worth and eternal significance'.[11]

At its first meeting in May 1956, the Council of Churches for Wales issued to the churches of Wales a message which emphasized this aspect of the ecumenical commitment:

> We confirm our belief that the Christian unity upon which we have set our faith and hope is rooted in the unity of God and his unique redemptive act in Jesus Christ . . . We are convinced that the Council of Churches for Wales will be an effective means of enabling the churches in Wales to witness together to their shared commitment to Jesus Christ and to co-operation in matters which call for joint action.[12]

During the years that followed, much energy was devoted to the search for Christian unity among the churches and denominations of Wales. The conversations between the Church in Wales and the Methodist Church, the four denominations scheme, *Tuag at Uno* (Towards Unity), and following the Faith and Order conferences in Carmarthen (1963) and Nottingham (1964), the process towards covenanting for union, took up a great deal of time in denominational committees and assemblies. During the 1950s and 1960s it is difficult to think of any subject that received more attention in denominational periodicals. For example, in *Y Dysgedydd*, the periodical of the Union of Welsh Independents, there were articles on issues relating to Christian unity and union in successive issues from 1954 until 1968 when it joined forces with *Y Drysorfa*, the Presbyterian periodical, to form *Porfeydd*, which continued the practice throughout the 1970s.

An outline version of the Scheme to unite the four Welsh-language denominations, *Tuag at Uno* (Towards Unity), was published in 1963 and the full Scheme in 1965, with a request that the denominations should respond by December 1967. Sales were high and discussion extensive, with many articles analysing the Scheme appearing in denominational periodicals. Meirion Lloyd Davies[13] concludes that 'all enthusiasm had disappeared (by 1967) and there was a general belief that there was no future for the Scheme'.[14] Although three denominations had responded positively, it was clear by the end of 1968 that there was no future in pursuing the Scheme. Working groups were set up to give urgent consideration to some controversial issues, and a report of their conclusions was published but there seems to be no account of the denominations' responses, nor a minute of a decision to terminate the Four Denominations Committee, but that is what happened. Meirion Lloyd Davies concludes that 'lack of enthusiasm for the Scheme and the fact that so many other discussions were going on at the same time led the committee to conclude that no purpose was served in continuing to meet'.[15]

In the meantime, other worldwide and British factors were at work. In 1961, the Third Assembly of the World Council of Churches in New Delhi agreed a statement that has had a formative influence on the understanding of the nature of 'the unity we seek':

> We believe that the unity which is God's will and gift to his Church becomes visible when all in each place, who are baptized into Jesus Christ, confessing him as Lord and Saviour, are brought by the Holy Spirit into one fully committed fellowship, holding the one apostolic faith, preaching the one gospel, breaking the one bread, joining in common prayer, and having a corporate life reaching out in witness and service to all and who at the same time are united with the whole Christian fellowship in all places and all ages, so that ministry and members are acceptable to all, and that all may act and speak together as necessary to undertake the work God calls his people to fulfil.[16]

When the significance of this statement for the churches in Britain began to be considered there was a feeling of new confidence, based partly at least on the united churches that had been formed in India and elsewhere. 'There is a real possibility of an "ecumenical breakthrough" in Britain in our time', wrote John Weller, Faith and Order Secretary of the British Council of Churches. Consequently, when the Faith and Order Conference of the World Conference of Churches, in Montreal in 1963, called on the churches 'to unite with us in our effort to subject all that our churches mean to us and all that we understand about other, to the judgement of Christ, who is Lord of us all', the British Council of Churches set about planning a preparatory process for a British Faith and Order Conference in 1964. The Council of Churches for Wales agreed to share in this process by convening a conference in Wales on the same theme, 'The Unity we Seek'. The purpose of this conference would be to consider the relevance of New Delhi and Montreal to the situation in Wales and formulate recommendations that would challenge Wales and contribute towards the search for Christian unity. This Welsh conference was also a preparation for the British conference to be held in Nottingham in September 1964. Huw Wynne Griffith agreed to act as secretary of the planning group and £400 was set aside to finance the event ('which is considerably more than the annual budget of the Council').

During the preparations, considerable emphasis was placed on local activities and centres were established in Bangor, Aberystwyth, Cardiff, Swansea and Wrexham. It appears that the response was most encouraging. For example, there were forty-five at the Bangor meeting, fifty-five in Llandudno, and the phenomenal number, according to the report, of 300 in Llangefni. In Swansea, the Blaendulais Ecumenical Centre was responsible for the arrangements. In January 1963 the annual conference of the Welsh Ecumenical Society was devoted to the theme, 'The Unity we Seek'.

The Welsh conference was held at Trinity College, Carmarthen on 9–13 September 1963, with the Bishop of Bangor, Gwilym O. Williams (later to be Archbishop of Wales), in the chair. Each tradition within the Council had been invited to appoint twenty-five delegates. As a result, this was one of the most representative events held in Wales. Its recommendations were therefore of considerable significance.

At the end of the conference delegates agreed a 'Message to the Churches of Wales', which expressed the heart of the search for unity: 'it is as we look to Jesus, the Head of the Church and its centre, and as the Holy Spirit takes from his own and communicates it to us, that we can grow into unity.'[17]

The message celebrated the unity which was already the experience of the churches – and of which the Council of Churches for Wales was a sign – and called for growth into fuller unity. It examined the challenge of bilingualism in Wales and believed that a bilingual approach could foster relationships among Christians in Wales and promote the growth of unity in all kinds of ecumenical work. It was particularly characteristic of this period that the message emphasized Christian unity not only as the goal of the Church but also as a sign of God's purpose for the whole world.

The recommendations to the churches included in the final report (presented to the Council in October 1963 by Huw Wynne Griffith) were practical on the whole, and included a further call for adequate funds to be made available for the Council's work and for greater efforts to establish local ecumenical groups throughout Wales. The conference and the Council also agreed on a principle that would play an increasingly important part in the Council's life, namely, that Welsh and English should be given equal status in ecumenical work in Wales in the future.

The message commended the New Delhi statement on 'The Unity we Seek' as an articulation of the fullness of unity because it expresses well 'the necessary conditions for portraying in the world the fullness of truth which was revealed in our Lord'. Consequently, the Council agreed to produce a study booklet on church unity to be entitled 'The Unity we Seek', so that those who were not at the Carmarthen conference could 'play their part in the (Faith and Order) campaign and in the search for true unity'. The booklet, which was edited by Huw Wynne Griffith, was based on the New Delhi statement. Its main contribution, typical of the early pioneers who were key figures in the faith and order process in Wales, was to adapt the vision and emphasis of the worldwide ecumenical movement to the Welsh situation. This had a notable effect some years later, in formulating proposals for the Covenant for Unity in Wales, which was, of course, one of the direct outcomes of this process.

A year later, in September 1964, the British Council of Churches convened the British Faith and Order Conference that was held in Nottingham, following the same theme, 'The Unity we Seek'. According to Adrian Hastings,[18] this was the most important ecumenical conference ever held in Britain. There were around 500 delegates, including thirty-two from Wales. It became clear on the first evening that a number of controversial issues were to influence the thinking of this conference. One key issue was the need to take specific steps towards inter-communion between the Anglican churches and the Nonconformist Churches. The opening communion service followed the order in *The Book of Common Prayer* (1662). According to the official report, neither the Salvation Army nor the Quakers were invited to the service, apparently because they do not practise sacraments. If this report is correct, this appears incredible over forty years later! Some Nonconformists were unhappy that the Bishop of Southwell had presided at the service in his episcopal robes ('it seemed to bring back a whiff of the medieval church which they found distasteful').[19] And some Anglicans felt uneasy that some representatives were present from churches that did not have a priesthood within the apostolic succession.

It is not surprising, therefore, that a discussion of intercommunion during the first evening session had revealed deep divisions. Professor A. H. Hodges (a Church of England layman) believed that the Church of England was right to refuse to be in communion with those churches 'which [we] believe to have departed from the given pattern of ministry and the sound practice of the sacraments'.[20] On the other hand, Professor Geoffrey Lampe from Cambridge called for intercommunion now amongst all churches that confess the apostolic faith on condition that they seek to be built by the Spirit into organic union. This debate led to a call to the member churches of the British Council of Churches (and therefore not including the Roman Catholic Church) to reconsider their practice and theology in relation to intercommunion.

One of the most important addresses was given by W. A. Visser 't Hooft, first General Secretary of the World Council of Churches. In a review of the worldwide ecumenical movement he had seen a deepening of churches' relationships with each other during previous years, a true solidarity and an increasing number of union negotiations. At the same time, he feared that union generally occurred between churches that shared the same ethos, and that few steps had been taken towards intercommunion or joint planning for mission and evangelism. He was particularly concerned that it had proved impossible to show within the local situation that the time for disunity was over and that the time for unity had come. For Visser 't Hooft, who had been one of the chief architects of the contemporary ecumenical movement, the greatest need was for repentance: 'We cannot expect real progress on the road to unity unless our churches go through a process of radical purification, a repentance in the biblical sense . . . a basic reorientation.'[21]

One interesting and significant aspect of the conference was the presence of a number of 'evangelicals'. They were given an opportunity to express their objections to the official ecumenical movement. In particular, they affirmed their belief that the priority was mission, that discussing unity was a waste of time and that faith in Christ already united Christians. They were also afraid that there was a danger of compromise on the authority of the Bible and that union ultimately led to Rome. Some, such as John Huxtable,[22] were very critical of the negative attitudes of the evangelicals, but their presence was an important contribution to the life of the conference, and it was noted by one commentator that the evangelicals among the Church of England delegates had voted almost unanimously in favour of the conference reports and recommendations.

Another important factor in the conference was the presence of six observers from the Roman Catholic Church. The third session of the Second Vatican Council was convened while the conference was in session and it was agreed that the following message be sent to the Council: 'Fellow-Christians gathered at the British Faith and Order Conference . . . send greetings and assurances of prayer for the new session of the Council; may the Holy Spirit grant you renewal in truth and holiness, in which we may all share.'[23]

One Catholic observer was invited to give a brief address and he received the enthusiastic response of the conference. One paragraph of his greeting was particularly significant, given that the Second Council had not finished its work nor published the reports that would transform the attitudes of the Roman Catholic Church in such dramatic ways:

> The differences that stand between us may be solved if we work at them together ... Human formulation of God's truth cannot be exhaustive, and no one would claim that a complete description of the nature of God's church had been achieved so far ... Let us work together in searching the Scriptures, pondering the meaning of Christian history and trying to appreciate different traditions.[24]

Most of the conference's work was done in sections on Faith (chaired by G. O. Williams), Worship, Membership, Ministry, and All in Each Place. Each section produced substantial and significant reports but this conference was mainly remembered for its call to the churches to seek union by Easter 1980. Some, including Edwin Morris, the Archbishop of the Church in Wales, believed that it was inappropriate to set a timetable for the work of the Holy Spirit, since the churches had not yet agreed on a pattern for reunion, and, therefore, that it was dangerous and impractical to make a commitment to a specific date. This was an unpopular view but the Archbishop received applause for expressing his views! Fundamentally, however, this was not a debate about the appropriateness of union, as such, but rather a debate about the 'spirituality of haste'. Norman Goodall[25] saw the setting of a date as a way of being obedient to the Word:

> ... it becomes symbolic ... a proclamation, splendidly irrational but authentic ... The issue before us is not whether the Holy Spirit may be offended by our daring hope and dated determination. It is whether the Holy Spirit shall continue to be grieved by our tardiness in giving expression to a unity which we all affirm to have been given us already in Christ.[26]

At the end of the debate the following statement was agreed:

> United in our urgent desire for One Church Renewed for Mission this conference invites member churches of the British Council of Churches, in appropriate groupings such as nations, to covenant together to work and pray for the inauguration of union by a date agreed among them.

We dare to hope that this date should not be later than Easter Day 1980. We believe that we should offer obedience to God in a commitment as decisive as this.[27]

As we shall see, it was this statement that led to the development of the Covenant towards Union in Wales.

One of the most influential recommendations called for the implementation of the Lund Dictum. This principle was formulated in the Faith and Order Conference in Lund, Sweden, in 1952, when the churches were challenged to consider 'whether they should not act together in all matters except those in which deep differences of conviction compel them to act separately'.[28] The Nottingham recommendations invited the British Churches to consider implementing this principle locally.

One example of this would be to set up areas of ecumenical experiment:

> [The conference requests member churches of the British Council of Churches] to designate areas of ecumenical experiment, at the request of local congregations, or in new towns and housing areas. In such areas there should be experiments in ecumenical group ministries, in the sharing of buildings and equipment, and in the development of mission.[29]

This recommendation was as influential as the Easter 1980 call, if not more so. It led to the formation of over 1,500 local ecumenical projects in the nations of Britain during subsequent years. And when the attempt at covenanting in England failed in 1982, it was the vision of this recommendation that ensured that ecumenical energy was directed into the local situation, where these projects and partnerships continue to be among the most creative aspects of the churches' life and mission.

The response to the conference amongst the Welsh delegates was very mixed. The first impression gained by M. Islwyn Lake[30] was that Wales: 'fell far behind in comparison to (England). Where we are conservative and static they are becoming more flexible in worship and are very familiar with experiments such as joint ministry.'[31] He welcomed the resolution about Easter 1980 as a goal, since the churches had 'talked so much about unity as the will of God and the pain of divisions. Sooner or later we have to ask, 'Are they serious? Are they ready to proceed immediately to take steps towards the goal? This is what 1980 achieves.' On the other hand, Trefor Parry (of the Methodist Church) was quite critical of the conference. He felt that 'the delegates had been drowned by the cold hailstones of the ecumenical saxophone and drum, and the leaders blew the same clichéd, pedestrian theme through their polished instruments'.[32] He feared that it was too great a feat for the Church in Wales, one of the children of a church 'which was married to the State, to shake herself loose from the unequal bond and develop into a powerful and revolutionary power in the land' Rather he commends a radical Non-conformity, since 'there is a new call and task facing the Church if she succeeds in freeing herself from the oppressive chains of the Establishment'. And, while he was prepared to accept Easter 1980 as a goal, he believed that there was a more important challenge facing the people of Wales than 'fiddling about again with our nice little theories about apostolic succession, free-communion, closed-communion, denominationalism ... In the meantime, Wales rushes towards moral and spiritual darkness'. E. Curig Davies[33] also felt that the churches were wasting their time on matters that were not relevant to the crisis facing the world. He was also concerned that there would be very little left to unite by 1980 'with the drift of things today'.[34] While he appreciated the contribution of the ecumenical movement to the task of presenting Christianity effectively in the modern situation, Iorwerth Jones[35] came away from Nottingham afraid that unity with the catholic tradition would mean accepting the traditional creeds as factual and sufficient statements of faith, accepting a hierarchical succession 'as the *sine qua non* of a united church' and accepting sacraments whose mediation of grace *ex opere operato* 'savoured of magic ... Few of us can accept all this.'[36]

When the Bench of Bishops of the Church in Wales discussed the Nottingham report they noted particularly the section on Worship: 'In view of the unanimity ... on the fundamental principles of Christian worship, we recommend that in the future liturgical revision be undertaken jointly or in close consultation with each other by the member churches of the British Council of Churches.'[37]

## THE SEARCH FOR CHRISTIAN UNITY IN WALES

The Bench requested that the Council of Churches for Wales should invite the Welsh denominations to form a Liturgical Study Group, which should include observers from the Roman Catholic Church.

When the Welsh delegates came together during the Nottingham Conference, the following statement was agreed: 'Meeting as delegates from Wales we believe that the resolutions of the Nottingham Conference challenge all the churches of Wales, and we call on the Council of Churches for Wales to develop its work in the light of the agreements and resolutions recorded at Nottingham.'[38]

The Nottingham resolutions were seen as a challenge to the Welsh churches 'to covenant together and to seek an united church for Wales' and the Council of Churches for Wales was invited to consider whether it should convene a consultation for the churches on the form of a covenant. In his report to the Council in Llwyngwril on 29 and 30 October 1964, Huw Wynne Griffith said:

> The date 1980 means that the matter of unity has become urgent, since any inappropriate delay or postponement would mean that the conviction which is expressed in the recommendation would be rejected. The Council of Churches for Wales should give serious consideration to the resolutions that are directed to the Council and should also study the implications of the '1980 resolution' for Wales and offer its services to the denominations and churches in preparing a covenant.[39]

This was the beginning of the Covenant towards Union in Wales. The first step was the setting up of a Faith and Order Committee for Wales as a standing committee of the Council. Its members would be the Executive Committee together with the Bishop of Swansea and Brecon (John A. Thomas), the Dean of Brecon (W. Ungoed Jacob – who was the general secretary of the Council at the time) and the Revds J. S. Williams (a Baptist minister in Swansea), Trebor Lloyd Evans (General Secretary of the Union of Welsh Independents), Erastus Jones and Huw Wynne Griffith, who would be Secretary.

So the period following the Carmarthen and Nottingham conferences was challenging and creative as far as the search for union in Wales was concerned (as in the other nations of

Britain and Ireland). The Faith and Order Committee was formed, and a group was convened to consider the invitation to produce a Covenant towards Union. A Department of Ecumenical Action was set up jointly between the Council and the Welsh Ecumenical Society, with specific responsibility for fostering local ecumenism. At the initiative of the Bench of Bishops of the Church in Wales, the Joint Group on the Forms and Principles of Christian Worship was established (later renamed the Liturgical Study Group, see Appendix II on p. 214). All of this sprang from Carmarthen and Nottingham and it would have an enormous influence on the ecumenical programme during the next period.

## ~ 2 ~
# The beginnings of the Covenant in Wales

In 1965 the Council agreed to form a Joint Covenanting Committee, to which every member denomination of the Council was invited to appoint four representatives. The invitation was accepted by the Presbyterian Church of Wales, the Church in Wales, the Methodist Church and the Union of Welsh Independents, and a little later, the Congregational Union of England and Wales. The Joint Committee would consider (in relation to Wales) the meaning and implications of the invitation which was given to the churches to work and pray to establish union by a date set by them through agreement.[1]

Three two-day meetings of the Joint Committee were held (chaired by the Bishop of Bangor, G. O. Williams) in the early months of 1966, and in April of that year it presented an unanimous report and recommendations to the churches and denominations which had appointed it under the title, *The Call to Covenant*. The report summarized the recommendations of the Nottingham Conference, outlined the discussion of faith and order issues that were initiated by the conference, and dealt directly with covenanting in Wales.

The question to be faced at the beginning was: 'Do our Churches in Wales share the same conviction as was felt in Nottingham, namely, that there is already sufficient agreement to justify taking the decisive step of making a commitment to each other in a Covenant which aims at union?'[2] The remainder of *The Call to Covenant* was devoted to a consideration of the implications of this question. It defined 'Covenant' in this context as: 'a solemn act by the churches to promise before God and one another to give such priority to working and praying for union so that it can be achieved . . . by a date which will be sufficiently near to have a firm effect on their life and work today.'[3]

It was the firm judgement of the Joint Committee that the agreement that already existed between the denominations, especially their membership of the Council of Churches for Wales, was such as to justify further searching. So it was recommended that the churches and denominations appoint a new Joint Committee to consider the terms of a Covenant, suggest practical arrangements to ensure that the Covenant would include all the members and ministers of the churches, and produce a statement on the effect of the Covenant on their churches' relationship with each other. It was suggested that the new committee should bring a report and recommendations to the churches by the spring of 1968.

The Church in Wales, the Methodist Church, the Union of Welsh Independents, the Congregational Church in England and Wales (Province of Wales and Monmouthshire) and the Baptist Union of Great Britain and Ireland (South Wales Area) appointed representatives to the joint committee. It had thirty-one members, and from 1967 there were two observers from the Roman Catholic Church. G. O. Williams remained as Chairman and Huw Wynne Griffith as Secretary. It published its first report, *Covenanting in Wales*, in March 1968.

The two parts of the final report on covenanting towards union in Wales that were published in February and October 1971 built on the previous reports and sought to respond to comments made by the churches. It included the terms of the Covenant and a commentary (as well as some papers on issues such as ordination, priesthood and sacraments). The churches and denominations were invited to decide whether these terms were acceptable to them as the basis for an agreement, and to adopt an explication and study programme to ensure that informed decisions were made. It was the Joint Committee's hope that the churches and denominations would reach agreement during 1974.

There were seven articles to the Covenant itself, each divided into two parts, the first acknowledging what the churches had in common and the second expressing a commitment for the future. There were articles on faith, mission, the church, membership, ministry, worship and sacraments, and church government. In each case, the text was based on what had been said in previous reports, in particular *Covenanting in Wales (1968)*. The most controversial article was the fifth on ministry:

(a) We recognise the ordained ministries of all our churches as true ministries of the word and sacrament, through which the love of God is proclaimed, his grace mediated and his Fatherly grace administered.

(b) We intend to seek an agreed pattern of ordained ministry which will serve the gospel in unity, which will exhibit its continuity throughout the ages and which will be accepted as far as may be by the Church throughout the whole world.[4]

The commentary on this article acknowledged that the ministry was 'a complex problem'[5] and that the wording did not go as far as some would have wished towards full recognition of each others' ministry. To a great extent, the arguments presented in the previous report are repeated and the principle which was fundamental for the Joint Committee set out, namely, that 'an *ad hoc* compromise should not be sought, but rather true continuity with the Church of the apostles throughout the ages'.[6] In this task the three basic principles of article (5) would be central: the ministry which was to be mutually recognized would have to serve the gospel in unity, display the continuity of the church throughout the ages and should be accepted by the church throughout the world. These principles continued to be fundamental in all subsequent work undertaken by the covenanted churches in Wales in relation to ministry. At the end of *Part II*, the question was asked: Can the various patterns of ministry which exist among the churches be brought together within the United Church? The answer given in the essay (which was not, necessarily, the official view of the Joint Committee) was that this could be done, by adopting a threefold pattern of the early centuries and adapting it for the purposes of mission and ministry in Wales in the twentieth century. This principle became fundamental in all the decisions taken by the covenanted churches in relation to ministry. It was this principle also (among others) that led to some churches rejecting the Covenant in 1974. Hitherto, however, while agreeing on the theological principles of the threefold ministry which includes the ministries of oversight, of the word and sacraments and of service, the churches have not succeeded in offering either a scheme of ordination or a pattern of ministry which proved to be acceptable to all the covenanted churches and met the requirements of this article.

The implications of covenanting received considerable attention in *Part II* of the final report.[7] In particular, it was claimed that the Covenant should not be a marginal matter but a commitment which is central to the whole life and work of the churches nationally and locally, and which touches every member and not only the leadership of the churches denominationally and locally. After all the explication and discussion, the challenge of the covenant was clear. Although the churches and denominations 'did not yet know what form unity would take',[8] and although they realized that they had to be 'open to the Spirit', the Covenant was nevertheless a call to 'a solemn commitment before God': 'Therefore, we make this solemn Covenant now before God and one another, to work and pray in common obedience to our Lord Jesus Christ, so that we may be brought through the Holy Spirit into one visible Church to serve together in mission to the glory of God the Father.'[9]

In 1972 *Why Covenant?* was published as a popular guide to the call to covenant. It included a brief outline of the background of the Covenant, a short commentary on the articles of the Covenant and suggestions about the practical consequences of such a Covenant. It summarized the issue before the churches in these words:

> In essence, covenanting means a new relationship between the churches. Each church would have to change to some degree. As the relationship developed, the consequences would become gradually more clear. And in the end, under the leadership of the Holy Spirit, the form of the united church would appear.[10]

All these reports published between 1966 and 1972 represented enormous work by the Joint Committee and the Council of Churches for Wales. 2,670 copies of *Covenanting in Wales (1968)* were sold, 5,500 of *Part I* and 2,765 of *Part II* of *Covenanting towards Union in Wales (1971)*, 15,000 of *Why Covenanting? (1972)* and 48,000 copies of the text of the

Covenant. All this represented an enormous effort to foster careful and wide-ranging consideration of the Covenant.

By 1974 four denominations had agreed to enter into Covenant, namely, the Church in Wales, the Methodist Church in Great Britain (the whole denomination and not only the Welsh Districts), the Presbyterian Church of Wales and the United Reformed Church in England and Wales (again the whole church and not only the Welsh Province). Twelve congregations of the South Wales Area of the Baptist Union of Great Britain and Ireland also agreed to enter the Covenant. Only 169 from a total of 750 congregations of the Union of Welsh Independents voted on the proposals. Of these, sixty-seven voted in favour, ninety against and twelve were divided. Since such a large majority of churches expressed no view it was judged, probably rightly, that they were either indifferent or against the proposals, and that consequently there was insufficient support for the Union to enter the Covenant. The Governing Body of the Church in Wales agreed the Covenant on condition that it would not take any decisions as a result of this covenanting commitment that would in any way change the fundamental principles of the Church in Wales. Naturally, there were those who were suspicious of this condition from the beginning, and who doubted that it would be possible to move into Christian union within the Covenant without some changes to denominational principles. But this was accepted at the time as a valid positive response.

On 18 January 1975 (at the beginning of the Week of Prayer for Christian Unity), 'a Service of Thanksgiving for the Covenant' was held at Seilo, Presbyterian Church of Wales, Aberystwyth, where Huw Wynne Griffith, who had been such a key influence in the process of the Covenant, was minister. As a sign of the commitment of the churches and denominations to the Covenant a signed authorized copy of the official resolution of the church was placed on the communion table during the service.

G. O. Williams, the Bishop of Bangor and chairman of the Joint Committee from the beginning, was the preacher. His text was Romans, chapter 15, verse 7: 'Accept one another, as Christ accepted you, to the glory of god.' He emphasized that Christian union meant: 'obedience to the Gospel . . . being one in worship, ... a ministry that is fully recognised by all, ... shared responsibility for mission, ... full communion with fellow-Christians in other places, ... practising responsible stewardship.'[11]

He emphasized also that church unity did not mean:

> inhibiting diversity ... taking responsibility away from congregations and members ... removing all authority to the centre ... uniformity in worship and church life ... The purpose of our unity will be to embody the vision [of one, holy, catholic and apostolic Church] to the utmost of our ability ... and that in turn will be a step, taken in faith, towards the highest goal of the glory of God who reconciles all his people into one whole fellowship.

The Joint Covenanting Committee's work came to an end with this momentous step and in 1976 the Commission of the Covenanted Churches was formed, with representatives from each Covenant Church and observers from the Union of Welsh Independents, the Salvation Army, the Roman Catholic Church and the Baptist Union of Great Britain and Ireland (representing the interests of those churches which were not among the covenanted Baptist churches). D. Huw Jones[12] was the first Secretary of the Commission, and within a year it was agreed to appoint, jointly with the Council of Churches for Wales, a full-time General Secretary.

From this point on, the Council of Churches for Wales, as such, would have no responsibility for promoting the Covenant. However, the joint appointment and the general interconnections between two bodies that existed to foster Christian union and unity in Wales, meant inevitably that the interrelationship between the Covenant and the wider search for Christian unity in Wales was always under consideration.

During the ensuing years after its inauguration the Commission, which was renamed Enfys (Welsh for rainbow) in 1990, developed considerably. In 1990, Gethin Abraham-Williams[13] was appointed General Secretary, a half-time post which was combined with the half-time post of Ecumenical Officer within the Church in Wales (although he was and is a minister of the Baptist Union of Great Britain). In 1998, Gethin was appointed the General Secretary of Cytûn in succession to the present author and in 1999 the Revd Dr Sion Aled Owen

## THE BEGINNINGS OF THE COVENANT IN WALES

was appointed to the joint post of General Secretary of Enfys and Local Ecumenism development Officer of Cytun. On his resignation in 2003, the Revd Gethin Rhys[14] was appointed to the post. In 2005, following a careful review of the Covenant commitment by the covenanted churches, Enfys was brought to an end and the work of coordinating the Covenant, to which the churches had reaffirmed their commitment, was incorporated into Cytûn. In July 2005, Siôn Rhys Evans became Associate Secretary of Cytûn, with particular responsibility for the Covenanted Churches within Cytûn.

The Commission made considerable efforts to promote the Covenant locally and nationally. In 1979, *The Principles of Visible Unity in Wales* was published, which sets out to paint a fuller picture of the implications of the seven articles of the Covenant (as another step towards the production of a comprehensive unity scheme for the covenanting churches). In 1981, *The Holy Communion* was published. This is an order for Holy Communion that is approved by all the covenanted churches for use in uniting services (and which is used by many ministers for 'denominational' services also). In 1986, *Ministry in an Uniting Church* was published, which was an attempt to present an understanding and pattern of ordained ministry which would reconcile the ministries of the covenanted churches in a Uniting Church. In 1990, an order for *Baptism* was published, to be used experimentally at appropriate occasions, together with a collection of essays on the meaning of baptism and membership. In 1995 services were published for affirmation and reaffirmation of faith (an attempt was made to avoid the terms 'receiving into full membership' and 'confirmation'). The churches were asked to examine these reports and services and to comment on them. They were all substantial contributions to a fuller understanding of the faith and order of the Uniting Church which was the goal of the Covenant but so far it has not been possible to ensure adequate agreement on these matters to enable the denominations to move forward together towards an union scheme on the basis of the 1975 Covenant. Indeed, Meirion Lloyd Davies judges that such a scheme is unlikely to appear for at least a generation. [15]

During this same period, as we shall see, attempts were made to foster local cooperation among the covenanted churches, and many believed that the Covenant would not succeed until there was much deeper commitment to local collaboration between covenanted churches.

To sum up, then, we can note a number of key reasons for the significance of the Covenant towards Union within the search for visible union in Wales. First, according to Paul Crow,[16] the Covenant in Wales was the first attempt to use the Covenant framework as a means of reconciling divided churches.[17] The Covenant was part of a worldwide search for union and it reflected some of the inherent priorities of that search.

Secondly, the covenanting discussions made a substantial contribution to theology in Wales. During the period under consideration, very little work was done in inter-church theology in fields such as faith, the nature of the church, the ministry and the sacraments, except for the theological work which emerged from the Joint Covenanting Committee. Its reports were a notable contribution to mutual theological understanding. However, there is cause to wonder whether the mutual understanding that became clear within the documents themselves had a substantial influence on the theological positions of the denominations as such. When the churches rejected some of the recommendations within these reports, they tended to do so because they were not consistent with the traditional position of the denomination. It would have been far more creative if the churches had asked themselves how the ecumenical recommendations challenged the traditional position of the church and how it could be changed so that it could be enriched through other traditions. This, of course, is the complex problem of reception, of integrating into the understanding and life of the churches insights and agreements that emerge from the ecumenical dialogue.

Thirdly, the Covenant was seen, from time to time, as a commitment that was the cause of local division as well as a means of enabling fuller unity. One of the reasons for this accusation was that some had assumed that the Covenant enabled cooperation and shared worship and prayer between covenanted churches which was not possible between some of these churches (primarily, the Church in Wales) and churches which were not within the Covenant. Often the greatest unease was felt in relation to the use of *The Holy Communion* (1981). To some extent, this fear continues today and there is therefore a continuing need to develop patterns of belonging which enable the covenanting churches to share fully and regularly with other churches in joint worship, prayer and action.

Fourthly, the commitment of the Joint Committee to bilingualism has been important, despite the fear of some that bilingualism threatened identity. From the beginning, Welsh-medium, English-medium and bilingual denominations shared in the discussions about covenanting. All the documents were published bilingually. The Joint Committee (and the Commission in the years after 1976) believed that bilingualism was one of the essential marks of the uniting church that was sought and, with this in mind, bilingual worship material was prepared for use locally. This was seen not just as fulfilling a practical need but also as a witness to the reconciliation between languages and cultures which is one of the gifts of the Gospel.

Fifthly, it may be that the chief contribution of the Covenant was to hold the goal of union before the churches and denominations. It has been Gethin Abraham-Williams's view that the heart of the Covenant is to be a bridge between 'chapel' and 'church'. In view of past divisions in Wales, the relationships which exist at the present time – however inadequate they may appear – are an important contribution to drawing into a greater integrity and wholeness our ecclesial, theological, historical and cultural diversities. The debates about the disestablishment of the Church of England in Wales were difficult and painful, and their effects remain today. The Covenant makes a notable contribution to overcoming these continuing effects by nurturing friendship, confidence and mutual understanding.

Over and over again in this story of the beginnings, we have seen that the greatest barrier to the Covenant has been the understanding of ministry in the different traditions. It could be argued, however, that ministry is not the key issue but rather the understanding of the nature of the church. Some have claimed that it is impossible to reconcile the three traditions within the Covenant, namely, Episcopal, Presbyterian and Congregational. They are, it is said, completely incompatible with each other and it is impossible to imagine a pattern of church life that can do justice to the three traditions. This incompatibility, they claim, is the cause of the failure so far to present a single pattern of united ministry which is rooted in the three traditions and which does not appear to deny some of the essential tenets of one or more of the traditions. It is doubtful, however, whether this is the sole, or even the main, reason for this failure. May it be not so much a matter of fundamental theological incompatibility as a failure to separate out what is of the essence of the church and what can be set aside in order to enable the church to respond more fully and obediently to the call of God to mission and ministry in unity in a particular period of history and within a particular social context? Is it not a failure of obedience to what is already possible rather than a theological failure to imagine a new pattern of church life and ministry?

For the truth is that the Covenant has offered to the churches creative possibilities for Christian union and unity locally and nationally. But they have not been grasped. When Martin Conway[18] was asked to evaluate the effectiveness of the steps towards unity taken by the churches by 1980 (the target date for union set by the Nottingham Conference), he wrote as follows about the Covenant in Wales:

> The opportunity for experiment and advance has been provided, but it has been all too seldom seized. At the local level, the inflexibility of inherited outlooks, and at the wider levels, an indifference and unreadiness to explore actual partnership, have been seriously crippling. A Covenant that is formally accepted but not put to use soon becomes an added cause of hesitation and mistrust between the churches.[19]

Many within the covenanted churches – and outside – would echo that judgement. These churches continue to express their commitment to the Covenant, at least in their public statements, and remain committed to taking steps locally and nationally to moving forward together towards the one visible church which remains the goal of the Covenant in Wales – a commitment recently reaffirmed by all these churches. This will demand the overcoming of cultural and historical obstacles as well as theological and ecclesiological differences. This will not be possible without the will to seek union that inspired the early pioneers in Wales.

## ~ 3 ~
## Fostering local ecumenism in Wales

Local cooperation predated the Council of Churches for Wales. The Second Assembly of the World Council of Churches (Evanston, 1954) called on the churches to move forward to deepen their unity 'by doing everything . . . to ensure that [their] neighbours hear the voice of the one shepherd calling every (person) to the same sheepfold'.[1] In an editorial in *Yr Efrydydd*, a periodical of the Student Christian Movement in Wales, Huw Wynne Griffith called on the churches of Wales 'to provide an opportunity for the congregations to consider this message'. A special conference was held on 28–31 December 1954 to enable 'the friends of the ecumenical movement' to consider the message of Evanston for Wales.

As a result of this conference, *Urdd y Deyrnas*, which had been fostering the ecumenical debate in Wales from the early days of the modern movement at the beginning of the century, was brought to an end and a new organization, the Welsh Ecumenical Society, was formed 'to promote an understanding of the ecumenical movement to provide an opportunity for fellowship to supporters of the ecumenical movement and to foster ecumenical links with other groups within and outside Wales'.[2] The founders of the new Society believed that 'God [was] working through the Ecumenical Movement in our day to guide and renew his Church'.[3]

The Society was based on an individual membership list, although some local churches were also in membership. By 1965 there were 218 members. They were energetic in their efforts to foster local cooperation during this period. Enthusiasts such as Abel Ffowc Williams[4] made an enormous contribution by travelling tirelessly to encourage local support for the work of Inter-Church Aid (the predecessor of Christian Aid) and to promote joint action and prayer through local councils of churches. As a result, a number of local Inter-Church Aid committees (which were often the nucleus for cooperation in other fields) were formed as well as some local councils of churches. The Society cooperated with the Joint Committee for the Promotion of Mutual Understanding and Co-operation between the Christian Communions in Wales, which concentrated on relations between denominations, until the Joint Committee was disbanded with the formation of the Council of Churches for Wales in 1956.

In the early 1960s, a Faith and Order Working Group was established by the Council to encourage discussions on the statement by the Third Assembly of the World Council of Churches (New Delhi, 1961) on 'The Unity we Seek', chiefly through the faith and order conferences in Carmarthen and Nottingham. A number of local groups and a few local councils of churches were formed as a result of this activity also.

The Welsh Ecumenical Society cooperated closely with the Council of Churches for Wales for nearly ten years, until the setting up of the Department of Ecumenical Action in 1965 brought the work of the Society to an end 'as the Council of Churches for Wales is seen to be growing and taking its responsibility seriously'.[5] The Department's aim would be:

> ... to promote knowledge and understanding of the Ecumenical Movement and most particularly of the work of the Council of Churches for Wales ... initiating local ecumenical action ... offering an opportunity for individuals and groups to support and share in the Council's work ... and initiating and promoting opportunities for research and experiment in church renewal.[6]

One of the consequences of disbanding the society was the formation of the Friends of the Council of Churches for Wales as a means of continuing the personal support that had been possible through the Society. Growth in membership was very slow initially, but by 1967 there were around 200 Friends of the Council. For a time this network proved to be very effective but in the course of time membership decreased and its work became less effective. There was some renewal towards the end of the 1970s and the beginning of the 1980s under the inspiration of Mrs J. T. Morgan, one of the generous and dedicated Christians of Swansea and later the Hon. Antony Lewis.[7]

Around £4,000 was raised towards the Council's work during that period and a small group of enthusiastic supporters was developed. But the Friends were disbanded also when the Council came to an end in 1990 and the funds transferred to Cytûn through the Council.

The Department undertook its work with enthusiasm, producing publicity leaflets, fostering relationships with the British Council of Churches (BCC) and the World Council of Churches (WCC), inaugurating and developing the activity of the Friends and 'presenting the Council to Wales'. But from the beginning it believed that its chief task was 'to foster every ecumenical development, whether it was a group or a council'.[8]

At this time, the Department worked mainly through a combination of regional groups and ecumenical centres. Within a year of its formation, the Department had sixteen regions, each with an organizer. The Blaendulais Ecumenical Centre was already in existence (as a result of the vision and energy of Erastus Jones, who was a Congregational minister there at the time) and an ecumenical centre was established in Bangor (under the title of the Gwynedd Forum) in 1967, on the same basis as the Blaendulais centre. In 1969 Tŷ Toronto was set up in Aberfan (with a substantial gift from Toronto) to be a centre for reconstructing and renewing the community following the terrible tragedy of 1966. Erastus and Lun Jones went there in 1968 and it became a centre that fostered local cooperation not only in Aberfan and Merthyr Vale but also throughout the Glamorgan and Monmouthshire valleys. During this same period, Trefeca College was opened as a lay training centre for the Presbyterian Church of Wales, and it served from the beginning as an ecumenical centre which was open to all denominations. The Department used this network of centres, together with the Collegiate Centre for Theology at University College, Cardiff, as an ecumenical network to promote and support local ecumenism, through study and action.

One of the most forward-looking and exciting programmes during this period was 'People Next Door'. This was a study programme developed jointly by the Conference of British Missionary Societies (CBMS) and the Education Department of the BCC in response to recommendations from the WCC Commission on Mission and Evangelism Conference in

Mexico in 1966 on the theme, 'The Missionary Structure of the Congregation'. The Department for Ecumenical Action agreed to promote this programme in Wales jointly with the United Missionary Council for Wales, with the support of *Wythnos y Gair* (an annual conference sponsored by the Bible Society and held on 22–9 July 1967) adapting the British materials for use in Wales.

In a letter to the *Western Mail*, the Council's officers explained the nature of this programme:

> It will not be an attempt to bring outsiders into the church but rather a sincere attempt by the church herself to understand the world and God's work within it . . . In *People Next Door* our primary concern will be the conversion of the church so that she may become a more effective part of God's answer to the needs of men. Consequently we are led to ask what new structures will the church need to adopt in order to participate faithfully in God's mission to his world.[9]

Naturally, therefore, establishing 'a dialogue between the church and the world' was a key aspect of the programme. As the introduction to the Welsh booklet stated: 'We have been invited to place "the People Next Door" at the centre and to keep them there.'[10] It was agreed that the programme would be followed for a period of six weeks during January to May 1967. It was supported by all the member churches and denominations of the Council, and an information leaflet was circulated to every priest and minister in Wales with a request that they initiate steps to follow the programme either by using a local council of churches which already existed or by setting up a planning committee. Special resources had been produced, including a Welsh-language booklet. *Church for All Men,* by Robert Latham, was available (extracts from which appeared in the Welsh-language weeklies), together with the Welsh-language daily Bible readings (*O Ddydd i Ddydd*) for spring 1967.

The introduction to the Welsh booklet acknowledges that it was a discouraging period for many within the churches of Wales, but:

> . . . there is an intellectual revolution on a par with the Protestant Reformation at work throughout the Church at the present time, bringing hope and renewal in its wake . . . the ecumenical revolution

> ... (The People Next Door Campaign) could be an instrument in God's hand to shape a new church for the end of the twentieth century.[11]

Although this appears to be, with hindsight, a rather exaggerated evaluation of the actual effects of the ecumenical movement at the time, there is no doubting the commitment of those in leadership within ecumenism in Wales in the 1960s or their confidence that through it the Spirit of God would transform and renew the church.

Groups in many areas followed the programme, although there is no detailed account of their number, and all groups were invited to send representatives to a conference either in Glynllifon or Rhoose, during the summer of 1967, to evaluate the activities. Thirty-three attended the former and thirty-nine the latter. Some of the insights gained through the programme became the basis for the booklet, *Uppsala and Wales*, which was intended to help Christians in Wales to prepare for the Fourth Assembly of the World Council of Churches in Uppsala in 1968, on the theme 'Behold, I am making all things new'. Two thousand copies of this booklet were published and six regional study conferences were set up by the ecumenical centres. Two conferences were held, again at Glynllifon and Rhoose, following the Assembly, and a leaflet was produced which gathered together the implications of Uppsala for Wales.

'Areas of Ecumenical Experiment' (more recently described as Local Ecumenical Projects or Partnerships) also received considerable attention during this period. As has already been noted, the Nottingham Faith and Order conference in 1964 approved a motion that encouraged the formation of such projects.[12]

This resolution was just as influential as the more famous Easter 1980 motion. It stimulated churches in many localities in England to consider establishing such experiments and they have been an important aspect of Christian mission, especially in new housing estates (where local authorities frequently allocated only one site for a church building).

Another development which had considerable local influence was the Sharing of Church Buildings Act 1969, which permitted denominations in membership of the British Council of Churches, and others, such as the Roman Catholic Church, to make legal agreements to share church buildings. For the first time, this law gave congregations and denominations freedom to agree to make effective inter-church use of local church buildings for mission, witness and worship.

Such was the growth of local ecumenism in England that it led to the publication by the British Council of Churches of *Areas of Ecumenical Experiment* (by R. M. C. Jeffrey) in 1968. This reviewed developments in response to the Nottingham resolution and offered guidelines to localities and denominations that were considering setting up such experiments.

These possibilities received very little attention by the Department of Ecumenical Action of the Council until September 1969 when the effect of the Covenant towards Union on local ecumenism was considered. The minute of the meeting refers to three areas only where such experiments were either established or being considered. These were at Penrhys (Rhondda), the Glenboy Estate in Mountain Ash and the united church in Baglan Moors, Port Talbot being planned by Wern Congregational Church, Aberafan. Four key issues were emphasized as churches moved towards ecumenical experiments, namely, ensuring that denominations authorized the continuity of the experiments, securing advance information about new housing estates and recognizing these from the beginning as areas of ecumenical experiment, convening a consultation on buildings which would be appropriate for contemporary mission, and encouraging theological colleges to explore these possibilities and include ecumenism in ministerial training courses.

Following this initial discussion, the Department set about, in 1970, to evaluate the Welsh experiments. A questionnaire was produced and sent to twelve areas, Newtown, Penrhys, Mountain Ash, Pwllheli, Llanedeyrn (Cardiff), Aberfan, Cowbridge, Croeserw (Cymer), Cwmbran, Baglan (Port Talbot), Llansannan and Llangollen. When the responses were analysed in a consultation in 1970, it became clear that there was considerable unease in some of these areas: 'church leaders who have long insisted that ecumenism should happen locally, are horrified when it does, in fact, happen. Their objection, in the form of hindering progress, usually has the effect of keeping rebellious churches safely within the institution.'

It is difficult to determine whether or not this was a fair conclusion but, as a result, it was resolved that ecumenical growth was unlikely until denominations acknowledged the validity of an experiment, fostered and supported it, and did so without waiting for the denominations to covenant together for union. The continuity of the experiment was also a matter of considerable concern in these areas. Often, the successors of supportive and enthusiastic ministers or priests did not show the same support as their predecessors. There were examples of this failure leading to the failure of the experiment. The Department believed that there was a need to develop a pattern of external, local supervision that could bring pressure to bear on denominational leaders either not to move a minister or to ensure a suitable successor. Finally, it was felt that the denominations needed to develop a way of recognizing and designating such experiments, since many of these experiments were very fragile and likely to fail without denominational support. It was agreed that this report should be the basis of a memorandum to be presented to the Council meeting in Merthyr in October 1971.

When this was considered by the Council alongside a report from the Theological Advisory Group, on the theology of experiment, the discussion focused on the tension between the radical and local thrust of the former and the conservative and centralist emphasis of the latter. The end result of these discussions was an agreement that any experiment had to go beyond regular cooperation within a local council of churches, that there should be full consultation between the local and the national, that the denominations should seek to ensure continuity of local leadership in these localities and that there was a need to define 'the limits of experiment'. It was further agreed that an ad hoc group should meet to consider these matters and to convene a meeting of the denominations to discuss areas of ecumenical experiment 'and to suggest principles and methodologies for experiment and cooperation in the future'.[13]

This meeting was held in Aberystwyth on 24 July 1973, with the chief officers of most of the denominations present. The memorandum which was to be the basis for the discussions noted a number of issues to be considered, including the continuity of ministry, team ministry, questions relating to membership, problems raised by discrepancies in denominational boundaries, issues of order and freedom in patterns of worship, the use of buildings (in the light of the Sharing of Church Buildings Act 1969) and the relationship of interdenominational congregations with the denominations. The initiatives taken by the Department were welcomed and it was asked to be responsible for advising local churches wishing to cooperate more fully. So for the first time in Wales, areas of ecumenical experiment were set on an official basis amongst the Welsh denominations and the Council was authorized to promote and advise them. Within two years, following the agreement by five denominations to covenant together, the Commission of the Covenanted Churches would also promote and advise such local experiments among the covenanted churches and mutual understanding between the Council and the Commission would become a natural feature of fostering local ecumenism in Wales.

However, the growth in the number of such experiments in Wales during this early period was slow. Some denominations complained about this and there was much discussion about where authority and responsibility for initiating experiments was located. For example, the Chairman of the Cardiff and Swansea District of the Methodist Church was worried that 'as yet no areas of ecumenical experiment have been *proclaimed* in Wales' (emphasis added) and he believed that there was a need to define areas of ecumenical experiment 'with all speed' so that the denominations could proclaim experiments in those areas where there was such need for them. In his response, the General Secretary of the Council, Meirion Lloyd Davies, emphasized that definition was not the issue but rather the need to ensure that local churches should be encouraged to apply for designation as areas of ecumenical experiment. Local ecumenism was not a matter of denominational proclamations but rather of fostering and developing the cooperation that was already happening, bearing in mind that the authority to initiate and designate ecumenical experiment lay with the denominations themselves, in consultation with each other, and not with any inter-church body.

By 1974, the description Local Ecumenical Project (LEP) had been adopted. They were defined as follows:

An LEP may be said to exist where there is at the level of the local church a formal, written agreement affecting the ministry, congregational life and/or buildings of more than one denomination, and a recognition of that agreement by the appropriate denominational authorities.[14]

*Adventures in Unity* reports that Wales did not have any LEPs, as such, in 1974, but Penrhys, Llanedeyrn, Baglan and Cowbridge are listed as ecumenical projects, and it is noted that there was sharing of buildings under the 1969 Act in Fairwater (Cardiff), Fairwater (Cwmbran) Risca, Barry Island and Penlan (Swansea), and joint ministry in Carmel, Caernarfonshire between the Presbyterian Church of Wales and the Welsh congregational church.

In 1978 the Department made a further effort to encourage the formation of ecumenical projects by convening a special conference for local councils of churches and local congregations which were interested in establishing projects in their area. Representatives from an LEP in Redditch in Worcestershire, together with John Nicholson, the ecumenical officer for England, were present at the conference to share information and experience about developments in England.

During subsequent years, a number of LEPs were established in Wales, some confined to the covenanted churches and others including non-covenanted denominations in membership of the Council of Churches for Wales. They varied in nature and location. Some were established in new housing estates, such as Pentwyn, on the outskirts of Cardiff, where the five covenanted churches had joined to form a united church that worshipped in the local school. In other areas, such as Llanuwchllyn and Bancyfelin/Carmarthen, an interdenominational pastorate was formed (in these cases between the Union of Welsh Independents and the Presbyterian Church of Wales) with one minister serving both denominations. More recently, these have been termed 'community ministries' *(gweinidogaethau bro)*. In Ruabon the Anglican parish church shared its building with the Roman Catholic Church within the 1969 Act, which resulted in occasional cooperation in worship, education and mission. In other areas, such as Llangollen, a united church was formed from long-established congregations. Elsewhere (for example, in Botwnnog, in Llŷn), the local Church in Wales priest was also the minister of the Presbyterian Church of Wales churches, on the basis of regulations drawn up specifically on the basis of the covenant towards visible unity in Wales. During the 1980s, efforts were made to foster the formation of community ministries, especially among the Welsh-language Nonconformist churches, with the support and oversight of the Free Church Council of Wales, which established an Inter-Church Joint Consultative Committee on the ministry specifically for this purpose.

Although these diverse projects developed gradually in Wales, they all sprang from the fragile beginnings through the Department of Ecumenical Action in the early 1970s. Whilst they varied considerably in nature, they possessed some common characteristics. Almost invariably, they included an element of shared ministry. Indeed, it could be argued that much of the steady growth in local projects in Wales was the result not so much of a vision of mission (which was the main impetus in England) but of a ministerial crisis, especially among the Welsh Nonconformist churches. Another common characteristic was that many of these projects were products of the efforts of denominational leaders rather than of a vision that had developed naturally within the local situation. In this regard, also, the LEPs in Wales differed generally from LEPs in England. Another tendency in these projects was their failure to face the burden of buildings, which continues to be one of the chief hindrances to creative mission and witness in Wales. One consequence of this is that many ministers have to lead worship in a number of worship centres Sunday by Sunday and maintain a church structure which insists on clinging to the separateness and identity of congregations rather than enabling churches to discover effective ways of sharing resources of experience, buildings and money for Christian mission.

These projects have been an important contribution to the Christian mission in Wales during the last twenty-five years. The denominations have continued to encourage the setting up of such projects through the Commission of the Covenanted Churches, the Council of Churches for Wales (and Cytûn after 1990) and the Free Church Council of Wales. When the Council undertook a review of LEPs in Wales in 1989 it found that more than sixty ecumenical projects of various kinds were in existence at that time. This was a much higher figure than was expected and a proportionately higher figure than in England, where around 700 projects were in existence but where the population and church membership were at least fifteen times greater that the population and church membership of Wales.

During the same period there was a growth in the number of local councils of churches in Wales. In 1969, sixty councils affiliated to the Council of Churches for Wales were listed. By 1978 the number had increased to seventy-nine, of which sixty-five were in urban or post-industrial areas and fourteen in village settings, fifty-seven in English-speaking areas and twenty-two in Welsh-speaking communities, forty-four in the south, eight in mid-Wales and twenty-seven in the north. By 1985 there were around ninety councils, between a third and a half of which made a regular financial contribution to the Council and could be assumed, according to Noel Davies, the General Secretary, 'to have a more active awareness of the wider ecumenical movement in Wales and more widely'. When Cytûn was inaugurated in 1990 there were 110 councils and by 1996 this figure had grown to 130.

Naturally, throughout these years the effectiveness of these councils varied considerably. Some concentrated only on occasional activities such as the Week of Prayer for Christian Unity and Christian Aid Week. Others held regular activities – some on a monthly basis – to foster friendship, mutual understanding and local cooperation. Others sought ways of deepening the relationship between local churches and consequently some LEPs developed within local councils. However, in some areas the council existed only in name and nothing was heard from them from year to year. As with individual congregations, local councils of churches varied considerably from place to place and their effectiveness was mainly dependent on local leadership, lay and ordained.

One very important aspect of the life and work of these councils was the presence of the Roman Catholic Church. From the late 1960s onwards, as has been noted above, local Catholic churches were encouraged, mainly under the influence of the Second Vatican Council, to share in ecumenical activities. In some areas, such as Swansea, the Roman Catholic

Church had been a full member from the beginning.[15] In other areas the Roman Catholic Church, although it was not a full member of the local council, shared in worship services, prayer and reflection groups (especially during the Week of Prayer) and contributed to social action, including Christian Aid Week (although their primary allegiance was clearly to their own aid and development agency, CAFOD). By 1990, it was estimated that about 75 per cent of local councils of churches in Wales included the Roman Catholic parish.

In England, local covenanting was one of the most significant means of deepening partnership with the Roman Catholic Church. Through these covenants churches, priests, ministers and members, in a particular area or community covenanted to share in joint worship (within the current discipline of the various denominations) and joint action in education, mission and witness within society. There was a considerable growth in the number of such covenants in England over recent years. However, this was not the case in Wales. Indeed, at the time of writing, only one local covenant has been inaugurated in Wales, in Dinas Powys near Cardiff, where the Roman Catholic Church, the Church in Wales and the Methodist Church are in covenant. This covenant (which is not directly based on the Covenant for Union in Wales) has been creative and constructive in many ways but has nevertheless faced difficulties, not least as a result of changes in clergy that have not always recognized the need for continuity of ecumenical commitment. It is a sad fact that no other churches in Wales have seen a local covenant as a way of deepening their mutual commitment in mission and unity within their local communities.

In 1985, *Views from the Pews* was published by the Inter-Church Process. It offered an analysis of the response of local groups to the Lent 1986 ecumenical study programme. It was estimated that around a million people had been members of about 70,000 groups in Britain and Ireland. A number of these returned questionnaires about their experience in the groups. 4,200 of the 100,000 questionnaires returned came from Wales. An analysis of a 10 per cent sample of these showed that 50 per cent were members of the Church in Wales, 50 per cent were over 55, 7 per cent under 25, 64 per cent were women and 92 per cent worshipped at least once weekly.

## FOSTERING LOCAL ECUMENISM IN WALES

In summarizing the contribution of local councils of churches, *Views from the Pews* notes: 'All too often the local council is little more that a meeting place for interested people rather than a proper forum which is representative of, and represents the commitment of, the local congregations.'[16]

According to one local council: 'The potential for greater things does exist . . . if only we could harness it properly . . . the strength of the council in terms of will and resources is not such as would enable us to strike out and map new territory.'[17]

But this is not the whole story. Throughout these years there have been lively, enthusiastic councils which won the commitment of local churches and which followed a regular programme of cooperation and joint worship that led to genuine ecumenical companionship. From the earliest days, many individuals within these councils and within the Council of Churches for Wales itself have been most energetic and active in the ecumenical enterprise. At their best, these local councils have offered a way ahead for the churches. Of course, renewal has always been necessary, and the expectation was that the formation of Cytûn in 1990 would be one way of enabling such renewal. But it cannot be denied that these councils have contributed significantly to the new relationship between congregations in most areas of Wales.

During the 1980s, local councils of churches (and individual local congregations where there was no local council) were invited to prepare for a special celebration. In 1983 the Council of Churches for Wales and the Commission of the Covenanted Churches in Wales (on the suggestion of the Commission's education group under the indefatigable leadership of Dr Gwyneth Roberts, Prestatyn) agreed to hold a festival, which came to be called 'God's Family'. Its purpose was to stimulate ecumenical work in Wales within the Covenant and more generally to celebrate the thirtieth birthday of the Council. It was agreed to hold the festival in Llanelwedd (at the Royal Agricultural Showground) on 24 May 1986 (thirty years to the day from the inaugural service of the Council), with Bishop Desmond Tutu (then Anglican Bishop of Johannesburg and later Archbishop of Capetown) as chief guest.

O. P. Jones, a lay Congregationalist from Port Talbot, was appointed as a part-time organizer and considerable efforts were made to promote the festival through publicity within the churches and the media. In fact, it was an enormous undertaking for such a small administrative organization as the council and commission possessed. Nevertheless, according to the officers of the showground between 15,000 and 20,000 attended. It was a great success, although some arrangements broke down completely because of the unexpectedly huge numbers that attended!

There was a range of activities for all age groups, including a pageant, work with children and youth, seminars on a wide range of topics (based on the study pack that had been published in 1985 to help local groups with their preparations for the Festival), a soccer competition and worship and prayer workshops. Naturally, Desmond Tutu was the highlight and his powerful address on the current situation in South Africa and his inspiring, lively and challenging sermon at the closing service were most memorable occasions. As the closing service came to an end, it began to rain and everyone will remember Desmond Tutu running light-footedly across the field, cassock in hand, to reach rapid shelter.[18]

The total cost of the Festival was around £25,000 and to everyone's surprise a profit of £2,174 was made. A number of denominations gave generous help, the Bishop's travelling expenses were paid by an anonymous gift (it can now be revealed that it came from the late Mr Keith Bailey of Swansea, a very committed member of the Friends of the Council), radio and TV companies paid fees for broadcasts from the Festival and £10,000 was received in entry fees on the day.

The God's Family Festival was one of the high points of the ecumenical enterprise in Wales. Its purpose was to give encouragement to ecumenical work through the Council and Commission. Many local councils and congregations were given new heart and they found new enthusiasm, confidence and joy. So much so, that the council agreed to hold another Festival in 1990. But although this Festival was a success in terms of programme and activity, attendance was around 3,000 only, largely because it was decided that no attempt would be made to invite a well-known personality. It made a financial loss.

So, in conclusion, fostering local mutual understanding, cooperation and shared worship has been central to the goals of the ecumenical movement in Wales, as elsewhere, from the beginning. It was the basis for the Welsh Ecumenical Society and the Council's Department of Ecumenical Action was established specifically for this purpose, as well as the centres in Blaendulais, Bangor and elsewhere. This work was at its best when a network of enthusiastic people worked energetically to foster cooperation. People such as Abel Ffowc Williams and Islwyn Lake gave generously and voluntarily of their time and enthusiasm to this task, because they were convinced that the success of the ecumenical vision called for priority to the local.

It must be said also that the Council had more success in this work than is often acknowledged (including during the latter years of the Council, which saw considerable growth in the participation of the Roman Catholic Church in local councils). While it is true to say that the ecumenical vision captured the imagination of local congregations in Wales rather slowly and that new efforts were constantly needed to awaken churches to the creative possibilities of joint action and worship, it must also be recognized that the local church scene has been transformed – in some ways, beyond recognition – in many areas, during the last forty years. There has been a growth in shared worship and action, and in friendship and mutual trust.

The Welsh response to the Nottingham motion on Areas of Ecumenical Experiment was slow in comparison to that of England. The initiative for many such projects in Wales came from church leaders and chief officers rather than as a consequence of local discussion and enthusiasm. This was particularly true in rural areas and in the south Wales valleys, where such experiments were often undertaken because congregations and churches had failed to secure ministry through conventional denominational channels. But, having taken the first step, the new partnership was warmly welcomed and the projects continued although they have had to face crises from time to time, as in all other kinds of pastorates. In locality after locality, churches testified to the enrichment that they had experienced as a result of these deeper ecumenical commitments.

In some areas there had been tension between Welsh-speaking and English-speaking congregations, usually around the language of joint worship and the meetings of the local council of churches. And while simultaneous translation facilitates meetings at national level, this has not usually been possible at local level. Surely, however, the promotion of true bilingualism within the ecumenical family at all levels in Wales must continue, not least within a nation whose new National Assembly Government functions bilingually. After all, mutual understanding between Christians of different languages and cultures is an important contribution to reconciliation between peoples of different languages and cultures within the wider society. This is one of the secrets of warmer ecumenical relationships: the nurturing of the mutual trust and friendship between churches and individual Christians which can help them to understand and appreciate the rich diversity which exists among them.

During recent years the Council (and Cytûn, since 1990), the Commission of the Covenanted Churches (later, Enfys, and now the Covenanted Churches within Cytûn) and the Free Church Council of Wales have made considerable efforts to foster local ecumenism. At the present time the denominations in Wales share the view that the local should be given priority, and that much more energy and resources need to be given to these efforts, since deeper denominational partnership will mean very little unless it is built on partnership in worship, Christian witness and service among local congregations.

## ~ 4 ~
# Relationships with the Roman Catholic Church

The Roman Catholic Church was never a member of the Council of Churches for Wales but the developing relationships with that Church became an important aspect of ecumenical growth in Wales. There were three key stages in the relationship. Mainly as a result of the Second Vatican Council, the Catholic Church became a Consultant Observer within the Council of Churches for Wales in 1968.[1] In the early 1980s, discussions were begun which were aimed at deepening the relationship and which proposed that the Church should become a full member of the Council (although that step was never taken). By the end of the 1980s, the Church had become a full member of the Inter-church Process which would lead in 1990 to the formation of Cytûn: Churches Together in Wales, of which the Church would be a founding member.

The first tentative steps towards relationships with the Church were taken in a very unpromising context. In May 1946 and again in May 1949 the Archbishop of the Church in Wales made statements on the rights of the Church in Wales as 'The Catholic Church in Wales': 'The Roman Clergy and the Nonconformist ministers are intruders . . . There may be historical excuse for their being here, but we cannot recognise their right to be here . . . '[2]

In an article on 'One Church' in 1961 even Erastus Jones acknowledges that:

> . . . on the world and national level it is the Roman Catholic Church which is most difficult to deal with. So far the Church has refused to have anything to do with the ecumenical movement, although individuals and small groups within the Church have shown considerable interest . . . we know that for the Catholics Church Unity clearly

## RELATIONSHIPS WITH THE ROMAN CATHOLIC CHURCH

means the return of the wandering Christians to the one Church, the Roman Church.[3]

Nevertheless, in that same year (and therefore before the Second Vatican Council was even proposed), a step was taken which would have far-reaching consequences in terms of inter-church relationships and cooperation in Christian witness. At the meeting of the Council of Churches for Wales in September 1961, it was agreed to invite the Roman Catholic Church to appoint two representatives to the Joint Committee for the New Welsh Bible, which had been established that year. Some of the Catholic scholars in Wales collaborated in the translation and *Y Beibl Cymraeg Newydd* (the New Welsh Bible) was used for the biblical texts in the new Welsh Missal that was published in the late 1980s.

These initial steps towards closer relationships in Wales were taken at a time when the Church's search for deeper relationships with other churches and denominations was developing rapidly at a world level. In 1952, the first annual meeting of the Catholic Conference on Ecumenical Issues was held. In 1960, the Secretariat for the Promotion of Christian Unity was established. In 1961, the Pope agreed for the first time to send five Catholic observers to the WCC Assembly in New Delhi. The following year, the Second Vatican Council was convened, and continued to meet until 1965.

One direct consequence of the Second Vatican Council was the publication in 1967 by the Conference of Catholic Bishops in England and Wales of *The Directory for the Application of the Decisions of the Second Council of the Vatican concerning Ecumenical Matters*,[4] on behalf of the Vatican Secretariat for the Promotion of Christian Unity. The Directory was intended to offer encouragement and guidance for the search for unity that the Council expressed in its Decree on Ecumenism, *Unitatis Redintegratio*. It emphasized that it was the bishops' responsibility to make decisions on ecumenical policy having taken the whole local context into consideration: 'Proper care must be taken in these matters so that the ecumenical movement itself is not impeded and the faithful do not suffer harm due to the danger of false irenicism and indifferentism.'[5]

## RELATIONSHIPS WITH THE ROMAN CATHOLIC CHURCH

It called for the establishment of Ecumenical Commissions either within a single diocese or for a number of dioceses if that would be more appropriate, and it recommended that these commissions should include lay people, members of religious communities as well as priests. The whole range of ecumenical responsibility that was emphasized by the Vatican Council would become the responsibility of these commissions and it recommended that they cooperate, in appropriate ways, with any councils or ecumenical bodies already in existence amongst the other churches and denominations.

The Decree on Ecumenism was equally influential in Wales. It was this Decree that unlocked the door to deeper ecumenical relationships. In October 1967, the Catholic Bishops in Wales published their 'ecumenical intention', which was to be read in every mass throughout the province on Sunday, 8 October 1967. It was significant in terms of the identity of the Catholic Church within Wales that this was a bilingual statement. Already the Church saw itself as an heir (along with others) of the Welsh Christian tradition. The statement was a deliberate attempt to interpret for Wales the intentions of the Second Vatican Council. It rooted the longing for unity in the life of the Trinity and reminded the churches that the Second Vatican Council had set a high priority on the search for Christian unity and that the Welsh bishops wished to give it the same priority.

One of the most significant sections of the statement was its recognition of the work of the Holy Spirit in the other traditions of Wales: 'we discern that God's grace has been powerfully at work in each Christian body, and we appreciate the practices and devotions through which their members have responded to His grace.'

It also acknowledged that Christian unity was essential to Christian witness in the spiritual crisis of the nation and the bishops therefore issued a strong call to the Catholic parishes in Wales to put every effort into the search for fuller Christian unity: 'let us all make every effort to be rid of the divisions which are caused by sin and human weaknesses; let us open ourselves to the purposes of Christ, so that He can gather together as one family around him all who accept him as true Lord and Saviour.'

Soon after this statement was issued, discussions were commenced (in January 1968) which would lead to the Roman Catholic Church being received as a Consultant Observer within the Council of Churches for Wales. The trigger for this process was a letter to the General Secretary of the Council (Erastus Jones) from Jo Brown,[6] reminding him of the discussions that had taken place between the Roman Catholic Church and the Anglican Churches at a world level, and with the Methodists in England and Wales. The letter suggested that 'the Catholic authorities in Wales should consider initiating discussions with those Christian bodies in Wales which are neither Anglicans nor Methodists'. Specifically, he asked whether an invitation from the Roman Catholic Church to the other churches to join in discussions would be 'to the benefit of Christ's cause in Wales'.[7]

In his response, Erastus Jones expressed his personal view that the Roman Catholic Church should reflect before holding discussions with the other denominations in their turn: 'They have not yet held bilateral discussions with each other and it is not with the great enemy, at its invitation, that such a process should begin . . .'[8] The Executive Committee of the Council agreed instead to appoint five persons, one from each of the larger denominations, to represent the Council in a meeting with the Welsh representatives of the Ecumenical Commission of the Roman Catholic Church in England and Wales. It appears that this suggestion arose from a conversation with Bishop Langton Fox, Bishop of Menevia, who, along with Erastus Jones, was a member of a joint commission of the Roman Catholic Church and the British Council of Churches. In welcoming the Executive Committee's decision Jo Brown made the interesting comment that he believed that:

> Rome is a hindrance even to Protestant unity. There *must* [Brown's emphasis] be some joint discussion. If everyone was willing to discuss their fears openly and not be hurt when others express their fears, then there could be movement. In one way everyone is too courteous at the moment.[9]

The resolution was officially presented to Bishop Langton Fox in a letter dated 8 January 1968 and in his response the Bishop commented:

## RELATIONSHIPS WITH THE ROMAN CATHOLIC CHURCH

The meeting could hardly have asked for more than your Executive is to propose to the Council. In my own mind, I do agree with you that in Wales the main ecumenical dialogue must take place at the level of local councils of churches . . . Our desire for dialogue at every level should be known to all our fellow-Christians here in Wales. There are those who might presume us unwilling.[10]

At its meeting in March 1968, the Council appointed Alun Francis,[11] Huw Wynne Griffith, Erastus Jones, W. Ungoed Jacob and M. J. Williams[12] (later replaced by D. Islwyn Davies) as members of the delegation. The Roman Catholic Church was represented by Sister Mary Anthony from Cardiff, Father Leo Caesar of Cardiff, Bishop Langton Fox, Harri Pritchard Jones[13] and Father Anselm Pulanevitch from Carmarthen. With the exception of Harri Pritchard Jones, the Roman Catholic delegation members had been formed into a Sub-commission on Ecumenism in Wales within the Ecumenical Commission of the Roman Catholic Bishops' Conference for England and Wales in October 1967 – the first time the Roman Catholic Church had appointed such a body within Wales.

The first meeting was held in Swansea on 24 May 1968 (interestingly, twelve years to the day after the founding meeting of the Council of Churches for Wales, also held in Swansea). The main outcome of this first meeting was to agree a statement on dialogue which had been drafted by Bishop Fox. It set out the foundations of any ecumenical relationship: 'We are all Christians. We are . . . bound together by baptism . . . We are members of one body.'[14] Looking back at the history of the relationship between member churches and denominations of the Council of Churches for Wales and the Roman Catholic Church, it acknowledged that:

> There are profound differences in what we believe about revelation, and we must respect them. Each church has a history of animosity and even persecution. Each needs, therefore, to repent for sins against unity and to replace them with humility and a fraternal attitude . . . The prerequisite for dialogue is the acceptance of the absolute demands of truth . . . and of the individual conscience. (In dialogue) each is looking for positive Christian values in the other . . . We must co-operate wherever conscience does not forbid us to do so.[15]

## RELATIONSHIPS WITH THE ROMAN CATHOLIC CHURCH

During discussions about future relationships at this first meeting, the Roman Catholic delegates indicated that the Church would be prepared to become members of the Council of Churches for Wales if that were possible and desirable, or to enter into whatever relationship with the Council as would appear appropriate at the time. Representatives of the Council were invited to attend meetings of the Menevia Diocesan Ecumenical Commission and it was agreed that observers from the Roman Catholic Church would be invited to attend Council committees and departments. The Church was already represented on the Joint Committee for the New Welsh Bible, the Liturgical Study Group and the Faith and Order Committee, and it had been possible to include the Church in the Council's discussions about setting up a Church and Society Department or Committee. These proposals were presented to the Annual Meeting of the Council of 24 and 25 October 1968, and it was agreed that the Roman Catholic Church should be invited to appoint four delegated observers (later they were to be called consultant observers) to attend the next meeting of the Council on St David's Day 1969. Bishop Langton Fox, Father J. C. Thomas (of Mountain Ash), Sister Brendan Joseph (of St Joseph's Convent, Llantarnam) and Dr J. P. Brown were appointed as the first consultant observers on behalf of the Roman Catholic Church.

This was a historic step in ecumenical relationships in Wales. It was seen at the time as 'reflecting a new ecumenical atmosphere'[16] and welcomed as 'a means of further developing ecumenical relationships locally and nationally'.[17]

During the same period, a Joint Working Group between the British Council of Churches and the Roman Catholic Church in England and Wales and in Scotland had been set up (with G. O. Williams and Erastus Jones as members from BCC member churches and Bishop Langton Fox as one of the Roman Catholic representatives).[18] Its formal and informal discussions contributed significantly to the success of the Welsh working group, not least because they had built up a deeper knowledge and trust among key ecumenical leaders in Wales. This was a notable example of the way in which the partnership between the British Council of Churches and the Council of Churches for Wales had a positive influence on ecumenical developments in Wales. Two reports were published, the first in September 1968 and the second in 1971.[19] W. Ungoed Jacob and Bishop Fox were now the representatives from Wales. The second report examined both structural and theological issues in relation to the Church's membership in the British Council of Churches.[20] Some key issues were addressed, such as the nature of the Church[21] and the acceptability of ecumenical statements on public and moral issues.

In summarizing its discussions, the working party report concludes that it was the leaders of the Roman Catholic Church (rather than the faithful) who were most enthusiastic about membership of the British Council of Churches and that a careful educational process would be necessary to help ordinary members to understand the significance of membership. It was envisaged that the majority of the denominations who were members of the Council would welcome Roman Catholic membership, but that there could be greater hesitation and disagreement within the Baptist Union of Great Britain and Ireland and the Scottish Baptist Union (the Baptist Union of Wales was not a member of the BCC) and the Presbyterian Church of Ireland. However, although it could well be that the Church's membership would make it difficult for all the churches to speak with one voice, it would make the Council more representative, it would enrich the Christian witness, strengthen cooperation and foster local relationships.

However, despite this positive report, the Roman Catholic Church did not become a member of the British Council of Churches and continued to be a consultant observer (as in the case of the Council of Churches for Wales) until the demise of the Council in 1990. Throughout this long period of nineteen years, collaboration and shared prayer, locally and nationally, were deepened, in Britain as a whole as well as in Wales. This collaboration continued to be the main emphasis until the end of the 1970s, when preparations were begun for a historic event in the life of the Roman Catholic Church in England and Wales:

> The Bishops resolved to convene a National Pastoral Congress in Liverpool on 2–5 May 1980 and to invite all the bishops, representatives of priests, orders and laity. It had an ambitious goal of taking

stock of the Church's 'life and work, to deepen and renew its prayer and spirituality and then to suggest a way forward for the future . . . If the Congress achieves its objectives then the Church in England and Wales will have taken a step forward. It will mean that we have tried to absorb the lessons of the Second Vatican Council and put them into practice.[22]

The main recommendation of the Section on Unity was that the Bishops should reconsider membership of the British Council of Churches:

Since our remaining outside the British Council of Churches puts a permanent question mark against the serious commitment of our Church in this country to the cause of Christian Unity, we strongly urge the Bishops to reconsider the question of the entry of the Roman Catholic Church in England and Wales into the British Council of Churches.[23]

But when *The Easter People*,[24] the Bishops' official response to the Congress' recommendations, appeared, many who had been present were deeply disappointed, not least in relation to this recommendation about entry into the BCC. The Bishops were able to rejoice in what had been achieved so far: 'We are becoming almost imperceptibly one community of reconciliation . . . We have achieved a reconciliation in charity.'[25] It is not clear what precisely this could mean. In Wales, whereas undoubtedly local Catholic churches were members of at least half of the local councils of churches in Wales and played a prominent role in many of them, the relationships and patterns of collaboration at national level did not merit this description. The Church's status as a consultant observer in the Council of Churches for Wales had not developed in any marked way since 1968 (i.e. over a period of twelve years), although some positive steps had been taken and discussions about deepening that relationship had begun, as we shall see. But it could hardly be claimed that the churches and denominations in Wales had attained reconciliation in love with the Roman Catholic Church. It is fair to assume that it was the situation in England that was foremost in the Bishops' mind. In England the situation had developed and by 1982 (two years after the Congress) a number of local covenants involving the Roman Catholic Church had been established, where congregations would cooperate closely with one another in areas such as education, service to the community, and pastoral care, and would also worship and pray together regularly. There were no examples of this at the time in Wales. One such covenant was established between the Roman Catholic Church, the Church in Wales and the Methodist Church in Dinas Powis, in the Vale of Glamorgan, but in recent years it has faced difficulties.

In their response to *The Easter People*, the Bishops were very hesitant about any steps towards unity that would mean compromise on doctrinal issues that were of the essence of the Catholic understanding of the fullness of the Christian faith. Rather they placed greater emphasis on cooperation in mission, in accordance with the commitment made by Pope John Paul II and Archbishop Robert Runcie.[26] However, their response was completely negative in relation to BCC membership. They suggested that more work needed to be done (although considerable work had already been done) on the status of statements on moral and social issues, and on matters of structure and finance. Until this was done, all they felt able to say was:

> The recommendation of the need here and now to make a convincing gesture is itself a welcome and precious witness of concern for advancing the cause of unity. It is sure of a place in our consideration of an issue . . . which . . . calls for a joint gift of light and warmth in its adequate solution . . . At this stage we commit ourselves to a re-examination of all these questions.[27]

Those who were eager to see the Church taking this step towards other churches, heard this response, despite the careful language, as 'No!' In reality, there would be a wait of another ten years, when the new ecumenical instruments were established in 1990, before the Roman Catholic Church in England and Wales (and in Scotland) became a member of the ecumenical bodies in these nations.

However, at the end of this section on Christian Unity, the Bishops endorsed the words of the Congress: 'We profess our growing conviction of the need for more profound unity with our fellow Christians and we will continue to search for more effective ways of achieving that unity.'[28] Despite the negative aspects of their response to the Congress' ecumenical recommendations, there was a movement afoot which would be impossible to resist.

In April 1980 (that is, one month before the Congress was held), discussions had already begun (on the initiative of the General Secretary, Noel Davies) between the Council of Churches for Wales and the leaders and ecumenical officers of the Roman Catholic Church in Wales with a view to establishing a joint working group between the Council and the Church. The Council's Executive Committee agreed to seek to establish a working group with the following four aims. First, it would enable a theological dialogue to continue at all levels of the churches' life and most especially to study recent publications on authority, ministry, sacraments and moral statements and their relevance to ecumenical relationships. Secondly, it would conduct 'a review of local ecumenism and make recommendations about deepening the partnership with the Roman Catholic Church'. Thirdly, it would assist the churches and denominations that were already members of the Council to appreciate the advantages that would follow if the Catholic Church were to become full members of the Council. And finally, it would share in the dialogue and deeper relationships between the Catholic Church and other Churches worldwide.[29]

These recommendations were accepted by the Council of Churches for Wales and the Welsh Bishops of the Roman Catholic Church and the first meeting of the working group was held in Shrewsbury on 4 February 1981.[30] The Council was represented by Bishop B. N. Y. Vaughan (Anglican Bishop of Swansea and Brecon, President of the Council, who would be joint chair of the group), Meirion Lloyd Davies,[31] Owen E. Evans,[32] R. O. Roberts and Noel Davies, General Secretary of the Council (who would be joint secretary). The Roman Catholic Church was represented by Bishop Daniel Mullins[33] (who would be joint chair of the group), Father Michael Tomkins (of Porthmadog), Father Clyde Hughes Johnson (of Swansea), Ron Howells,[34] Wing-Commander E. Ryan (of Cardiff) and Miss Joy Abbati (Secretary of the Cardiff Ecumenical Commission, who would be joint secretary). Considerable time was spent during the first meeting discussing the aims set out above and agreeing on a pattern of work, but time was given also to considering the significance of the task entrusted to the working group for the interrelationship and mission of the denominations in Wales. In his report to the joint meeting of the Ecumenical Commissions of the Roman Catholic Church in Wales, Ron Howells quoted the opening words of Bishop Vaughan in the first meeting, that at this critical time in the history of the Church of Christ in Wales, the churches needed 'to repent and be renewed together as we confess our common faith, if the world is to believe': 'It was considered that there was a real need for the Roman Catholic Church in Wales to have a much closer relationship with the other Welsh Churches since the situation is often quite unique in matters ecumenical – tradition, language, culture &c.'[35]

In a comprehensive and perceptive paper to the working group's second meeting (on 10 September 1981), Ron Howells quoted Bishop Alan Clark:[36] 'The Catholic Church is pledged to achieve, by every means in its power, doctrinal unity with other Christian communities as the growing expression of the unity of faith which is the mark of Christ's Church . . . [and] at the same time, to express in practice the degree of unity we have already achieved.'[37] He ended with a reference to *Unitatis Redintegratio*, the Second Vatican Council's Decree on Ecumenism, and gave particular attention to the bond of baptism which unites all Christians and to the report's view that divisions between Christians were the result of sin on both sides. He also drew attention to its emphasis on the Church, as a pilgrim people, moving towards Christ rather than returning to the Roman Catholic Church.[38] He suggested that full membership of the Council of Churches for Wales could be an expression on the part of the Roman Catholic Church of the unity already fulfilled and of their eagerness to be seen alongside other denominations in a common witness to the Gospel in Wales.

There was a clear theological foundation, therefore, for the group's discussion and this was seen to be a key aspect of the ecumenical pilgrimage to which the Roman Catholic Church was called. But other more practical questions had to be faced also. Four meetings were held during 1982 and 1983. At the end of the process, there was unanimous agreement on recommendations which were drafted by Bishop Mullins. They proposed that the Church should move towards applying for full membership of the Council, defined 'the limits of what the Council can achieve' and set Pentecost 1985 as the date for 'a firm and binding decision'.[39]

Later in the year, Bishop Mullins gave an address to the Annual Meeting of the Council.[40] He believed that there was a new awareness of Wales within the Church, 'her mission was here' and in order to prepare the Church for this mission in Wales a new diocese was in process of being established. Examining the recommendation of the working group would be an important aspect of these developments. In the discussion that followed, it became clear that the Roman Catholic Church's full membership in the Council 'would certainly be of the greatest significance for the Council's life and would challenge the Council and its members'. The Bishop believed that the Roman Catholic Church 'would be a friend . . . but at times an uncomfortable friend', if it became a Council member. However, there was no doubt that the Council itself was keen to see the Church becoming a full member.

By November 1983, the working group had completed its work and no further meetings were held. It was now a matter of waiting for a decision, in the first instance, by the Roman Catholic Church in Wales. A number of other developments influenced this process. Archbishop John Murphy announced his retirement in 1982 and it was believed that no decision should be taken on such an important matter until his successor has been appointed and he had had time to give the matter careful consideration. In 1983, Bishop John Aloysius Ward, the Bishop of the then Diocese of Menevia, was appointed Archbishop of Cardiff. The Bishops, and others who were committed to seeing further ecumenical progress being made, believed that a great deal of education would be needed among members and priests of the Roman Catholic Church in Wales before there could be confidence that the whole Church was behind this historic step of becoming a full member of the Council. While these matters were being considered in Wales, similar discussions were being held about the membership of the Roman Catholic Church in England and Wales in the British Council of Churches. While the Welsh bishops had the authority to make their own decision, nevertheless the wider discussions did influence them, since they were members of the same Bishops' Conference. Although many were still eager to see the Church becoming a full member of the BCC, gradually it was decided that the Church could not take this step unless the Council changed substantially.

As a result of all this, the decision about membership of the Council of Churches for Wales was delayed. In the meantime, the BCC and the Bishops' Conference of England and Wales agreed that the next step for them would be to provide an opportunity for the leaders of all the Churches and denominations to meet in two retreats, one at the invitation of the Catholic Bishops and one at the invitation of the Archbishop of Canterbury as President of the BCC. The former was held at New Hall, near Chelmsford, on 10 and 11 January 1984 and the latter at St Augustine's College, Canterbury from 6 to 9 April 1984. The fruit of these retreats was the gradual realization that it was not by membership of the current ecumenical bodies that the Roman Catholic Church could best express its ecumenical commitment. Rather it became clear that much more far-reaching steps would be necessary which would mean radical changes in the life of Councils of Churches. So the idea of an Inter-Church Process for these nations began to be formed, particularly in the mind of Philip Morgan,[41] who was General Secretary of the BCC at the time. Following extensive consultation, representatives of thirty-two Churches and denominations in Britain and Ireland met at Lambeth Palace on 7 May 1985, when it was decided to launch an Inter-Church Process 'on the nature and purpose of the church in the light of its mission in and for the world'.

The Roman Catholic Church in England and Wales and in Scotland were full members of this process from the beginning and it soon became clear to the Welsh Catholic Bishops and the Council of Churches for Wales that it would be inappropriate, in the light of this Process, to implement the recommendations about membership of the Council of Churches for Wales. Committed involvement in the Inter-Church Process was now the way forward. And, of course, this led, as we have seen, to the demise of the Council of Churches for Wales and the British Council of Churches (as well as the Scottish Churches Council) and the establishment of Cytûn: Churches Together in Wales

## RELATIONSHIPS WITH THE ROMAN CATHOLIC CHURCH

and the other ecumenical instruments, with the Roman Catholic Church in full membership. In many ways this historical step was the fruit of the discussions, collaboration and shared worship of the previous twenty years, and it changed the ecumenical climate in these nations.

In the meantime, Pope John Paul II had visited Wales. In the summer of 1980, it was announced that he would visit England, Scotland and Wales in the summer of 1982. In a letter to Archbishop Murphy, the General Secretary, Noel Davies, welcomed the visit on behalf of the Council of Churches for Wales:

> I am particularly encouraged that Pope John Paul has himself stressed the ecumenical dimensions of this visit. The first steps which we have taken recently to deepen relationships between the Roman Catholic Church and the Council of Churches for Wales, and the proposed joint dialogue on theological and moral issues will mean that we too will be strengthened by his visit.[42]

There would be three elements within his one-day visit to Wales: he would celebrate mass in Pontcanna fields in Cardiff in the morning; in the afternoon he would meet with leaders of all the denominations in Wales; in the evening he would address a youth rally in Ninian Park, Cardiff.

The Pope visited Wales on 2 June 1982. His homily at the mass in Pontcanna fields opened with the greeting: 'Today the Bishop of Rome greets the people of Wales for the first time in their own beautiful land . . .'[43] He recalled that there was in Wales a long tradition of faithfulness to Christ and that he wished to proclaim the same Gospel. The central theme of the Pope's homily was the place of the eucharist in the life of the Church, based on a reading from the Gospel of St John, chapter 6. He greeted most particularly the children who were to receive their first communion at the mass, their parents, teachers and priests, praying that 'this great mystery' would be for them and for the whole of the Church 'the centre of their life and the way to eternal salvation in Christ Jesus our Lord'.[44]

The meeting with denominational representatives in Cardiff Castle during the afternoon of the visit was intended to be the main opportunity to consider Welsh ecumenical issues. Unfortunately, the meeting was curtailed to twenty-five minutes, mainly because the Pope, on the last day of his visit to Britain, was over-tired and under strain following all the meetings which he had attended and addressed. Two representatives of each church and denomination in membership of the Council of Churches for Wales came to meet him. He was greeted by Bishop B. N. Y. Vaughan, the President of the Council, and the Revd Frank Lee, President of the Free Church Council for Wales led a brief bilingual act of worship. In his response, the Pope welcomed the emphasis on prayer during the meeting: 'all our efforts to do his will are vain if they are not rooted in change of heart, in holiness of life and in prayer for unity: these are the very soul of the ecumenical movement.'[45] He went on to welcome the cooperation between Roman Catholics and other churches and communities in Wales, and the Church's growing participation in the Council of Churches for Wales. This was not an opportunity for dialogue (as originally intended) but for prayer, and this was its main ecumenical significance. His friendship and humanity also made a considerable impact. At the end of the meeting he was presented with a copy of the New Testament in the New Welsh Bible translation.

## *Conclusions*

At the beginning of the twentieth century, there were 65,000 registered Catholic worshippers in Wales, ten times as many as in 1851 and the great majority of these were descendants of Irish immigrants. By 1982 there were 129,000 members, approximately 25 per cent of the total church membership in Wales.[46] By 1990 this figure had increased to 150,000, approximately 30 per cent of the total membership. During this period of growth, the proportion of members who were descendents of Irish immigrants declined – although it remained high – and the proportion of indigenous Catholics increased. The number of Welsh-speaking Catholics was (and remains) low. Nevertheless, it is natural that the Church, especially amongst its leaders, has developed a deeper sense of its Welsh identity. One consequence of this was a greater awareness of its partnership in Christian mission in Wales with other churches and denominations. For example, when a new Diocese of Menevia was established in 1987 (by dividing the former diocese of the same name which was focused on Wrexham and served north and south-west Wales to form the new Diocese, covering south-west Wales, and a Diocese of Wrexham, covering north Wales), one reason given for the change was that it would strengthen and facilitate this partnership in Christian witness in Wales.

During the same period, there was a substantial growth in the number of local councils of churches in which the local Roman Catholic Church was a full member. It was estimated that this was around 75 per cent of all councils in 1990, the year in which the church became a full member of the new ecumenical instrument for Wales, Cytûn: Churches Together for Wales. An inevitable consequence of this was that a growing number of Christians from other churches experienced worship in Roman Catholic churches – especially during the Week of Prayer for Christian Unity – and from time to time were also present in celebrations of the Mass. There was a small number of shared church building schemes involving the Roman Catholic Church (e.g. in Ruabon, near Wrexham, and in Pontardawe, near Swansea) and one example only of a local covenant (in this case involving the Roman Catholic Church, the Church in Wales and the Methodist Church). However, in general, despite growing friendship and cooperation through local councils of churches, there was very little growth in participation in local ecumenical projects (now called local ecumenical partnerships) involving Roman Catholic churches, a development which would have signalled an official commitment to local partnership by the Church. It was the hope of the Welsh leaders of the Church that the formation of Cytûn would foster such projects.

However, during this period there had been a dramatic change in the attitudes of the other denominations, nationally and locally, towards the Roman Catholic Church. Inter-church relationships in Wales had come a long way since the Archbishop of Wales declared in 1949 that: '[t]he Roman Clergy are intruders . . . We cannot recognise their right to be here' (*see above*). Now Cytûn's constitution declared that one of its aims was 'to bring the churches together in all the richness of their present diversity ... so that they can learn from and appreciate one another's traditions'.

There were already examples of this mutual enrichment at work. Catholics had come more and more to appreciate the importance of Scripture in any Christian renewal. And, ironically, at a time when they were on the wane in Welsh Nonconformity, Catholic churches were establishing bible study and prayer groups. At a world level, there had been an extensive process of liturgical renewal, which had deeply influenced churches and denominations in Wales, such that their patterns of worship had more and more in common. The Roman Catholic Church had been at the heart of this liturgical renewal, especially in the area of the eucharist. These developments had their effect on churches in Wales too.

Another important aspect of international inter-church relationships had been the growing number of bilateral dialogues involving the Roman Catholic Church since the Second Vatican Council. The best known of these had been the Anglican-Roman Catholic International Commission which had issued reports, for example, on the eucharist, ministry, authority and justification. One of the weaknesses of the relationships with the Roman Catholic Church in Wales was that little attention was given to these bilateral dialogues and that there were no substantial theological discussions among the churches and denominations on the fundamental issues that divided them. One of the intentions behind setting up Cytûn was to provide a forum for such theological encounter.

There is always the danger within inter-church relationships that churches and denominations avoid the difficult questions that divide their members. This was a danger in the developing relationship with the Roman Catholic Church in Wales. Whilst there was substantial agreement on the wording of eucharistic liturgies, for example, little attempt was made to grapple with the deep theological disagreements on the meaning of the eucharist which were hidden behind the common wording. Nor was there an acknowledgement that the churches' understanding of the mystery of communion was constantly changing and developing.

The churches' responses to the WCC report, 'Baptism, Eucharist and Ministry'[47] clearly show this conflict and the 'development' that had occurred in the understanding of all the Christian traditions in Wales. In particular, the doctrine of trans-substantiation was studied extensively within the Roman Catholic Church during the twentieth century and there have been changes in the way in which the doctrine is expressed, but without any substantive changes of understanding.[48] Aspects of this discussion were reflected in documents produced over the years by the Council of Churches for Wales' Liturgical Study Group and these in turn influenced the theology and liturgical patterns which the group presented from time to time. But this doctrine remains one of the main stumbling blocks to relations between the Roman Catholic Churches and other denominations and demands further study by the churches and denominations in Wales.

Similarly, while accepting each other as partners in Christian witness in Wales, adequate attention was not given to deep differences among the churches on the nature of the Church. Intercommunion with the Roman Catholic Church is unlikely until agreement is reached on this very difficult issue and at least some in our denominations would claim that such agreement cannot be possible without such fundamental theological changes as would mean a revolution in denominational self-understanding.

But other divisive aspects of the Church's doctrine received very little ecumenical attention in Wales during this time, issues such as papal infallibility and the role of Mary – a question that has received considerable ecumenical consideration in recent years.[49]

It should not be a matter of surprise, therefore, that a minority within all the churches and denominations believed that to be fellow members along with the Roman Catholic Church of Cytûn would be a denial of the scriptural and theological foundations of their traditions and that such a step should not be taken. It would deny their Christian identity and hinder Christian witness in Wales. This was not a minority view among the member churches in Wales of the Baptist Union of Great Britain, which decided – partly on this basis – not to become a member body of Cytûn. There was a difficult debate also within the Baptist Union of Wales (which had Welsh- and English-language churches) and they agreed to become members of Cytûn for a trial period of three years. However, at the end of the three-year period, following a referendum of all the churches (in 1993) it was agreed to remain in membership of Cytûn. Similarly, there was a minority within the Presbyterian Church of Wales who shared this view, but they did not affect the decision of the General Assembly in 1990 nor in 1991, when the matter was raised again, that the church should unconditionally become members of Cytûn.

During the period prior to the formation of Cytûn, inter-denominational statements on moral and social issues continued to cause concern, and for at least two reasons. First, the leaders of the Roman Catholic Church had considerable doubts about the authoritative status of ecumenical statements on such matters. They had (and still have) grave doubts about whether an inter-denominational body has the right either on its own behalf or (and this causes even deeper concern) on behalf of its member churches to make public statements. In their view (a view that is clearly not limited to the Roman Catholic Church), only the churches and denominations themselves have this right. Even if there is general agreement across the denominations on a particular issue, they question the authority of a statement made on behalf of all the churches. Secondly, there was (and is) considerable disagreement among the denominations on a range of moral and social questions, such as abortion and contraception, on the one hand, and war and defence, on the other. There was a fear that disagreement on such 'public' issues could harm the Christian witness and lead to superficial statements which would not do justice to the fullness of Christian moral teaching. This tension continues to be an issue for the ecumenical movement in Wales (and elsewhere).

The response that was presented by the Roman Catholic Church in England and Wales during the Inter-Church Process makes the following claim about their involvement in the ecumenical pilgrimage:

> We come to the work of ecumenism not with the intention of trying to achieve an amalgam of Churches but of working with others to build up into its proper fullness the one Church of Christ. We accept

that within the Church of Christ there will be legitimate diversity, and different expressions of the same faith which illuminate the one truth . . . This is an urgent task because the present situation openly contradicts the will of Christ and provides a serious stumbling block in the mission given by Christ to his Church.[50]

It continues to be necessary, twenty years later, for the churches in Wales to engage in serious theological reflection on these fundamental questions as they seek to build a deeper partnership with the Roman Catholic Church as fellow-members of Cytûn: Churches Together in Wales, on the basis of the dramatically changed relationships that have developed over the last forty years.

# ~ 5 ~
# *The churches and society: beginnings and foundations*

A large part of the energy of the ecumenical movement has been directed to the search for a common Christian witness to the problems of modern society. Indeed, for laymen [sic], most of the attraction of the ecumenical movement is in its creativity and vitality in facing social issues and in the challenge they have posed to Churches.[1]

Throughout the years of the Second World War and the formation of the World Council of Churches (established in 1948), leaders such as George Bell (Bishop of Chichester), William Temple (Archbishop of Canterbury), J. H. Oldham and the first WCC General Secretary, W. A. Visser 't Hooft, emphasized that the Council, and the ecumenical movement in general, were called to a prophetic ministry and a ministry of reconciliation. The first Assembly of the World Council of Churches (Amsterdam, 1948) offered the following definition of a 'responsible society' as a suitable framework for understanding the Church's responsibility in society:

> Man [sic] is created and called to be a free being, responsible to God and his neighbour ... A responsible society is one where freedom is the freedom of men who acknowledge responsibility to justice and public order, and where those who hold political authority or economic power are responsible for its exercise to God and the people whose welfare is affected by it ... For a society to be responsible under modern conditions it is required that the people have freedom to control, criticize, and to change their governments, that power be made responsible by law and tradition, and be distributed as widely as possible through the whole community. It is required that economic justice and provision of equality of opportunity be established for all the members of society.[2]

If the main impetus for the formation of the Council of Churches for Wales was the desire to see Welsh denominations and churches pursuing the goal of church unity more energetically, another important factor was the need to develop an effective instrument to enable them to cooperate more fully with each other in witnessing to a just and free society in Wales and worldwide. Over the years, the Council devoted increasing effort and vision to this aspect of the ecumenical agenda.

In these early years, the Council gave attention to a number of burning issues in Wales which called on Christians to offer guidance and leadership to the people of Wales. Thus, among other issues, the Council considered broadcasting (in a period when television was beginning to reach Wales), laws governing the opening of public houses on Sunday (at the time of the first vote on this issue in 1961), and unemployment and the closing of coal mines (with the National Coal Board threatening to close a number of pits in the south Wales coalfield).

The question of land use in Wales attracted most attention at the beginning. In its meeting on 7 October 1955 the Joint Committee for Mutual Understanding and Collaboration between Christian Communions in Wales stressed that people in rural Wales should be defended 'from the increasing tendency to turn to Wales for land for waterworks and other schemes while ignoring the historical, religious and cultural realities of their communities'.[3] In the same meeting it was agreed to invite the Council, at its first meeting in May 1956, to set up a Commission on 'our activity in rural areas'. This was a response not only to the social and religious crisis in rural Wales but also to the report of the Commission on Land in Mid-Wales. A number of prominent figures were appointed to the Commission (including Professor E. G. Bowen, Professor of Geography in University College, Aberystwyth) which would be convened by Principal W. R. Williams (Principal of the United Theological College, Aberystwyth and Secretary of the new Council). In establishing this Commission, the Council called the attention of all religious bodies in Wales to the report it would study, since its recommendations would mean far-reaching changes in the pattern of the social and economic life of Mid-Wales and raise very important questions for all who had an interest in the cultural and religious life of Wales.

The Commission's final report was presented to the Council in October 1960.[4] Its starting point was the need to accept the economic, agricultural and social changes as inevitable and as demanding transformation within the communities themselves:

> ... it is fairly clear that reasonable home and social amenities can only be provided if the community becomes much more compact than the scattered pattern which has characterised rural Wales ... Local Authorities and other organisations must, in planning for the future, look forward to an increasing concentration of population in the most favourably situated villages and to strengthening of community life.[5]

While accepting that efforts were needed to secure light industries in rural Wales, the Commission recognized also that transport questions would need to be tackled. It called for issues around the Welsh language and culture within the region, especially in relation to education and broadcasting media, to be given attention. The formation of the Mid-Wales Development Association, the forerunner of the Development Board for Rural Wales, was welcomed.

The second part of the Commission's report was devoted to a survey by Professor E. G. Bowen of the churches' role in these changes: 'The Churches and Changes in Social and Economic Life'. Professor Bowen came to two main conclusions on the basis of his analysis. First, that there was more than enough space for everyone in the places of worship even if the whole population were to attend public worship. Secondly, that the present distribution of places of worship did not match population distribution, apart, perhaps, from the coastal catchment area where the population continued to be pretty dense and showed signs of increasing.

He made three recommendations on the basis of his analysis. He believed, first of all, that the Council should accept the recommendations of the public Commission, that the denominations should 'amalgamate many of their churches and so concentrate their resources in those churches and chapels which are situated along or near the main roads, or in the smaller villages' and that such a plan would require improving transport provision among farmers and inhabitants of rural areas.

The Council's response to the Commission's report made extensive use of Professor Bowen's work. However, it began with two fundamental principles:

> The Christian Communions in Wales have a responsibility in matters social and economic that affect the life of Wales. Individual members of Christian Churches who are members of public bodies have likewise a responsibility and an opportunity for Christian action in public life.[6]

The Council's recommendations focused on the need to collaborate on community youth activity and on fostering the Welsh language in the region. However, there were few signs that the denominations' consideration of its analysis and recommendations had much influence on their policy. The churches have not found it easy to face the questions of Christian witness and community engagement in rural Wales although there have been some notable initiatives.

Another subject that had priority in these early years was broadcasting, especially early developments in television broadcasting. In 1959 the Council passed the following resolution which was proposed by T. I. Ellis:

> Having regard to the potent influence of Television upon our people, and particularly upon children and those of an impressionable age, this Council is glad to lend its support to those who are pressing for an arrangement which will give Wales a Television service of its own.[7]

The aim was to secure control over TV provision for the people of Wales, especially in the Welsh language. At the beginning (in the early 1950s), the BBC provided the only Welsh channel, but in 1955 the independent television services were established and Wales became part of 'the territory of *Television Wales and the West* (TWW) – "the kingdom of King Arthur" once again – although viewers in the north-east could receive the programmes of Granada from Manchester'.[8] Being aware of considerable dissatisfaction about this, the Council attempted to get the Government to receive a delegation from among the churches of Wales, but to no avail. In the meantime, the Lord Mayor of Cardiff convened a National Representative Conference to consider the matter, and representatives of the

Council attended. This Conference called – as the Council had done earlier in the year – for a television service for Wales, and to this end, a Continuation Committee was appointed.[9]

In 1960, the Pilkington Committee was set up to consider the future of broadcasting in Britain and at its meeting in October of that year, the Council pressed for Wales to speak with one voice in the evidence which was being submitted to the Committee. Its resolution called for:

> ... every opportunity to be taken to try to secure for Wales a television medium for itself ... to meet its own special needs. In the opinion of the Council, the chief medium should be the responsibility of the BBC and Wales should enjoy control of Programmes and policy and, apart from this, have the same right as the rest of the country to an alternative service. The Council also commends making every effort to get more time for religious programmes as well as more consideration of Wales' needs in general.[10]

However, the Committee asked rather for the Council's permission to publish the memorandum presented to it as an appendix to the Pilkington Report that was published in 1962. Its recommendations led to the setting up of BBC Wales and the Television Company of Wales (which collapsed a year later, and its responsibility taken over by TWW). At least some of the battles on behalf of broadcasting in Wales – in which the Council shared – were being won gradually.

However, broadcasting standards as well as provision became an issue of ecumenical concern. In 1964, a resolution from the Union of Welsh Independents was approved, calling for the setting up of a Committee within the Council of Churches for Wales to consider the whole field of broadcasting:

> Being aware of the influence and potential of radio and television in our day, we desire that a group be set up with sufficient expertise to be able to offer advice and review developments in the mass media.[11]

An Advisory Committee was set up to consider the effective use of the media, to explore appropriate training and to collaborate with the advisory committees already in existence. Professor Mansel John (Baptist Union of Wales), the Revd Derrick Childs (the Church in Wales, later to become Bishop of

Monmouth and Archbishop of Wales), the Revd Wyndham Bold (later to become Chairman of the South Wales District of The Methodist Church), the Revd M. R. Mainwaring (Presbyterian Church of Wales, later to become Secretary of its Mission Board) and the Revd Emlyn Jenkins (Union of Welsh Independents) were appointed as members. This committee was responsible for the Council's engagement with broadcasting and the media throughout the sixties until the Department of Christian Communication was set up in 1974, with similar aims.

This is another example of the leaders of the Council in the early days being alert to the opportunity and challenge of a completely new and revolutionary medium, and being able to act on behalf of the denominations and the churches on an important national issue, so that they could speak with one voice when the need arose.

In 1960, the possibility of changing the law (which had been in force since 1881) concerning the opening of public houses on Sunday in Wales began to be explored. This was opposed by most of the denominations – and particularly the Welsh-speaking Nonconformist denominations. In its meeting on 19–20 October, the following resolution was passed by the Council:

> ... in the opinion of the Council no change in the law of Sunday opening in Wales should be made without an enquiry by means of a Royal Commission or other appropriate body to ascertain the state of responsible opinion in Wales on the matter.[12]

A referendum was to be held. On the eve of this referendum (in October 1961), the Council issued the following statement:

> The Council of Churches for Wales strongly urges members of the Christian Churches in Wales to act in accordance with their Christian and civic duty when they come to use their vote in connection with the provisions of the Licensing Act, bearing in mind the importance of this vote, particularly to the youth of Wales, in view of the moral dangers which they have to face.[13]

This was a response primarily to the declaration by the Archbishop of Wales, Dr Edwin Morris, in the *Western Mail* on 13 September 1961 on 'The Christian Use of Alcoholic

Beverages', when he went so far as to defend Sunday opening although he argued that four hours each Sunday would be enough for anybody.[14] The South Wales Synod of the Methodist Church asked the Council to issue a statement that would give a lead to the Christians of Wales. The above resolution was the result. The annual report of the Council for 1960–1 repeats the opinion that 'the chief duty of the Welsh nation on Sunday [is] to worship the Lord God'.

The result nationally was a split vote. The industrial, anglicized regions in south, south-east and north-east Wales voted in favour of opening. The rural, Welsh regions in north and west Wales voted against Sunday opening. This meant that 72 per cent of the population of Wales now lived in 'wet' areas. During the next few years, this percentage would increase in every referendum, and by 1982 there were only two regions, Ceredigion and Dwyfor (together representing about 3 per cent of the population), which were 'dry'.[15]

According to Kenneth O. Morgan,[16] the 1961 referendum was:

> ... a somewhat pathetic commentary on the waning authority of organised religion ... [T]he chapels and their ethos were retreating to the rural fastnesses, setting their face against secularism and materialism which flew against all their deepest and most cherished convictions ... [A]nother permanent nail was laid in the coffin of Welsh puritanism and those social and institutional symbols which served to perpetuate it.

Whilst this analysis is certainly true to some extent – this result was an obvious sign that the influence of the churches and chapels on the life of the inhabitants of Wales had waned – it may have also been a sign of a change in the priorities of the churches and their understanding of the Christian values which it was their responsibility to promote. Without a doubt, this was true of the Council itself, because this matter was never raised in its meetings again. Other social issues became the main focus of its attention from this point on.

In the early years of the Council, a number of other issues arose also, including most particularly unemployment and pit closures. But it was the three issues examined above – namely, land in Wales, broadcasting and Sunday opening – which received most attention. And at the end of the 1950s and the beginning of the 1960s, these three struggles had significance not only in themselves but as symbols of struggles for national identity. In different ways, there was a sacred aspect to each of them. Throughout the centuries, the land of Wales had been perceived as sacred. Costly battles had been fought to keep it under Welsh control so that it could shape future generations. Radio and television represented modern means of nurturing, renewing and handing down the cultures that had given Wales its identity. Sunday (understood in the past as 'the sanctity of the Sabbath') was a powerful sign of the loyalty of the Welsh people, over the previous century at least, to the Christianity that had been the 'soul' of the nation. Now they were all under threat, not only from within Wales (even though internal threats were often more savage than the external ones), but, perhaps chiefly, from outside. Others wanted to drown and trample the land, take control of the broadcasting media, and secular cultures were threatening Wales' loyalty to the symbols of its old religion. The churches and the denominations felt obliged to join the fray. In the early days, the Council and its leaders saw that it was necessary for the Christian witness to society and nation to speak to the heart of those symbols which made it a nation. But, of course, with the passing of the years, those symbols would change because of internal and external influences, and part of the task of the Church in every age is to comprehend these changes and find new ways of enabling the churches – in this case, together, through the Council – to understand the challenge of Christian witness in a new age.

That is what happened in the case of the Council. Partly as a result of the address by the General Secretary of the British Council of Churches, Bishop Kenneth Sansbury, in the annual meeting of the Council of Churches for Wales in Holyhead on 6–7 November 1967, it was decided to consider 'The Council and social responsibility'. This was done in the awareness that there was 'one obvious defect in [the Council's arrangements] ... there is no provision for witness to society'.[17]

In the meantime, the results and recommendations of the first worldwide conference of the World Council of Churches on Church and Society (Geneva, 1966) were beginning to penetrate the life and work of the Welsh denominations. It had considerable influence on the preparations for a Welsh conference. According to Paul Abrecht,[18] the Geneva Conference was 'the most serious attempt by the WCC to understand the revolutionary realities that shape the modern world'.[19] In order to help the churches and denominations worldwide to prepare for the Geneva conference, four volumes of essays were published on *Christian Social Ethics in a Changing World*, *Revolutionary Government in a Revolutionary Age*, *Economic Growth in a World Perspective*, and *Man in Community*. Subsections of the conference reflected these headings and there was an attempt to see them in the light of three other themes which influenced the whole field, namely, theological issues in social ethics, the potentialities of the modern technological and scientific revolution and the Church's work in society. It had a considerable effect on every aspect of the ecumenical movement, but Abrecht emphasizes three aspects.

First, it set before the churches the challenge of Christian responsibility for economic and social development worldwide. On the basis of this challenge, the Third Assembly of the World Council of Churches (Uppsala, 1968) called on the churches:[20] 'to go beyond the charitable understanding to the need for fundamental social changes based on a new urgent concern for social justice in a world perspective'.[21]

Secondly, basic agreement was reached that the Church had to realize the need for revolutionary changes in social and political structures, and the Uppsala Assembly believed that those should be founded on principles of non-violence. A consultation on violence and non-violence was held in Cardiff in September 1971, under the auspices of the World Council of Churches, as part of a two-year process of study which led to a very important report on 'Violence, Non-violence and the Struggle for Social Justice'.[22] During this consultation, an open meeting was held at which Margaret Mead (the well-known anthropologist) and James Lawson (from Memphis, Tennessee) spoke. One of Lawson's chief contributions was to welcome the Programme to Combat Racism[23] that had been adopted by the World Council of Churches in 1969 (see Chapter 9). He saw it as a symbol of the love that seeks to challenge governments and individuals who oppress and use violence, and that wishes to be in solidarity with those who suffer violence and repression at the hands of institutions of all kinds. A number of supporters of the ecumenical movement in Wales took advantage of this opportunity to attend one of the few worldwide ecumenical meetings ever held in Wales.

Thirdly, it was realized that the World Council of Churches and the Roman Catholic Church were in close agreement on some specific points and that these should be a basis for further collaboration.

In weighing up the contribution of the World Council of Churches up to 1968, Abrecht concluded:

> Despite the achievements in recent years, ecumenical social thinking remains a precarious exercise ... Up to the present [i.e. 1970], ecumenical consensus on Christian social responsibility has been limited, experimental and provisional and with relatively slight impact on the action of the churches in society ... Possibly, the most significant achievement of the ecumenical movement has been its ability to encourage and nourish that dialectic of obedience and unity, even in situations where opposing points of view seemed to make real encounter impossible.[24]

In Wales, at least, the National Conference on Social Responsibility which was to be held in Carmarthen in 1970 would make a substantial contribution to the 'ecumenical mutual understanding on Christian social responsibility' which Abrecht longed for. In preparing for this Welsh Conference, the Geneva Conference and W. H. Pritchard's analysis of the social witness of Welsh denominations contributed extensively to its content and pattern. A paper which was presented to the meeting of the Council[25] reflects this combination of influences. One key theme was 'Revolutionary changes in society' and included technological and scientific developments, the continual widening of the gap between rich and poor in the world, and the worldwide struggle for public participation in political decisions rather than imposition by a minority. Another key theme was 'Revolutionary changes in Wales' that included relationships with England, nationality, violent and non-violent action, unity and diversity in Wales (including the place of the Welsh language), industrial changes, depopulation and the Welsh Sunday. It was suggested that the Conference should consider these issues in the light of work already being done in Wales, in Britain and through the World Council of Churches.

Analysis of the Pritchard survey led to three conclusions about the attitude of the denominations in Wales to social witness. First, they all recognized their social responsibility. Secondly, they all recognized their failures with regard to this responsibility. Thirdly, by concentrating on traditional social issues, they tended not to give sufficient attention to the main contemporary issues: 'Much of their witness is in the field of individual morality, or constitutes a defence against attacks on traditional ways of living.'[26]

'After a long discussion', it was agreed to hold a conference along the lines suggested. The invitation to the denominations to participate in the conference noted that the Council, on the basis of the analysis of their social witness, believed '[that] the time is ripe for the churches of Wales to move together towards a common approach to social questions'[27] and that, therefore, the aim of the conference would be '[to] survey the scope of Christian social responsibility in Wales and advise the Council on a permanent mechanism for effective co-operation in this field'.[28]

The letter concerned quotes from the Uppsala report:

> Through the scientific discoveries and the revolutionary movements occurring in our time, new possibilities and dangers are opening up to men [sic]. Man is lost, since he does not know who he is. But God acts anew.

The denominations were invited to appoint a total of 105 delegates and a number of Welsh bodies and movements such as the Welsh Council, the Welsh Joint Education Committee, the Welsh Office and the United Nations Association, as well as local councils of churches, were also invited. Seventy-nine people attended the conference.

Specialist papers on the themes of the conference were produced in preparation for the event. The paper on 'Technological, economic and social change' (prepared by a group in Aberystwyth) set the topic in its worldwide and national context and then reviewed the changes under three headings, namely, faith, personal and social morality, and the

Church and society. It maintained that the challenge to faith was just as great as the moral and missionary challenge:

> A result of the success of science, and particularly the success of the scientific method, is the undermining of the Church's authority . . . Many believe that the churches do not understand, let alone be able to direct, the powers which, for good or ill, mould society.

The paper on the second topic, 'Decision-making in economic and political issues', was prepared by a group in the Swansea area. For them, the root of the matter was that there was 'a huge challenge to bring more justice, and greater love, into the lives of people within and between the nations'. It was necessary, therefore, to consider questions concerning food and population control, the ways in which Christians could influence society, the effectiveness of the media in sharing information, the pressure on the welfare society and the need to reconcile 'the demands of local [rural] societies and those of large civic and technocratic societies'.

The group which prepared the paper on the third topic, 'Nationality and the Unity of Mankind', suggested that it was necessary to understand the unity of humankind and Welsh nationhood in terms of the coming and presence of Christ: 'If we are to say and do specifically Christian things in the situation of Wales and the world . . . it is necessary to base it all on the truth of Christ.'[29] They saw two dangers in Wales. On the one hand, there was the danger of 'exalting nation above moral law' and, on the other, 'behaving as if the hope for the unity of man meant destroying the variety of culture which characterizes creation'.[30] It was suggested that the Conference should concentrate on three aspects, Welsh Nationhood, the Welsh Language, and Methods of Fostering Change (namely, the tension faced in the World Council of Churches Conference in Geneva in 1966 between constitutional methods and revolution).

The fourth topic was 'Participating in decision-making and in community'. It was suggested that the complicated question of power and authority be explored. Three basic principles were suggested with reference to the contribution of Christians to society: the responsibility of every Christian to be informed and to think about the issues which face contemporary society; the responsibility of appropriately qualified and experienced people to contribute to political life and action; the responsibility of the Churches together to try to act politically in order to create a more Christian society. (These were accepted by the Conference as a basis for the churches' involvement in politics.)[31] It was also suggested that Welsh democratic patterns, both local and national, should be examined since these patterns were of key importance if people were to have a voice in decision-making.

This was an ambitious agenda which sought to face up to the fundamental questions and to root the questions and answers of the Geneva World Conference in Welsh soil. The Conference was held at Trinity College, Carmarthen on 14–18 July 1970. There were seventy-nine present, including twenty-four from the Church in Wales, eighteen from the Presbyterian Church of Wales, thirteen Welsh Independents, four English Baptists and one from the Baptist Union of Wales, four from the Roman Catholic Church (in attendance as full members of the Conference), two from the Methodist Church and two from the Religious Society of Friends. It was thus broadly representative of the denominational pattern in Wales. Amongst these, thirty-seven (about 47 per cent) were lay people and eighteen (about 23 per cent) were women. The fact that the conference had attracted such a good representation is one sign of its importance and significance in the expectations of the churches.

One key indication of its effectiveness was the final message and recommendations. The message rejoiced that the delegates discovered considerable agreement on social, economic, political and moral issues. They had also realized 'that the extent, the rapidity and complexity of the changes that are taking place in society demand a rethinking by our churches of Christian social responsibility and we are convinced that such study should be done by them together'.[32]

These two conclusions were important in themselves and, as a result, the main recommendation of the Conference was that there should be progress without delay towards establishing a Department of Social Responsibility within the Council of Churches for Wales, and that for three reasons.

First, there were a number of key tasks that called for the concerted attention of the denominations and churches, such as the need for dialogue with public bodies, to consider the question of national and social change such as the future of rural Wales, and the continuing issue of the role and future of the Welsh language. Secondly, delegates agreed that there was a need to foster social action locally, especially through local councils of churches. Thirdly, it was suggested that special attention be given to two 'public' issues, namely, broadcasting and the call for a Welsh Language Act (which was backed up by a conference statement setting the concern for language in a theological context).[33]

This Conference had a key influence on the Council's own social responsibility programme and on the denominational partnership that it fostered. It affirmed that responding to social, economic and political issues was essential to Christian witness in Wales and that only through partnership with each other could the denominations discharge this responsibility effectively. The conference also recognized that there was considerable agreement among the denominations on theological, moral and practical issues in these fields. As a result, it should be possible to collaborate on these matters through the Council for Churches in Wales. And although the focus for ecumenical engagement in social responsibility should be Wales and its people, the worldwide changes raised through the WCC conference (Geneva, 1966) and the social and economic injustice within developing nations were also central to the churches' concern.

The inevitable conclusion was that setting up a Department of Social Responsibility was regarded as an urgent matter and, in view of the pressing need for this initiative, the denominations were called upon to make a substantial increase in their contributions to the Council in order to secure a full-time General Secretary, an administrative assistant and an office. It was also believed that the agenda set by the Conference was so large and important that it would soon be necessary to appoint a full-time secretary to the Department. All this was seen as a venture of faith:

> [The Churches] will be setting out on a new and difficult journey which will make great demands on their resources. We judge, however, that it will be a journey of faith – faith in the victory of Him to whom belongs all power in heaven and earth.[34]

Nevertheless, the Council did not get a full-time secretary until 1977, and there were never enough resources to secure a secretary, either full-time or part-time, for the social responsibility work of the Council. However, a Department of Church and Society was formed. This was the main consequence and contribution of the historic Carmarthen Conference. The first meeting of the Department was held on 12 March 1973 with the President, W. Ungoed Jacob, in the chair. During the first months, it focused on laying the foundations of the work, on the basis of the recommendations and reports of Carmarthen 1970.

There were two main intentions behind the setting up of the Department: 'a conviction of the world's need for the freedom and fullness of life which Christ brings. Each of our churches in the past has seen social responsibility as an essential part of its witness' and 'a conviction that our churches should rethink together the nature of Christian responsibility and, where possible, act together on such issues'.[35]

It was realized from the beginning that it would not be easy to set priorities, since the field was so wide. In the words of the memorandum: 'The tithing of mint and anise has always been easier than pursuing the mightier matters of justice and mercy.' There was agreement, nevertheless, on three areas of work for the Department. First, worldwide issues, including 'One World' issues (this was the time of the report, *Limits to Growth*) and development, the search for world peace, and the effort to achieve a just political and social order in states such as South Africa and Rhodesia (later to achieve independence and be renamed Zimbabwe). Secondly, Wales would be a focus, especially on questions of nation and language, participation in local and national government, Wales and the European Community, education policy, employment, economy and the environment, the mass media, licensing laws and rural depopulation. Finally, it would be necessary to consider personal issues such as care and welfare, drugs, sexual morality and censorship, and Sabbath observance.

A broadcasting Committee was already in existence and some of these issues would be part of its responsibility. The Council had had an Industrial Committee since 1965 that had undertaken significant work in its field and would continue to shoulder the main responsibility for Welsh industrial and economic issues. During the following years, the Department concentrated its attention on some of the other topics, including self-government and the Welsh language,[36] economic and industrial issues,[37] racism and South Africa,[38] and war and peace.[39] To these we must now turn.

# ~ 6 ~
# The churches and self-government in Wales

> It is a noteworthy fact that nationalist thought in Wales has been guided by men [sic] with strong Christian convictions . . . [who] have all developed their nationalism on the basis of specifically Christian presuppositions . . . wishing to understand their political commitment in the light of the Christian revelation . . . [Yet for many] this line of thought [is] a perversion of Christianity. For them nationalism is a direct contradiction of the Gospel emphasis on the centrality of love, a pernicious undermining of the true internationalism of Christianity, a retreat into a nasty chauvinism, an attempt to transform Jesus Christ into a national mascot and plain treason against the message of reconciliation.[1]

This paragraph sums up key ways in which the relationship between Christianity and Welsh nationhood were understood during the last century. First, most of those who made a significant contribution to an understanding of Welsh nationhood, and the place of self-government for Wales within that understanding, did so from a fundamentally Christian perspective. Secondly, they believed that their understanding of nationhood sprang directly from their Christian faith and the testimony of Scripture. Thirdly, others believed with the same passion that nationalism – and, therefore, any efforts towards self-government for Wales – was in complete conflict with their Christian understanding that God's purpose is to unite the whole of humankind into one family in Christ, and that there is no place for nationalism in this divine purpose. As we shall see, these issues will appear repeatedly as we survey the way the churches dealt with self-government for Wales during the years in question.

In this chapter, some of the Christian interpretations of nation, government, language and identity will be considered and we shall also examine some of the joint responses of the churches to key events in the struggle for self-government in Wales during the last half-century.

In his essay in *This Land and People*, quoted above, R. Tudur Jones describes the national struggle as a liberation struggle which was:

> ... concerned with releasing the creative energies of the Welsh people so that they may live a fuller, more humane, more democratic life and so contribute responsibly to the making of history ... The struggle for a Welsh parliament provides some hope of giving structural expression to the deeply held conviction of the Welsh people over the centuries that the maximum diffusion of power amongst citizens and amongst the various societal structures that comprise the nation is greatly to be desired.[2]

Again and again, it was emphasized that the aim of the struggle was not independence but freedom: 'And the meaning of freedom in this matter is responsibility. We who are Welsh people claim that we are responsible for the civilisation and ways of social life in our part of Europe.'[3]

In an article in 1973, the then Archbishop of Wales, G. O. Williams, made the same point:

> If we care for our heritage in Wales, we have to concern ourselves with political questions. There is a place for the kind of nationalism that seeks to secure for Wales whatever degree of autonomy is needed to control vital decisions affecting the life of the nation. 'Independence' is a concept that seems to me to have little relevance ... The proper debate is about where the particular decisions ought to be made – the degree of devolution that the Welsh situation demands.[4]

It is fair to say, nevertheless, as we have already seen, that many influential people and 'ordinary' members of our churches rejected this standpoint completely. Consider, for example, this quotation from the work of Daniel Jenkins, a native of Dowlais, who spent virtually the whole of his career in England:

> A Christian interest ... [would predispose us], other things being equal, to support a wider and more inclusive loyalty rather than a narrow and sharply defined one ... The Ecumenical Movement

arose at least in part as an attempt to express Christian repentance for having so uncritically baptized national movements in the past [a reference to the two wars] and many older ecumenists find it depressing that the same is being done again in many parts of the world.[5]

If we look back at the period of the Second World War, we see that there had been very lively discussion concerning the relation between the struggle for self-government and what was going on at the time in Germany. One of the most notable Christians in these arguments was Professor J. E. Daniel, Professor of Christian Doctrine in Bala-Bangor (Congregational) College. In considering the dangers facing civilization at that time, he wrote:

> From the right and from the left, by international capitalists of the city of London and by international Moscowpolitans of the Labour Party, it is proclaimed that the chief cause of wars is Nationalism. The main cause of wars and the chief danger of civilisation today are the increased powers of the large states which have within them no true democracy. The only hope for civilisation is to curb them and the only weapon it has is Nationalism.[6]

Again and again, he declared his belief that any concept of self-government means:

> the subservient nature . . . of the state, the need for self-subsistence or 'economic nationalism', rejection of the capitalism of the free market, the call to defend the welfare of the family, the right of the common people to their own land, the importance of agriculture as a foundation for the economy of the nation, as well as the ideal of de-industrialising the South.[7]

During this period Daniel was very severely criticized – including by those within the churches – for refusing to condemn what the Fascists were doing in Europe and to support the military struggle against Hitler. For him, the great arch-enemy was Communism and therefore, he says, 'whatever the enmity between Fascism and Democracy, it turns to friendship in the face of the great enemy, Communism'.[8] This argument was a public and bitter one, with the correspondence between Daniel and the editor of *Y Llenor*, Professor W. J. Gruffydd, being particularly bitter and personal. Daniel defended Plaid

Cymru's policy of neutrality during the war because: 'the aim was not state tyranny, be it Fascist or Communist, nor the central power of a democratic government like England's. "Our aim is to make Wales self-governing . . . by so diffusing property that Welshmen rule themselves".'[9]

Densil Morgan concludes, in the light of this amazing correspondence, that the divide between the two 'Christian' attitudes was complete: 'On the one hand, enlightened humanism and its horror of political and religious absolutism of every kind, was the standard by which to measure everything, and on the other, the basic right of Wales to determine its own fate.'[10]

These are just a few examples of the obvious commitment of many of the church leaders in Wales not only to nationalism but also to self-government for Wales. As we shall see, these were also reflected in denominational and interdenominational decisions. It should be noted that some interpreted this support for nationalism, self-government and the Welsh language, not as part of the social witness of the denominations but rather as a (self-serving) aspect of their Christian mission to strengthen the churches in a period of decline. In a study which concentrates on analysing the response of the political parties and the Welsh institutions to the 'Welsh Question', Alan Butt Phillips came to the conclusion that nationalist movements had often received considerable political support from the Christian churches and indeed that the continued survival of the denominations and churches had been connected at times with the political success of the nationalist movement:

> In most cases it does not appear that support for the nationalist and linguistic movements among priests and ministers of religion is entirely disinterested. While many have an intellectual commitment to nationalism and a strong interest in the cultural development of society, many are too aware of the general decline of the hegemony of organised Christian sects and see in nationalism a way of restoring or preserving their social control over the populace, especially the young and thus arresting the decline of church influence.[11]

It is difficult to find any evidence which supports this thesis, namely, that Christians took up positions with regard to self-government and the Welsh language on any basis other than a genuinely Christian and theological concern. Nor is there any evidence for the claim that restoring the authority of the Church within Welsh society was in any way the impetus for the campaign. Indeed, it had been realized for decades that no political stances or changes in political institutions were likely to transform the churches' position within society or lead to an increase in their membership. Such changes, if they came, would be the consequence of totally different factors!

Naturally, there has always been a relationship between self-government and the Welsh language in the mind of the denominations and churches in Wales. Over the years, these two campaigns have gone hand in hand. Indeed, in analysing denominational responses, many believed that responses to the Welsh language were a measure of commitment to nationalism and self-government. This is a questionable conclusion. Without any doubt, for most of the period in question it would have been easier to secure interdenominational agreement on campaigning for the language than for self-government. There was considerable agreement on the one but considerable disagreement on the other. (It may be worth noting, however, that the establishment of the National Assembly for Wales in 1999 has created a greater sense of confidence among many, both within and outside the churches, that a strong element of devolution, if not of self-government, is greatly to the advantage of Wales and her people.) In this connection, it is interesting to note that Saunders Lewis, in his Radio Lecture 'Tynged yr Iaith' in 1962, gives priority to campaigning for the language:

> Perhaps the language would bring self-government in its wake – I do not know. The language is more important than self-government. In my opinion, if any kind of self-government for Wales was achieved before permitting and using the Welsh language as an official language . . . in the Welsh speaking regions of Wales, then the language would not have official status at all.[12]

On the whole, the churches and denominations in Wales have not accepted this reasoning. While recognizing the association between the language and self-government, campaigning for these two aspects of the life of Wales was kept separate, without in any way trying to decide priorities between the two issues.

## THE CHURCHES AND SELF-GOVERNMENT IN WALES

We will consider the inter-church responses to self-government in Wales by focusing on some of the key events of the last decades of the twentieth century, namely, the setting up of the Crowther Commission and its report as the Kilbrandon Commission in 1974, discussions concerning devolution at the time of the 1979 referendum and the discussions on democracy in Wales in the 1990s, prior to decisions being made about a Welsh Parliament or Assembly. A survey of the extensive denominational and interdenominational discussion at these times will give us a clear picture of the response of the churches to these crucial issues for the future of Wales.

Before going on to these responses, however, it should be noted that there was a special section on 'self-government and unity of man' in the Council's Carmarthen Conference on the Church and Society in 1970 (see Chapter 7). The section report reflected the division which was inevitable among the denominations in Wales, with some declaring that 'some form of self-government is necessary to ensure the greatest benefit to the people of Wales' and others urging caution until the churches had gathered 'all the information, economic and other, and had gathered a team of experts to examine these issues',[13] with a view to taking a report to the Crowther Commission.

The Crowther Commission was set up in 1969 as a Royal Commission on the Constitution of the United Kingdom, with very wide terms of reference, including every aspect of central government and local government activity. It had two Welsh members, Sir Ben Bowen Thomas and Alun Talfan Davies – both having considerable sympathy with self-government for Wales, and having close connections with the churches in Wales. All the denominations in Wales, with the exception of the Roman Catholic Church, presented evidence to the Commission. Not unexpectedly, the Union of Welsh Independents was supportive of the principle of self-government, as was the Baptist Union of Wales (which stressed that this did not mean separatism or insularity). The Presbyterian Church of Wales, in its evidence, emphasized that: 'only one thing would meet all the demands and give Wales the opportunity to live as a nation. Only the authority of the people of Wales over their own lives would be able to sustain and foster the values which the

## THE CHURCHES AND SELF-GOVERNMENT IN WALES

Calvinistic Methodists (Presbyterians) have tried to develop within the nation over the centuries.' [14]

In its response, the Church in Wales said that: 'disestablishment had been a blessing to the Church in Wales. The Welsh language had the same status as English in the Church. Any Council or Parliament should be an elected body.' [15]

The Commission worked extremely slowly. According to Kenneth O. Morgan, '[it] pursued its slow and deliberate path between 1970 and 1973, with only vague hopes that a new step forward towards self-government might result'. [16] Its report was published in 1973, the Commission having been re-named the Kilbrandon Commission by then, since Lord Kilbrandon was now the Chairman following the death of Lord Crowther.

> Every one of the thirteen commissioners agreed that the current situation was unsatisfactory; two of them advocated a system of regional councils for the kingdom in its entirety, while two others wanted the Welsh and Scottish Offices to have greater powers. The rest recommended an elected assembly for Wales, and six of them – the two Welsh members among them – wanted that assembly to have legislative powers.[17]

A working party was set up by the Council of Churches for Wales to formulate a response to the report. The report of this interdenominational working party recommended three general principles as a basis for their views:

(a) Churches have an interest in fostering a healthy and responsible sense of citizenship and a responsibility for encouraging this attitude amongst their members.

(b) [The importance of] the identity and distinctive character of the society and its people and a desire to see institutions which will sustain these qualities and which will be effective instruments for dealing with the problems peculiar to Wales.

(c) [A] responsibility to ensure that constitutional changes lead to improvement in service and do not hinder effectiveness in meeting needs.[18]

The working party believed that the setting up of an elected Welsh Assembly would be a considerable step forward and that it was to be welcomed, but it would not be enough unless the Assembly had appropriate powers and was more than an advisory body. There was agreement that the Council of

Churches for Wales should support administrative devolution to a Welsh Assembly. The working party was more uncertain with regard to the recommendations to transfer legal powers in some fields and the right to distribute financial resources but without the right to raise taxes. It had no opposition in principle to these arrangements, but it could not give its full support, because it did not believe that a sufficient majority in Wales was in favour of this arrangement. It feared that transferring these powers would be a complicated and slow affair. The working party believed rather that it would be better to delay with respect to this and seek ways of enabling the Assembly to influence legislation. This would enable quick action on the fundamental recommendation of an Administrative Assembly, while giving time to consider carefully the necessary steps towards an Assembly that would have more substantial powers. (It should be noted that the Council also gave considerable attention to the recommendations on local reorganization and the changes in equality of representation suggested by Kilbrandon and recommended that elections to the Assembly should be on the basis of an adaptation of proportional representation.)

This report was adopted by the Church and Society Department of the Council of Churches for Wales in July 1974 and sent to the Welsh Office and the denominations in Wales.

It took some years for the Labour Government to present legislation to Parliament to enact these recommendations. When it came, it led to the 1979 referendum. In the meantime, the British Council of Churches and the Council of Churches for Wales had considered devolution and had agreed on clear resolutions in its favour. In March 1977 the Assembly of the British Council of Churches received a report on 'Devolution and the British Churches' which was written by the Archbishop of Wales (G. O. Williams), Bill Johnson (Church of Scotland) and W. D. Pattinson (Secretary General of the General Synod of the Church of England).

It was the report's view that 'devolution for both (Scotland and Wales) is necessary now and . . . legislative devolution for Wales [is] as necessary as for Scotland'.[19]

It believed that the Assembly should have sufficient authority to have a real influence on the life of the nation, and that the

Wales and Scotland Bill fell short of these demands, seriously so on some issues. It saw the establishment of such an Assembly as an opportunity to create new social patterns (most particularly in the fields of industrial relations, social responsibility and education). It also hoped the Assembly would be able to raise its sights above the demands of nationalism 'to look to the developed and developing world. Christians whose first loyalty is to the man who died for all mankind cannot be simply, uncritically, nationalists and will always watch out for the dangers of any less inclusive loyalties.'[20]

In a letter to the Secretary of the Council of Churches for Wales during the period of preparation for the discussion by the Assembly of the British Council of Churches, Harry O. Morton, who was General Secretary of the British Council of Churches at the time, wrote: 'The significance of this occasion is to engage the English in having to think seriously about their future relationships with Wales and Scotland.' In his Foreword to the Report, he underlines this point: 'What will not do is for residents in England to continue ignoring the plain will of the majority of the Scottish and Welsh peoples. A change of heart among the English will greatly help all the major political parties to move quickly to an acceptable consensus and early legislation.'[21]

At the end of the BCC Assembly discussion of the Report, a resolution was accepted which recognized the need for devolution legislation to meet the special needs of Wales and Scotland, pressing for the powers which would be devolved to Assemblies to be sufficiently substantial to give them a significant place in the life of Wales and Scotland, and expressing concern that the unity of the United Kingdom be preserved. This was the first time, indeed the only time, that a British interdenominational body made such a clear and firm commitment to devolution. It was, therefore, a historic resolution.

Nevertheless, it must be asked how many of the Council's member churches and denominations outside Wales and Scotland would have passed a resolution in these terms in their own denominational assemblies. There is reason to believe that the British Council of Churches was ahead of many of its members, at the time, on this issue as on many others.

## THE CHURCHES AND SELF-GOVERNMENT IN WALES

In October 1977 the Council of Churches for Wales also agreed a resolution on Devolution:

> The Council of Churches for Wales . . . confirms anew its conviction that an Elected Assembly is essential to securing good government in Wales, to giving the necessary measure of devolution and democracy and to safeguarding the national identity of the people of Wales.
>
> The Council is concerned at the delay in establishing the Assembly and urges Her Majesty's Government to press ahead as soon as possible on this matter, since it believes that delay will make the situation worse.
>
> . . . The Council urges the Churches of Wales to do everything in their power to remind the political parties that this is an urgent matter, and calls on every Christian to contribute to this discussion in a reasoned and conciliatory way.[22]

This resolution was welcomed by a number of the denominations, particularly the Welsh Nonconformist denominations. After all, it represented the position of very many of them and it was good to have an inter-church expression of their stance. However, although the leaders of a number of the other denominations were supportive of the main thrust of the resolution, it did not represent the official view of these denominations. One letter was received from a priest in the Church in Wales – who had been very supportive of ecumenical activities – responding very harshly to the resolution:

> . . . the resolution on devolution I personally find totally unacceptable and believe to be unrepresentative of the opinions of the majority of my congregations. Therefore . . . I would prefer to have no further dealings with the (Council of Churches for Wales). Both the issues of language and devolution are extremely divisive, and in my opinion, it would have been wiser and more charitable to have kept them separated from a movement specifically designed to heal the breaches of the past and intended to bring separated people together.[23]

The reply which was sent at the time by Noel Davies, the General Secretary of the Council, sought to set out the ecumenical task in such a situation:

Any church council which does not tackle [divisive issues] is lacking ecumenical obedience . . . The ecumenical vision embraces the whole of life and involves an evaluation of and concern for the whole of society . . . On many points there will be agreement. On some matters, we will disagree and on those occasions we will wish to state our criticisms and seek in mutual love to clarify the issues, absorb the tensions and continue to grow together.[24]

In March 1979, the referendum on Devolution was held which totally failed to secure a sufficient majority in favour of the Bill among the voters of Wales (only 12 per cent voted in favour). According to John Morris, the Secretary of State at the time: 'When you see an elephant on your doorstep, you know that it is there.'[25] The general response of the churches and denominations in Wales, and that of their members, was no different from the response of the voters. Some who were enthusiastic about self-government supported the Bill and others, who were just as supportive of self-government, rejected the Bill because it did not meet the requirements at that time. Others, of course, were opposed to self-government, and therefore rejected the Bill. The truth was that the range of opinion within the denominations and churches was not very different from general public opinion.

The fundamental question for the Council of Churches for Wales was: What was to be done now? This question was discussed at its meeting on 21 and 22 March. Huw Wynne Griffith, who was Secretary of the Church and Society Department, wondered whether the results shed light on the churches' views on this matter. He questioned too whether the way in which the Council (and its member churches) drew up statements on public issues such as these and, indeed, the statements themselves, were effective as means of deepening understanding and developing the views of local churches. A former Secretary of the Council, Meirion Lloyd Davies, believed that the problems to which the Bill attempted to offer answers still persisted. He feared that the results could be misused with regard to future attitudes towards the Welsh language. He also believed that the campaign had not wrestled with the real problems, and that greater public education in political problems was needed before a referendum could be an effective means of evaluating public opinion. The Bishop of Swansea and Brecon[26] stressed the need to keep three things in mind: that the people of Wales have their own identity, that Welsh culture and the Welsh language have an essential place, and that securing the economic future of Wales was most important.[27]

In the meeting of the Council on 24 April 1980 (that is, one year later), a report on the situation in Wales was discussed and it was agreed to send it to the churches and denominations for discussion – even though it had not been accepted as official policy by the Council. It was a comprehensive paper which took a very broad perspective on the situation. It noted, for instance, that there was a growing threat to the future of Wales, that the Government could take advantage of the referendum to neglect Wales economically. The paper expressed the fear that Wales would be regarded as a marginal region unless there was a body that would represent the whole of Wales. Principally, it recognized again 'that struggling for national self-government and cultural identity are consistent with the claims of the Kingdom of God'. It should be noted, too, that, while it emphasizes the rights of the small nation, it lays the same stress on creating a multicultural society: 'it is necessary to strive for the political, economic and cultural needs and rights of a small nation in its relationship to a large nation . . . it is also necessary to work to make inter-cultural dialogue possible in Wales at every level of the nation's life.'

This was the last statement on self-government made by the Council for some years. The struggle for the Welsh language and for the expansion of Welsh-language broadcasting provision, most particularly through the fourth channel, continued. During this period, some of the denominations were continuing to make statements from time to time to remind their members, the nation and the Government that the problems had not yet disappeared and that there was still a need for a political structure that would effectively meet the needs of the people of Wales.

Ten years passed before the question of self-government received any substantial treatment again. By then the Council of Churches for Wales had ceased to exist and Cytûn: Churches Together in Wales had taken its place, with the Roman Catholic Church, for the first time, in full membership of the ecumenical instrument (see Chapter 11 below). But this change was more than a change of name and a widening of membership. It was also a fundamental change in the nature and purpose of the inter-church body in Wales. Cytûn would not usually make statements in its own name, and even less often in the name of the denominations and churches. Cytûn's basic task would be to foster a partnership between them and to enable them to come to an agreement with each other on policy and action. This was severely criticized by some, particularly the Welsh Nonconformist denominations which would have been willing to see Cytûn offer much clearer leadership on the issue of self-government for Wales than it did. On the other hand, it was welcomed by other denominations that had been very uncomfortable with some of the statements made by the Council of Churches for Wales in the past. There is no avoiding this tension.

With this in mind, in July 1992 it was agreed to initiate a process which would urge all the churches to give 'careful consideration, as a matter of urgency, [to] the whole question of democracy in Wales, so that we can set out clearly to our members and the public what are the theological foundations of the different viewpoints which exist among the churches and the denominations'.[28] The task of Cytûn in this matter was defined as:

> ... to try to give expression to united Christian opinion on the essence of democracy in Wales at the end of the twentieth century; ... to do this in an European context and in the light of the consciousness of our Christian partners across the world of their national and political identity; ... and to be prepared to co-operate with other bodies in Wales in relation to these issues.[29]

It was envisaged that this would lead to a report which would summarize the different viewpoints of the denominations on democracy in Wales and towards a national Consultation with the Welsh churches and denominations which would enable them to discern whether a 'united Christian view' on self-government for Wales was possible. It should be noted that this process had begun to some extent as a result of the annual meeting of the Campaign for a Welsh Assembly, and the invitation to Cytûn to be a member, along with the Welsh TUC and the Campaign for a Welsh Assembly, of a committee to organize a national conference to consider the next steps with regard to self-government.

In the meantime, a statement was made by the President and Vice-President of the Free Church Council for Wales, which was commended by the Presidents of the Welsh Nonconformist denominations and confirmed by the Free Church Council for Wales at its spring 1994 meeting. In it they called on:

> ... our brothers and sisters in all the churches of Wales to join in the campaign, through every legitimate means, to free the nation of the injustice and oppression of the colonial system which exists in Wales and to support unsparingly those movements which are working for the dignity and prosperity of the Welsh nation and for the justice of its claims to express and realize its will, through its institutions and its own parliament, within the community of nations.[30]

This statement was welcomed by many within the Welsh Nonconformist denominations and it was perceived as giving a lead to the other denominations and churches in Wales. The editor of *Y Tyst*, for example, supported it enthusiastically, regretting that Cytûn had not taken a similar stand and expressing the hope that Cytûn would accept a lead from the Free Church Council for Wales in this matter. But when the Cytûn Council met on 12 May 1994, it could do no more than agree to summarize these different viewpoints in order to discover whether there was a united opinion among the churches on the issue.

In the meantime, another process had begun. In October 1993 Cytûn had responded positively to an invitation by the Secretary of State for Wales, Mr John Redwood MP (issued during an interview on the HTV programme, Wales on Sunday). Mr Redwood indicated that he would be prepared to meet 'the spiritual leaders of Wales' to discuss with them 'the moral fabric of Welsh society'[31]. Following such a meeting (on 23 March 1994), a process was inaugurated by Cytûn which was coordinated by a Steering Group chaired by Dr Rowan Williams (who was then Bishop of Monmouth) and which led to the publication in June 1996 of *Wales: A Moral Society? (An ecumenical response to some moral questions in Wales).* Chapter 6 of that report focused on 'Governance' and included a wide-ranging exploration 'of the moral basis of governance and the effectiveness of current patterns of government at local, national and European levels in providing an adequate moral foundation and framework for individuals and communities in Wales'.[32]

Its examination of theological perspectives on governance suggested a number of 'guiding principles of a responsibly Christian theory of governance'.[33] These principles included: governments as 'servants of God . . . and communities . . . not masters'; the priority of maintaining human dignity and respect for persons; enunciating the absolute principles of peace, justice, mercy, love and forgiveness while recognizing that the means of their embodiment 'in civil life in a particular context are always relative'; dialogue with those in authority should always reflect specifically Christian attitudes and patterns of behaviour; collaborating in appropriate partnerships with other agencies; spirituality and social/civic regeneration are inseparable within the Christian mission.

The report also concluded 'that there would be agreement on a number of fundamental principles in relation to governance in Wales (which, for many within the churches, but not all, would imply the possibility of an Assembly for Wales)'.[34] Among these principles were the need to avoid absolutism, the importance of being broadly inclusive and accountable, the need to foster partnership and power sharing at all levels of national life, the centrality of the Welsh language and the importance of bilingualism and the goal of justice and peace, not only within Wales but worldwide. On the basis of these principles, the report recommends that: 'H. M. Government, and the other Parliamentary parties, should reconsider the case for a Welsh Assembly, on an equal footing with any Scottish Parliament, with legislative and fiscal authority, based on the principles outlined above, and set in a pattern of power-sharing within the United Kingdom.'[35]

When the newly elected Labour Government called a referendum on a Welsh Assembly and a Scottish Parliament in September 1998, this chapter from *Wales: A Moral Society?* became the basis of a Cytûn pamphlet offering guidance to Christians and churches in the run-up to the referendum. During this period also the Government had set up a

Consultative Group on the National Assembly. In May 1998, the General Secretary of Cytûn, Noel Davies, issued a response to its Consultative Paper, which examined the detail of possible legislation. Although Cytûn's response made a number of detailed comments, it generally welcomed the Group's recommendations:

> We welcome the Consultative Paper and, in general, agree with its main recommendations. We believe that an Assembly set up in accordance with these recommendations would be an effective and representative body and that the suggested committee structure would enable it to deal effectively with the range of responsibilities which it will have.
>
> We also appreciate the process of wide consultation . . . undertaken through the Paper and through the series of regional meetings throughout Wales. All this indicates that the Government and the Consultative Group takes public opinion seriously as it makes crucial decisions about this historical step in the nation's history.[36]

In the event, there was a sizeable majority in favour of a Scottish Parliament but a very narrow majority in favour of a Welsh Assembly. Nevertheless, on this basis, the Government proceeded with a Bill and the National Assembly was inaugurated on 26 May 1999 in the presence of Her Majesty Queen Elizabeth II. The events on that day included a service of celebration, organized by Cytûn, at Llandaff Cathedral, Cardiff.

In the run up to the inauguration of the Assembly, Cytûn convened a conference on 'Wales: A New Society', at Gregynog in April 1999, which brought together wide representation of church and national life in Wales. Its aim was to reflect on the importance of this highly significant step in the history of Wales and to seek to bring into focus, for those who would be closely involved in the Assembly, elements of Christian vision, principles and policies. In his keynote address on 'Democracy in Wales Today', the former General Secretary of Cytûn, Noel Davies, considered 'The Opportunity and Challenge of the Assembly for Wales'.[37] He highlighted three key values, namely, that it should be an inclusive Welsh community, that it should be a holistic and participative nation, and that it should foster a just society. In examining characteristics of the political process to be adopted by the Assembly, he highlighted principles which were developed in *Wales: A Moral Society?*, namely, taking relationships between different levels of government seriously, rejecting the methods of attack and confrontation, being open and transparent, and giving a voice to minorities. He outlined, finally, a theological and moral framework for the new society in Wales:

> Christians . . . will need to develop a theology of public life in Wales, a morality of civil society. In doing so, we will wish to elevate the value of the individual, created in the image of God, without denying the centrality of a flourishing sustainable community; we will wish to build a nation that is in communion with the earth, where humankind and the environment are interwoven; we will wish to develop a morality which binds the local and the national and the international, which binds Wales to the world; it will give greater emphasis to just relationships between peoples than to the needs of the market . . . The final test for every political system, every moral framework, every Assembly, is the effectiveness of what is done to strengthen the poor, to include those who are marginalized and give a voice to those who are voiceless. These must be the true characteristics of the new Wales.[38]

How does one weigh up the contribution of the Welsh churches and denominations to the struggle for Welsh self-government? Without a doubt, prominent Christians throughout the twentieth century offered to this struggle vision, devotion and leadership. The nationalist movement and the struggles for self-government would have been much the poorer without this leadership by prominent Christians. Indeed, it is doubtful whether the struggle would have continued at all – at some periods during the nineteenth century and early twentieth century – without their commitment.

It is just as true to say that a number of the denominations – most particularly the Welsh Nonconformist denominations – have been consistently and zealously supportive of self-government for Wales. It should also be remembered that the Welsh language would have died long since in many areas of Wales without the total devotion of these Welsh churches to its support and maintenance – a fact which it is easy to forget in these days of church decline, when the focus of Welsh life has shifted from the churches to other cultural institutions.

## THE CHURCHES AND SELF-GOVERNMENT IN WALES

On an inter-church level – through the Council of Churches for Wales and the Free Church Council for Wales – clear leadership was given in favour of self-government, in statement after statement. Through these bodies and their member denominations and churches, continual pressure was placed on government after government in order to ensure that the issue of self-government was kept on the political agenda.

It became clear that the aim of these denominational and interdenominational discussions was not political independence but freedom for the people of Wales to take responsibility for their future and the future of their nation. It was also emphasized that neither the churches nor their leaders had a vision of an insular, self-satisfied, inward-looking nation, but of a people who would work for freedom, justice and peace in their own land and for brothers and sisters in the family of nations in Europe and worldwide. Theirs was not a narrow-minded nationalism but rather a desire to see the Welsh nation make its contribution to the cultural richness of the nations.

The final paragraph of the chapter on Governance in *Wales: A Moral Society?* expressed the vision which had been central to all these efforts:

> A society which is built on growing individualism, self-centredness, unjust competitiveness and material greed is bound to disintegrate. Governance is fundamentally about developing responsible and accountable instruments which can create and establish communities of justice and mercy, where all belong, where personal dignity is affirmed, and where all are cared for *(worldwide as well as in Wales)*. This is not solely a task for government. We believe that the churches have a key role, as partners with local and national government, in developing this renewed sense of community in Wales.[39]

# ~ 7 ~
# The Christian witness in industrial society

The story of the involvement of the Council and its member churches, with the problems and challenge of industry, especially in Wales, reveals a number of very important aspects of the Christian witness, at a time in Wales – and in the nations of Britain and Ireland – when significant changes took place in employment and economic patterns within society in general and in the lives of individuals and families. Christian witness in industry was seen as an intertwining of pastoral care, prophetic response and partnership between the churches and industrial and economic life within Welsh society. This engagement led to a new theological understanding of the place of work and economy in God's creation and in human society.

Very early in its history, the Council agreed a resolution on unemployment in Wales to be sent to the denominations. Its main message was a concern for the pastoral care of people who were already suffering from the results of increasing unemployment in Wales:

> As representatives of the Churches of Wales, the Council wishes to declare its sympathy with all who are suffering in any way because of unemployment. The days are weary and full of anxiety for many. It is proper for us to call to mind the promises of God to his people in times of need.
>
> A special responsibility rests on clergy, ministers and officers of the Churches in these areas to keep in close contact with the inhabitants of the area, to care for those in need and seek help for them, to seek to safeguard social and cultural life and above all to bring to the people the comfort of the Gospel.[1]

A year later – in November 1959 – a resolution on pit closures was discussed which was introduced by the Union of Welsh

Independents, through Alban Davies (a congregational minister Ton Pentre) and Curig Davies (General Secretary of the Union). The resolution expressed a desire for vigorous campaigning on behalf of the coal-mining areas:

> ... we are very much aware ... of the dire effects of ... closures on our living communities, with the threatened recurrence of unemployment on an alarming scale ...
>
> ... [T]he churches ... should make representations to the Government for the extension of the economic basis of these affected areas on the basis of our deep conviction that the churches are deeply aware of their responsibility for the material and spiritual welfare of our people.[2]

This pastoral concern for industrial regions and the unemployment which was threatening them, became one of the main currents of the life and work of the Council during the next few years. This led to the calling of the first Welsh inter-church conference on 'Church and Industry', in Coleg y Fro, Rhoose, from 15 to 18 July 1962.[3] Sixty people from the churches and industry attended. There was a programme of lectures, group discussions and visits (to Guest, Keen and Nettlefold's steel works in Cardiff, where everyone was given a foot-long nail by which to remember the occasion). The total cost of the conference was £175, including accommodation for three nights for delegates and the cost of the speakers!

The opening lecture, on 'The Industrial Scene in Wales', was given by Brinley Thomas.[4] He believed that an 'exchange relation' dominated industry. It is something amoral and morality should not be forced upon it: 'We are all used as economic means ... in ways that do not harm us morally.'[5] He believed that one of the fundamental problems of the churches in their relation to industry is that coalfield workers still had a rural image, and when the rebellion against capitalism came, 'it was the non-Welsh, non-chapelgoing leaders who became prominent ... The chapels, with their rural spirit, did not have an answer to offer.'[6] But he also believed that churches had a relevant mission: 'There is an economic area which is not an area of concern for the Church ... but wherever man is used as a mere means, the Church should get involved and stand up for him.'[7]

## THE CHRISTIAN WITNESS IN INDUSTRIAL SOCIETY

A number of speakers made a significant contribution by exploring, in theological terms, the place of the Christian faith and the Church in industry. One of the main contributors was R. S. O. Stevens.[8] According to Islwyn Lake:[9] 'he stressed that there is one world and God has united himself with it . . . Within this same world one can discover God . . . The Christian is called upon to be Christ here in the midst of the situation where God is working out his purpose.' An extension of this was the assertion by David Lee (the first full-time industrial chaplain in Wales, serving in the Margan plant of the British Steel Company) that the important thing 'is that the Church shows that it is there and gives a new impression to people. It shows that it is flesh and blood and that its concern is flesh and blood.'[10]

This Christian principle of 'presence' was fundamental to the industrial mission of the time. Indeed, it remained so throughout the remainder of the century. This is the mission of God (*mission dei*), a God who is present in the world and Lord over it. It is the Christian's privilege to witness to this presence and to seek to enable the industrial forces of the world to recognize its authority over them. It was on the basis of this belief that industrial mission encouraged and enabled the churches to serve industry and strive for the welfare of those who work within it and the communities which are dependent on its prosperity. Because of this belief, Glyn Simon,[11] in his conference summing up, doubted 'whether it is true to say that there are areas of activity in industry which are "autonomous" and for that reason beyond the concern of the Church'.[12] He urged everyone to realize: 'that there is a gulf between church and industry. We cannot expect a quick cure for a process that has been going on for 180–200 years. It will be necessary to stock up Christian capital before it disappears completely.' He believed that the Church had a very important contribution to make given the alarming nature of the huge industries that were in Margam (British Steel in Port Talbot) and similar places: 'When a person is a prey to impersonal and pitiless powers, then our only hope is to safeguard the dignity of man as a child of God.'[13]

In his report to the Council, K. B. Thomas[14] recommended that the group which had been responsible for organizing this conference become an Industrial Committee of the Council of Churches for Wales and that a similar conference be held every two or three years, as well as one-day courses to train ministers and lay people in industrial mission. This recommendation was approved and implemented.

The Industrial Committee was formed in 1965 and in time adopted the following aims: to relate to relevant denominational committees (in Britain and abroad), to encourage discussions on the relevance of theology and Christian ethics to industrial questions, and to facilitate discussions on the mission and responsibility of the churches in relation to industrial society.[15]

In the period after the conference, the question of industrial chaplaincies came to the fore. Some chaplaincies had already been established, for example in Margam in 1960 (with a priest of the Church in Wales working with the support of the local free churches – the attempt to finance the appointment of a chaplain on behalf of the free churches was initially a failure) and in Newport in 1962 (with a priest of the Church in Wales and a minister of the free churches as part-time chaplains). The Mission to Seamen had been organizing a chaplaincy for the oil refineries of Milford Haven since 1954. By 1964 the denominations had collaborated to appoint an ecumenical chaplain in Wylfa (a nuclear power station on Anglesey) during the building period. As a result of these developments, the question of the ecumenical implications of such chaplaincies began to be considered and the matter was raised in the Council by the Standing Committee of the Methodist Church. The Church in Wales also was concerned that receiving a number of applications for financial assistance would force the Church to review its policy. It was noted in the discussion[16] that the Nottingham Conference on Faith and Order[17] had foreseen situations similar to Margam and Wylfa and had urged cooperation.

As a consequence, the Executive Committee of the Council[18] welcomed the opportunity to give its seal of approval to a meeting of full-time and part-time industrial chaplains to be chaired by W. Ungoed Jacob. The meeting[19] requested that it be recognized as a sub-committee of the Industrial Committee and stressed that there was a need for cooperation on chaplaincies and appointments in Wales in future.

The immediate consequence was to convene another national conference in October 1967, once again in Coleg y Fro, Rhoose, to consider 'The Churches' Industrial Work – a Pattern for Wales'.[20] The introductory paper to the conference, prepared by David Lee, was heavily dependent on the World Council of Churches' Commission on World Mission and Evangelism Conference in Mexico City in 1963. The theme of that conference was 'Mission in Six Continents' and radical suggestions were made in relation to structures for mission, particularly as a result of the worldwide study 'The Congregation's Missionary Structures'.[21] Lesslie Newbigin, who was the director of the Commission for World Mission and Evangelism of the World Council of Churches at the time, believed that the most influential sections were those on 'The Christian Witness to Men in a Secular World' and 'The Witness of the Congregation in its Neighbourhood' which emphasized that the churches' mission was indeed 'to six continents'.[22] Under the influence of Asian theologians, the belief 'that God is somehow at work in the secular events of our time, beyond the bounds of the Church' began to influence missionary thinking.[23] As a result, according to the report of Section II: 'The pattern of Christian mission in the secular world must therefore be one of constant encounter with the real needs of our age. Its form must be that of dialogue, using contemporary language and modes of thought, learning from the scientific and sociological categories, and meeting people in their own situations.'[24]

As will be seen, this understanding of mission would be fundamental to the further development of industrial mission in Wales for the rest of the period in question.

Thus, the starting point for David Lee's paper[25] was that the Mexico City conference had opened the way to a new understanding among the churches of the structures that are necessary for mission in modern society. He suggested that a number of elements should be considered in constructing suitable patterns, including the traditional structures (which could no longer support all the Church's mission), the human zone, specialist ministries and ecumenical projects ('industries are responding to mission approaches by saying that they can accept ecumenical rather than denominational work').[26]

## THE CHRISTIAN WITNESS IN INDUSTRIAL SOCIETY

Patterns of industrial mission in Wales were already developing along ecumenical lines, with the last to be formed (in Wylfa in 1964) having been planned and established ecumenically from the beginning. Whilst there was a need to consider the requirements of industrial mission when new industries are established, it was also recognized that the heavy demands of sustaining the traditional pattern of ministry put a strain on the resources and energy of the churches.

No one was in any doubt about the difficulties of this work. Since December 1964 efforts were made in Port Talbot to secure sufficient resources to appoint a full-time chaplain on behalf of the Free Churches, but, as noted, the efforts were a failure, and in March 1967 the endeavour was brought to a close. In a letter which was presented to the conference,[27] the secretary of the local committee, Ivor T. Rees,[28] expresses disappointment that the intention had failed, but reiterates his basic belief that it is necessary for industrial mission to be ecumenical in its nature and pattern.[29] He also stresses that all the local churches consider that the Chaplain (David Lee) represented the whole Church in his work: 'He possesses the full confidence of Anglicans and Free Churches alike, and his work is regarded as being fully ecumenical in its nature.'[30] It is also noted that Port Talbot's problems were not only local in origin. Rather, they derived from the attitude of the churches in Wales towards the Church's mission as such, of which industrial mission is a part. He therefore calls for a national scheme for Wales to be drawn up and supported by all the denominations.

The Rhoose conference in 1967 made a major contribution to this task. Eight recommendations were adopted, among them one which asked for urgent attention to be given to establishing industrial chaplaincies in Cardiff, Pontypridd and the East Glamorgan Valleys, Swansea and Wrexham. Numerous possible patterns were suggested, including the pattern adopted in Wylfa, namely, that one denomination (in that case the Presbyterian Church of Wales) paid the salary and the other denominations had a shared responsibility for the remaining costs. It was also recommended that setting up a local inter-church committee in support of the chaplaincy was absolutely essential and that the Industrial Committee of the

## THE CHRISTIAN WITNESS IN INDUSTRIAL SOCIETY

Council of Churches for Wales should be responsible for drawing up policy, promoting effective cooperation between the chaplaincies, organizing training, and taking initiatives towards establishing new work in this field. For the first time, representatives of the denominations and the churches in Wales, as well as specialists in the field of industrial mission, had adopted an action plan for industrial mission in Wales and recommended the most effective means of facilitating the work.

This conference was a turning point in the history of industrial mission in Wales. Soon after, the committee was strengthened in order make its work more effective. But there was one fundamental weakness – and this was a weakness in the constitution of the committee from the beginning (a weakness which was later reflected in the Network of Industrial and Economic Issues of Cytûn, which was the successor to the Industrial Committee). Membership consisted of specialists in the field chosen by the committee itself. There was never an attempt to ensure direct denominational representation. This was an intentional decision, as there was a desire to ensure that members of the committee had an expertise in this specialist field. The weakness, however, was the committee's failure, at key periods in its history, to ensure that the denominations owned and supported the excellent work that it did. A denomination could not be expected to support pioneering work like this without having a voice in the decision-making. This is a fundamental ecumenical principle. But the committee was strengthened from time to time by co-opting experts from among the churches as well as Christians who had responsibilities within industry, either as trades unionists or as managers.

Within a year, in October 1968, directly as a consequence of the Rhoose conference, the committee was informed by Morgan Mainwaring[31] that the Presbyterian Church of Wales was prepared to support a chaplaincy somewhere else when the Wylfa scheme came to an end with the completion of the building of the Power Station. In accordance with the recommendation of the conference and in consultation with the Board of Mission of the Presbyterian Church of Wales, it was agreed to recommend an appointment in north-east Wales, in Deeside and Wrexham. This was the beginning of the North

East Wales Industrial Mission, established in July 1969 with Arthur Meirion Roberts,[32] who had been the chaplain in Wylfa, as the first chaplain. For the first period of five years, the Presbyterian Church of Wales was responsible for the salary and a house for the chaplain, and the other denominations (in this case the Church in Wales, the Methodist Church, the Congregational Church of England and Wales, the Union of Welsh Independents and the Baptist Union of Great Britain and Ireland) were responsible for paying the other costs. As in the case of the Wylfa chaplaincy, it was thoroughly ecumenical from the start, with the Council of Churches for Wales being responsible for ensuring and facilitating denominational support and relationships. This pattern continued throughout subsequent years, with two chaplains, Michael Williams and Richard Kilgour, being priests in the Church in Wales, and one, Marcus Robinson, being a Presbyterian minister. Its ecumenical nature was also reflected in the joint trusteeship of the President of the Council and the Bishop of St Asaph. This was the general pattern commended by the Rhoose conference. But the other chaplaincies established in Gwent and Glamorgan did not adopt this structure, despite being thoroughly ecumenical.

In its report in October 1969, it was admitted that the attempt to establish a chaplaincy in Swansea and in Cardiff – jointly between the Congregational Church and the Methodist Church – failed 'due to lack of support within Wales at the local level'. The report recognized that '[d]espite the Rhoose recommendations of 1967 – ratified by the Council – which sought to develop industrial work in key areas, the commitment of the churches to this work remains as it was five years ago'.

At the same time, however, in his summer 1969 report, Arthur Meirion Roberts, in summing up his period as chaplain in Wylfa, wrote:

> ... greater understanding now exists between the churches in Wales, particularly in the establishment of future industrial work and in the deployment of manpower and financial resources ... [There is] a growing awareness of a changing social and economic pattern in Wales and the need for the Church to consider its responsibilities within such a situation.

While this was true – amongst those who were close to the industrial scene there *was* more awareness of the challenge of industry and a deeper commitment to Christian witness within industry – the fact is that there was no success in establishing chaplaincies in Swansea and Cardiff (which should have had priority as the two largest industrial and commercial cities in Wales) despite assiduous efforts for more than two years. In his report to the Council in October 1971,[33] the secretary, David Lee, wrote: 'The Committee records its disappointment that the churches in Wales are not responding to the challenge of mission in an industrial society, especially in the region centred upon Swansea.' Those words, written in 1971, reflect what was a continuing failure among many of the churches to engage with industrial and economic issues in a structured way, either locally or nationally and, in subsequent years, no new industrial chaplaincies were established in Wales and no new approaches to the challenges and needs of industry were developed. Indeed, those that currently exist are now themselves under threat.

In this same Committee report, the Council's attention was drawn to the growing problem of unemployment in Wales and it was agreed that the Committee should instigate a special consultation which would draw together experts from a number of related fields to examine the situation and bring recommendations to the churches. It was held in Cardiff in January 1972. Two approaches to unemployment were suggested, to be coordinated by the Committee. First, a group should be formed within the Committee to gather information from local and central government about planned industrial changes in Wales and the social effects of unemployment. Secondly, the Committee should act as a think-tank to examine long-term industrial planning in Wales. As a result, on 20 May, a delegation from the Council met with the Secretary of State for Wales, Peter Thomas (Conservative). It was led by W. Ungoed Jacob (Dean of Brecon and President of the Council), and the other members were Arthur Meirion Roberts (Chairman of the Industrial Committee and chaplain to the North East Wales Industrial Mission), Michael Williams (Secretary of the Industrial Committee), Ray Taylor (a Baptist minister who was an industrial chaplain in Gwent),

T. R. Coughtrie and S. Killen (who were industrial managers in Newport and Cardiff), and Erastus Jones (General Secretary of the Council). The aim of the meeting was to discuss some basic priniciples in relation to unemployment in Wales. The substantial presentations made during the meeting are indications of the direction of the Industrial Committee's thinking on the issue of unemployment, its causes and the appropriate response to it. In presenting some basic considerations, Erastus Jones began in a way wholly typical of his standpoint over the years: 'We are concerned with Wales.'[34] This led to the key considerations:

> Wales is in a condition of permanent differential vulnerability ... this produces (within our Welsh communities) alternatively acquiescence or lack of self-confidence and deep reaction ... It is the concern of the church not only to comfort the victims but particularly to pose radical questions to our society ... e.g. Can the will to create a worthwhile society in all its aspects be caught by the people themselves, so that they can discover how to participate in their own destiny. [35]

Michael Williams spoke on 'Wales within the European Community': 'We need to be sure that adequate representation is made regarding Wales as a "Regional Development Area".'[36] He believed that confidence in Wales was essential if it was to commend itself for European aid. Ray Taylor outlined the principle of 'total cost', which became one of the fundamental principles deployed in the Committee's analysis during the next few years when dealing with the Christian response to unemployment. Ray Taylor was responding to the increasing tendency that he saw in industry and government to make crucial decisions merely on a commercial basis, without giving adequate consideration of the human cost of these decisions. So he recommended adopting what he called a 'social audit': 'the costing [of closure operations] should become more comprehensive and inclusive ... the write-off of human capital investment in skills and the debilitating effects of continuing unemployment should also weight the account, even if they are not precisely costed.'[37]

In a statement immediately after the visit, the Secretary of State said: 'all the signs [are] of a resurgence of industry and this should make the employment situation easier in the future . . . He shared the concern of the council at the social effects of unemployment and would welcome the possibility of further contacts between his officials and representatives of the council.'[38]

The fuller response of one of the officials of the Welsh Office[39] was interesting. He recognized that the idea of total cost was important because it emphasized social aspects of unemployment, and difficult 'because it raises judgements about the balance and aims of economic organisation'. Furthermore, he believed it would be difficult for the Government to carry out policies based on this principle because the attempt by the Government to influence company decisions on the basis of such broad studies would mean 'a greater degree of state intervention than has been practised hitherto or indeed regarded as generally acceptable'.

During the same period, work was initiated to foster a relationship between the Committee and other industrial institutions in Wales. The Committee was represented by Arthur Meirion Roberts in a meeting which established the Welsh Trades Union Council, and George Wright[40] welcomed the opportunity to discuss common issues 'reflecting the ways in which the Church can make a real contribution in the industrial priorities of the Principality'.[41] In addition, conversations were held with the Secretary of the Welsh CBI. There was also an opportunity to discuss with the managing director of the British Steel Company in south Wales the company's plans for Shotton, Ebbw Vale, Newport and East Moors (Cardiff). According to the report: 'Our presence was welcome and productive.'[42]

The mid-1970s were a comparatively quiet period of relationship building, when the bulk of the work was done through the industrial missions. In 1974, Arthur Meirion Roberts was appointed Warden of Trefeca College and considerable difficulty was experienced in appointing his successor as chaplain in north-east Wales, and that, according to the Committee,[43] 'despite considerable effort on the part of the Council'. Michael Williams, his successor, did not start on his chaplaincy there until 1977. This was another sign of the lack of suitable people to serve in a specialist field such as this.

By the end of the 1970s, however, unemployment was critically high, and the Committee asked the Council for permission to start a research project on the problems of unemployment and the place of the Church in creating and changing attitudes to work, including the place of the Protestant work ethic. As part of this project, a national conference was held on the theme *Why Work?* in October 1979.[44] The fundamental questions were: what place was there for work in the life of individuals and society in the future? Did the churches have a responsibility to consider their place and responsibility within a society that was facing a new future when the old preconceptions about work would be either invalid or irrelevant? Some of the experts who were present foresaw a rapid increase in the number of unemployed in Wales during the next decade, from 80,000 in 1979 to 230,000 in 1991. (In fact, by 1984 – i.e. half-way through the period – 163,000 had registered as unemployed.[45] By 1988, however, the number had fallen, rather than continued to rise, to 113,000.[46]) The conference attempted to set these threats to Welsh society within a world context, and the trends in Wales were compared with economic trends in poorer countries of the world.

There was no doubt among the delegates that Wales was facing a crisis and that a swift response was needed. The TUC recommended steps to lessen the effect of these changes, such as reducing working hours, more holidays, sabbatical periods and more training in new skills. But another reform would be needed too, according to Clive Jenkins, namely, a reform of leisure. This crisis was seen as an opportunity to review the behaviour of society towards work, the place of work in human life and the standards of living which should be aimed at in the face of such poverty worldwide: 'that 90% of the world's population is living in poverty is an affront. Putting it right may mean a lowering of our own standards. What use can we make of the benefits (technology) can bring both . . . here and in the third world?'[47] Another consequence of this conference was to establish a working party to consider the theology of work and, as a result, a very significant volume, *Towards a Contemporary Theology of Work,* was published in 1982 (see below).

When the Industrial Committee met in January 1980 to evaluate the conference, it was believed that the beginning of the

Thatcherite era boded ill for the economic future of Wales. Already monetarist policies were seen which did not consider 'the social cost', and which encouraged a policy of conflict rather than cooperation and social planning. 'The consequences for Wales as a whole, its culture and national identity, (will be enormous) if its industrial base is destroyed.'[48] It was felt that the situation was hopeless: 'There is no light at the end of this tunnel.'[49] The Committee met again within a fortnight and it was again stressed, chiefly by Erastus Jones, that this crisis would have: 'consequences for the whole of Wales . . . [T]here is need . . . for the "prophetic word" which has its sources in something deeper than current economic or political ideologies and which can see further than the pundits.'[50] There was also concern about the political doctrine which was the basis of the economic strategy: 'the return to an emphasis on the competitive society, rather than the cooperative ideal; a pessimistic view of man as motivated entirely by self-interest, as against a possibly over-optimistic view which expected too improved [sic] social conditions, education, etc.'[51]

But there was a much more hopeful note in the report of the Committee to the Council in April 1980,[52] and that, not because the political and economic situation had changed, but because the Gospel offered signs of hope: 'It is not the business of the Church to sing laments; in the presence of death we are committed to preach resurrection . . . If deindustrialisation is inevitable and employment is no longer so readily and universally available, we may regard it as a problem – or see it as an opportunity. The Church must look for signs of hope.'

It sought to present a new vision for Welsh society:

> Christians need to have a clear view of the kind of society to which we should be working and the description of that society as 'just, participatory and sustainable'[53] is one which we commend for consideration. The Christian voice must surely be heard resisting a purely monetarist approach: the Bible sees wealth in God and in people, rather than in money and commodities, and we must insist on reckoning 'social cost' as a factor in any adequate evaluation. Certainly the social cost for the people of Wales of the sudden and huge addition to the unemployment queue will be considerable and in some respects [will] have consequences which are both damaging and irreversible.

## THE CHRISTIAN WITNESS IN INDUSTRIAL SOCIETY

Alongside these national efforts to understand and interpret the industrial and economic situation in Wales, the Committee was very busy calling regional consultations in a number of centres in Wales that brought together representatives of the local churches, local industries (managers and unions), statutory and voluntary bodies as well as politicians. These were held in Gwynedd (Caernarfon), Powys (Newtown), Clwyd (Wrexham) and Dyfed (Llanelli). An attempt was made through these events to urge local churches to be more aware of industrial developments in their areas and to be ready to respond appropriately: 'We believe that the Church has a decisive role in helping to restore to economic and industrial man a sense of his intrinsic worth, not as worker or consumer, but as "child of God". It can only do so by entering into the industrial world and finding people there.'[54]

But that was not the only pastoral contribution of the Committee during these years. In 1975, *Redundant! A Personal Survival Kit* was published (largely under the influence of Ray Taylor), and a second edition appeared in 1980. This was chiefly intended for individuals who lost their jobs. In 1979, *Redundancy: The Last Option* was published. It offered guidance to industrial managers and union officials when dealing with unemployment problems. A total of 20,000 copies of these publications were sold and *A Personal Survival Kit* was translated into a number of other European languages. It also led to the Manpower Services Commission's leaflet *Out of Work?* Over 500,000 copies of this were distributed free through Job Centres across Britain.

There is no doubt that the industrial chaplains and those who assisted them provided a very important Christian service to the world of industry and unemployment at a critical time in the recent history of Wales. By being at the heart of the situation, they were a presence and a voice of the Gospel in places where others in the churches had not dared to venture. They took every opportunity to interpret to others in the churches what was happening, and to urge them to be prepared to act 'prophetically' and 'pastorally' within their areas. And in all this, the Council of Churches for Wales was very supportive of these individuals and of the Industrial Committee which was a forum for them in their difficult and often discouraging work. However, few people in the churches heard their appeal during this period and the mission and financial priorities of the churches and denominations in Wales did not change very substantially as a consequence of industrial mission. There was continuing need for efforts to help the churches and Christians generally to understand better what was happening in industry, its effect on our whole society, and the challenge to our Christian theology. This became a priority for the Committee for the next period.

It was mainly achieved through three activities. In November 1980, a conference was held in Trefeca College, under the auspices of the Industrial Committee, on the theme *Wales – Making a New Future*. In 1982, *Towards a Contemporary Theology of Work* was published as an attempt to reconsider the theology of work in the Welsh context. In 1985, a leaflet on *Privatisation – A Dangerous Trend in British Society* was published, causing much discussion and disagreement at the time.

The main speakers at the 1980 conference were Charles Elliott[55] and Harold Carter.[56] Charles Elliott's topic was 'Wales in the World'. He attempted to compare what was happening in Wales with what was happening in the poorest countries of the world, basing his interpretation on the model of the centre and the periphery:

> Putting the national and international applications of the model together, we can say in Wales that at the national level we are victims while at the international level we are beneficiaries. We are both exploited and exploiters . . . There is a lot to be said for not being caught up in the centre and to maximise the satisfaction that can be found on the periphery. Can this make sense in Wales?[57]

In looking to the future, Harold Carter presented a mixture of problems and opportunities. For example, he believed that we were facing continual change in industrial patterns, that there was a need for entrepreneurial talent, that priority should be given to producing a workforce with the necessary skills rather than seeing education in terms of producing 'teachers and preachers', that it was necessary to realize that in-migration within Wales had its social consequences – such as estrangement from the local community – and that the changes seen were fundamentally inimical to the maintenance and development of the Welsh language.[58]

The conference emphasized Christian values and the need to focus on practical steps. A Christian is called to be realistic and hopeful. There was a danger 'that we could depress ourselves by our own analysis . . . But we wish to affirm that there is a future to be made . . . There is a need for realism but part of that realism must be confidence in what we have.'[59]

In Andrew Morton's words:[60] 'while resurrection faith is optimistic, crucifixion faith is realistic.'[61] There was also an emphasis on the quality of life: 'For the Christian . . . the industrial/economic process is not just about the creation of wealth but about the creation of worth . . . We have to ask how, in a society which has largely learned to value people by the work they do, people are to be given "worth" without work.'[62]

Practically, in the short term, there was a need to establish local plans to support the unemployed at a time of crisis; in the medium term there was a need to improve conditions on the periphery by enabling local people to participate more fully in planning; in the long term it would be necessary to develop 'life skills', since there would be no need in future for what we used to call 'work'.[63]

This conference – like its predecessors – represented a notable effort not only to interpret the situation in 1980 but also to point to a way ahead: 'The churches must recognize their responsibility to contribute their insights and thinking on these and many other questions if they hope to participate in making a new future for Wales.'[64]

Unfortunately, only a few listened to this call, partly because there was a continual failure to develop patterns of communication which would bring such issues to the attention of the churches and denominations in effective ways, and partly because the churches and denominations in Wales had not developed effective means – either denominationally or inter-denominationally – of responding to the challenge that the huge changes occurring within society during the period in question posed for Christian mission.

We have already seen[65] that one of the basic conclusions of the detailed consideration given to unemployment in Wales

## THE CHRISTIAN WITNESS IN INDUSTRIAL SOCIETY

was that there was a need to look afresh at the theology of work, and particularly at the Protestant work ethic which was the basis for the attitudes of post-Christian society in Wales and in Western Europe. A working party was set up which consisted of academics in theology and other fields, industrial chaplains and others with extensive experience in industry. The task of the working party was 'to examine the Christian understanding of work in human society'. Its report, *Towards a Contemporary Theology of Work*,[66] was published in March 1982. In his foreword to the document, the General Secretary of the Council wrote: 'This is no academic exercise; theology and action are interwoven and the author gives us an essential foundation for our search for new directions for the Churches' mission in our day. Furthermore, it is a significant contribution to the shaping of our society, in Wales and worldwide.'

In the same way, the author, Paul Ballard,[67] saw that here was an attempt to face 'all the symptoms of industrial decline and change, and the need to discover, often by painful experience, slowly and painstakingly, the shape of the future in our society: the nature of industry, the patterns of employment, the alternatives to presently assumed lifestyles'.[68]

The document stressed that this was a task in Christian morality with the chief aim of sharing general information which would provide 'the parameters of Christian judgement and a sense of direction'.[69]

There were five chapters: 'Development of Industrial Society and Work'; 'Concepts of Work, theological and ideological'; 'Biblical Perspectives; A Theme for Variations': 'God, man and work'; 'Indications for Variations on a Theme', and a final summary of the main conclusions.

In assessing the biblical testimony with regard to work, Ballard concluded that a new definition was called for. The following was offered as a starting point:

> Work is given to and for man, not man for work. The existence of man must not be defined by work or made dependent on work, however essential and proper work is, but he must be understood and evaluated as God's creature who can find meaning and reward and identity in the relationship of love that draws out adoration, fellowship and service.[70]

The attempt to deal with the main theme, God, man [sic] and work, which followed, took as its premise the fundamental ambiguity already noted. There was an inherent tension throughout the document between 'the ambiguity of human existence and the possibility of hope'.[71] These two currents ran through the 'variations on the theme' that were offered in the fourth chapter when considering the relationship between the individual and work, work and the community, and work and eschatology. The biblical vision of *Shalom*[72] was the key: 'Shalom . . . is the harmonious interweaving of responsibility and pleasure in and with and for each other in which work is not a burden . . . but a fulfilling necessity . . . Shalom holds the vision of prosperity . . . Wealth, not for its own sake, but as a condition of peace.'[73]

In a period of uncertainty and pain, the Christian faith emphasized two fundamental truths, according to the author, namely, that God identifies himself with the poor and deprived (so, Christians should be dealing with the challenge of unemployment and all its consequences), and that the Gospel is relevant to our strength as well as our weakness: 'It is therefore just as important for the Christian presence to be found (within rapid developments of technology . . . and economic points of growth) as anywhere else.'[74]

One of the main conclusions was that it was impossible to renew our theology for a new age without such involvement in the decisive issues of our time 'of which the problems of work, unemployment and economic change are some of the most crucial and immediate'. The conclusion represented a challenge to the churches and to individual Christians: 'It is absolutely essential that the word of judgement and hope which is the Gospel be heard. Christians know and will continue to strive to discover how it is that the heart of this secret is found in the cross and resurrection. And part of this will be to stand in and for the world in service, offering life through patience, love, caring and suffering.'[75]

The main contribution of this document was its very existence! A theological exploration of these themes had not previously been published in Wales. It offered a framework for constructing a Christian theology of work for a new age, an age which would bring in its wake enormous changes, beyond the imagination of those, in earlier centuries, who shaped the traditions outlined in the document.

It may be doubted still, almost twenty-five years later, whether the churches in Wales, either denominationally or on an inter-church level, have really tackled this problem. The world of industry, which has seen enormous changes, of course, during the last quarter century, especially in the heavy industries upon which south Wales depended, remains foreign to the churches, theologically and missiologically, and the faith, worship and mission of the churches in Wales are the poorer for it.

By 1984 the Tory Government under Mrs Thatcher's leadership had been in power for five years, with the free market economy and privatization (in industry and commerce as well as in the life of individuals and families) on the increase. In addition, the summer of 1984 saw the beginning of the dispute in the coalfield that had such a devastating effect, not only on the coal-mining districts but on society in general.[76]

Therefore, the Industrial Committee presented a paper to the annual meeting of the Council on 13 October 1984[77] on 'Dangerous Trends in British Society'. It led to a difficult debate within the Council. It was rejected and it was agreed rather to invite a small group to redraft the paper. In the end, it was published, not in the name of the Council itself but in the name of the Industrial Committee with the revised title, *Privatisation – A Dangerous Trend in British Society*. The *Western Mail* got hold of a copy of the original document and published a substantial article on its contents under the unhelpful headline 'Churchmen slate "menace" of Tories' social divide'[78] – and that in the middle of a miners' strike and the churches' attempt to contribute to resolving the dispute.

It concentrated on the two aspects of privatization noted above, namely, privatizing industries and public services (which was Government policy at the time), and the tendency (in the attitude of the 'right') to think that the fundamental principle in our society was the freedom, right and ambition of the individual (and his or her family). The heart of the leaflet's criticism were the references to the observation of the Prime Minister in an address to the General Assembly of the Church of Scotland, based on the parable of the Good Samaritan, that there was no such thing as society, and that the Samaritan would not have been able to help the traveller had he not amassed the personal wealth which enabled him to satisfy his needs:

> It was meant to legitimise selfishness, though not for its own sake but as a means to an end ... It was no less than cynical to use a biblical parable, which many of those most troubled would regard as authoritative, as a political lever ... It is indeed a dangerous trend when those who claim the moral right to govern are knowingly involved in subverting moral values and standards of behaviour, turning them upside-down and saying that bad is good. These changes in attitudes and values ... we judge to be the main aim of the Government's present policies.[79]

What did Christian tradition have to say about these tendencies? On the basis of key Christian principles, it drew the conclusion that the Bible offers us a vision which combines the personal and the social:

> ... we cannot ... find biblical support for a world view which equates the spiritual with the individual and ignores the ways by which the spiritual values are incorporated into our social structures. Nor can we find support there for policies which exempt the individual from responsibility for society, isolate the individual from others or ignore the biblical insight into the integration of the personal with the social.[80]

This leaflet was prepared by the Committee during the miners' strike. That was no accident. What was happening to the coal industry was seen as the most powerful example of the tendencies discussed in the leaflet which gave considerable space to analysing what happened. It will be instructive, therefore, to examine the churches' response to this crisis in the mining industry.

# ~ 8 ~
# The churches and the dispute in the coal-mining industry

The response of the Welsh denominations to the 1984–5 dispute was a notable, if not unique, example of Christian witness in a social crisis during recent times. It is very doubtful whether this response would have been possible had it not been for the contribution of the Industrial Committee to the Council's and the denominations' understanding of the challenge of Christian witness in the world of industry over the previous twenty years. There was deeper consensus and broader common action than at any time since 1956, and no joint action by the churches received so much media coverage. Consequently, it deserves special study in order to interpret the lessons learnt, not only with respect to the churches in the coal-mining areas in particular but also in relation to the way in which the churches' partnership in response to the challenges of community and nation could be strengthened.

It must be admitted that the churches entered into the situation rather slowly and that, in the beginning, there were few statements from churches and denominations. The first step for the Council of Churches for Wales, as such, was the resolution in the Annual Meeting of the Council in Aberystwyth on 12 October 1984 on 'The Future of the Coal Industry within the Future of Wales':

> In view of the importance of the coal-mining communities within the life of the whole of Wales, the threats to communal unity, justice and compassion within our society, the churches' involvement in those communities over a long period, and their fundamental task of trying to discern the will of God for Welsh society, we believe that the future of the coal industry should include the following:

It calls for a broad debate about energy policy, concentrating on one of the most natural sources of energy, coal. The debate should be not only about profit but about the stewardship of God's natural gifts for the benefit of all.

In this debate, particular note should be taken of the wisdom and skill which the miners have acquired over a century and a half. The calamitous parable of Aberfan, where the experts were wrong and the local people were right, is a permanent warning. There is no satisfactory future for the industry without full and responsible partnership between the miners and their representatives.

In assessing the future of the mines, the total costing must be considered. If the word economic (or uneconomic) is used, it should include the high cost of unemployment, which also includes the costs of health, housing and education. The Council of Churches for Wales has debated this at the Welsh Office in an earlier era of unemployment.

Compassion has characterised the main direction of Britain's social policy since the last war. It needs to be reasserted here, since the total cost must include the intangible elements of personal and interpersonal unhappiness.

When, by mutual agreement, mines have to close, there should be a firm policy of investing in new industries in the coalfield in order to secure jobs within this generation and the generations to come.

[We recall that a Conference of Christian Denominations in South Wales, during the depression, initiated an idea and campaign which led to the establishment of the Treforest industrial estate, the first predecessor of the Welsh Development Board. It was never enough – but it was the basis of further developments.]

An urgent national effort is essential to confront questions about the future of the coal industry and the coal-mining areas, within the context of the economy of Wales. In this we are confident that Welsh leaders of the National Coal Board and Welsh leaders of the National Union of Mineworkers are loyal to Wales, and we believe that there is here a basis for co-operation, and the co-operation of the wider society, including the churches, which have a commitment to Wales through the Council of Churches for Wales, is central.[1]

This resolution was drawn up by the officers of the Industrial Committee of the Council and it reflects many years of industrial experience in Wales through industrial chaplains and centres such as the Blaendulais Ecumenical Centre and

Tŷ Toronto in Aberfan (both under the direction of Erastus Jones). The reference to the 'significance of the coal-mining communities within the total life of Wales' and the 'fundamental task of trying to discern the will of God for Welsh society' expressed what was fundamental to the work of the Industrial Committee from the start, namely, that this activity had to do with the mission of the Kingdom in Wales. This was the answer to those who complained (as did someone from Llanishen) that 'the proper job of the Church is to worship God and proclaim the Gospel' and that consequently it should not be involved in such a dispute. This statement was also significant in that it raised the long-term as well as the short-term questions that were capturing the headlines at the time. Such expressions as 'energy policy', 'compassion', 'investing in new industries', 'the total cost', and 'the future of the coal-mining communities' would be of key importance in later discussions and statements.

Although this resolution was passed unopposed, not everyone in the churches was comfortable, and it was interpreted in a headline in the *Western Mail* a few days later as 'Churches side with miners'. The response of the Secretary of State for Wales, Nicholas Edwards, in a letter on 6 November 1984, was an interesting one:

> These are the natural worries of those whose future and way of life is linked to the future of the mining industry and your Council's resolution properly highlights major issues ... [T]he dispute has shown the harsh reality of what is possible when the pursuit of economic objectives by leaders of the NUM is carried to extremes and breeds violence, intolerance and intimidation ...
>
> We are fully committed to a strong and viable coal industry and are prepared to see substantial levels of investment ...
>
> Investment in new industry is the way forward ... These are acts of economic planning. They are also acts of compassion and caring ... But in (turning to the future) let us not forget that the actions of the current NUM leadership are ... threatening many of the values on which our social and religious structure depends.

On 19 November, in response to the invitation of the National Union of Mineworkers to churches (among other movements) to be more proactive in the dispute, Gronw ap Islwyn and Noel Davies (ministers with the Union of Welsh Independents),

Douglas Bale and John Morgans (ministers with the United Reformed Church) accepted an invitation to hold secret discussions with the south Wales branch of the National Union of Mineworkers (NUM) and the South Wales Director of the National Coal Board (NCB). The aim of this meeting was 'to listen to the opinion of the two bodies with respect to the current state of the dispute, to discover how they saw the possibilities of moving towards agreement, and to assess whether the churches had a role to play'. They were there as individuals and in no way as representatives of their denominations or organizations.

After these visits, some days were spent evaluating the significance of what was discovered and trying to draw conclusions which would offer a way ahead. Three conclusions were arrived at. First, one could discern common ground between the NCB and the NUM in Wales on a number of key issues. These included confidence in the future of the coal industry in Wales, the need for disciplined, skilled and loyal workers, the need for experienced and compassionate managers, the interdependence between the coal industry and the coal-mining communities, the need to secure agreement through negotiation, and that the future of the industry was bound up with the decisions of wider society. Thus, on the basis of this understanding, the group urged that the British talks between the NCB and the NUM should restart speedily. Secondly, it was believed that the situation called for setting up an Independent Review Body 'to consider carefully the future of the coal industry in the United Kingdom and to present their conclusions to the British Coal Board, to the National Union of Mineworkers and the Government, so that they might take responsible decisions together'. It was believed the Review Body should be asked to examine long-term energy policy and the needs of the communities which buy and produce coal. Thirdly, the churches were called upon 'to co-operate with each other and the wider community . . . in the task of bringing healing and reconciliation.' It was believed that these conclusions had general relevance and they were shared with the denominations, the inter-church bodies in Britain and other bodies that were involved in the dispute.

A statement by the group of four was released at a press conference in Cardiff on 3 December 1984. There were six journalists present, and the group was accused of being naive and ignorant! This was not an encouraging beginning.

Simultaneously, the conclusions of the group were shared with the Secretary of State for Energy, Peter Walker MP. In his reply dated 21 December, he noted that independent reviews had already been held and they were in agreement that there needed to be a reduction in the industry's ability 'to bring their capacity more into line with present and foreseeable demand levels and to make the industry more efficient. The NCB's proposals are intended to secure for the industry a viable and long-term future.' While welcoming any steps which would ensure that the miners return to work, 'it must be on a basis that can offer the industry a healthy and viable future. So far, Mr Scargill [president of the National Union of Mineworkers] has not shown himself to be interested in such a settlement.'

On 30 November David Wilkie was killed. He was driving a vehicle that usually took strike-breaking miners to work. He was killed when a large piece of concrete was dropped from a bridge across the Heads of the Valleys road near Rhymney in south Wales. Everyone was shocked. This was one of the most terrible and violent tragedies in the whole dispute, certainly in south Wales. How were the churches to respond to such a tragedy? Was not any hint of support for the miners' cause a sign that the churches were siding with violent men who had no respect for the value of the life of individuals? These were difficult days.

The Bishop of Llandaff, the late John Poole Hughes, was one of the first to respond publicly. In his sermon at David Wilkie's funeral at St Mary's Church, Glyntaf, Pontypridd, on 11 December, he said:

> The best we can do now is to dedicate ourselves anew to repairing the evil that has arisen among us. That evil is the result of intransigence in *many* quarters and the tragedy is the inevitable result of escalating violence once the path of negotiation seems closed . . .

> Would it be possible for some sort of moratorium to be agreed, allowing for an immediate return to work without prejudice to tactical gains so far achieved . . . ? Then an impartial board might be set up to look at the wider issues involved in an energy policy for the whole country.

There was a report of the Bishop's words in the *Western Mail* on 13 December and it was noted that this recommendation stemmed from the document which was presented by the group of four. In the same report the following observation was made: 'a major church initiative to try to break the deadlock is gathering momentum and could be taken up at the highest level nationally.' This was the first reference in the Press to the recommendations of the churches. From now on these efforts would attract considerable attention. One of the main reasons for this was that the Council of Churches for Wales and the leaders and chief officers of the denominations adopted the recommendations. On 6 December, unanimous support for the recommendations (including the call for the setting up of an Independent Review Body to examine the future of the industry) was given by the Executive Committee of the Council. In a letter to the denominations on 12 December, it was noted that experts supported this recommendation 'in the belief that it is one of the ideas that could make a key contribution to the much-needed discussion about the future of the industry'. In the same letter, the leaders and chief officers of the denominations were invited to give their personal support to the Executive Committee's resolution. It was believed that 'such a lead by leaders of the churches would be a great help towards ensuring that those who have responsibility for the future of the industry take effective note of these recommendations'.

By 14 December, the leader or senior officer of every member church and denomination of the Council, as well as the Roman Catholic Archbishop of Cardiff, had agreed to the resolution. On the basis of this agreement, a letter was sent to the Prime Minister – outlining the agreement which had been reached – in the name of the ten denominations. This was no longer an unofficial campaign by a group of four ministers but a concerted effort by leaders of all the denominations to speak with one voice in the name of the denominations in a dispute which was having an increasingly deleterious effect on individuals, communities and the nation. The letter was sent on 14 December in the belief that the recommendations could 'offer a constructive framework for restarting negotiations'.

The response of the leader of the Opposition, Neil Kinnock MP, was very positive. He applauded the recommendation for an Independent Review Board, since the Government did not have a composite strategy for the energy industries and the communities which were dependent on the coal industry. Unfortunately, the Prime Minister's response was not so positive. In an interview with the *Western Mail* (15 January 1985), she was asked for her response to the letter. She refused to comment directly on its contents. Rather, she believed that the next step in the dispute would be that more people would return to work and confirmed that there was no intention to hold another review. When she was asked a second time, her reply was the same: 'The real way to end the strike is the way that is happening' (by the middle of January, people were beginning to return to work), 'and it is very encouraging indeed.' And there was no change in the Government's attitude towards the efforts of the denominations for the remainder of the dispute.

Meanwhile, a start was made on implementing the third element of the group's recommendations, namely, promoting and supporting the pastoral work of the churches in the coal-mining communities. Nationally, the main vehicle for this was a hastily convened conference in the Town Hall, Merthyr Tydfil, on 14 December. About forty ministers and priests came together from mining areas in south Wales to share experience and to learn from each other. In his opening address, the Archbishop of Wales, Derrick Childs, said that the churches and their ministers were involved in this crisis, locally and nationally, 'because the pressure of the Christian Gospel is on us'. He saw this particular dispute in the context of the revolutionary changes which had happened to our society since the Second World War. He believed that these changes were behind much that had happened in south Wales, as in other regions. Pastoral care of individuals and communities would call for sensitivity to these influences on individuals and families:

> Are we not witnessing not only the end of a particular industrial phase in human history but also the exposure of the exhaustion in our own day of the spiritual capital created and bequeathed to us by those who have gone before us?

He went on to note the steps in pastoral care of communities: earnest and continual prayer that people listen to the call of the

Prince of Peace and proclaim, through actions, a spirit of compassion and support in suffering that could lead to a readiness to forgive.

One of the most important conclusions of this conference was that one could not separate the pastoral from the political; the one depends on the other. Providing care requires a common striving to alter causes of individual and community suffering. It also called for the development of a network of community care in order to share experience and gain a common understanding which would be a basis for the future. These networks would include not only churches but groups of all kinds which would offer care in the community. Most of all, the ministers who came together in Merthyr stressed that the chief need was hope for the individuals and communities who were at the end of their tether. Fundamentally, this could well be the greatest contribution of the churches in Wales. In his sermon (on the theme 'The Cost of Hope') in Durham Cathedral on the day of his enthronement as bishop there (during the dispute), David Jenkins said: 'There is the power and possibility (under the almightiness of God and through the down-to-earth presence of God) of hope in our present discontents.'[2] He went on to say that 'a negotiated settlement which is a compromise and demands of us all further work on the problems both of the miners and of society at large is the only hopeful thing'.[3] In these terms, the recommendations of the churches did express hope, even if they were not fruitful in other ways.

The period over Christmas and the New Year was very quiet as far as the churches' efforts were concerned, but on 8 January 1985 the churches' plan was backed by the National Executive Committee of the NUM and, on the same day, the *Western Mail*'s editorial gave it enthusiastic support:

> The proposals [of the Welsh churches] . . . take an impressive look at the problems facing the industry after the strike has ended . . . The churches' proposals rightly call for a broadening of coal policy to take in the full scope of the country's long term energy needs and resources . . .
>
> It is possible to hope . . . that the churches' leaders' far-seeing proposals may not be totally at cross-purposes with the Government's and Mr. McGregor's thinking.[4]

Two days later, an article by Mike Smith, Industrial Editor of the *Western Mail*, spoke of the growing support for the plan amongst members of parliament and noted that an early day motion in the House of Commons supported it. It was also reported that the President of Plaid Cymru, Dafydd Ellis Thomas MP, had called on the Prime Minister to act on the basis of the churches' proposals, calling them 'the collective view of Wales'.[5]

During this period, the campaign was gathering strength day by day, with frequent mention in the press and broadcasting media, and numerous meetings with individuals and key committees in Wales and London. On 15 January, a meeting of Welsh denominational leaders and senior officers was held to receive reports on the latest developments and to plan the next steps. The following day, the *Western Mail*'s editorial announced: 'It is vital that hopes of a negotiated peace in the coal industry should be kept alive. Those hopes have had the biggest stimulus in months from initiatives by the leaders of the churches in Wales.'[6] The editorial next day expressed considerable concern that Peter Walker, the Minister of State for Energy, had rejected the proposals, in spite of the expert advice obtained when drawing them up. At the time, it was unbelievable that measures which had attracted so little attention at the beginning of December 1984 had become one of the most central elements in the Press's treatment of the dispute by the middle of January 1985.

The consequence of this was that, on 16 January 1985, a basis for negotiations between the National Coal Board and the National Union of Mineworkers based on the proposals and discussion of the Council of Churches for Wales was made public. The substantial support received from a broad representation of public opinion in Wales, and to some extent in the rest of Britain, gave the churches the confidence to offer three steps towards a just resolution of the dispute. First, the Government was called upon to establish an Independent Review Body. Secondly, it was suggested that no coal mine should be closed until a report of the Review Body was presented, except on the basis of safety or because the supply of coal had run out. Thirdly, it was recommended that the Review Body should present its report by a date to be agreed by the parties in the dispute. It was believed that this would be a sufficient basis to restart the negotiations between the Board and the Union and could lead to ending the strike.

On 23 January, representatives of the churches (the Anglican Archbishop of Wales, the Roman Catholic Archbishop of Cardiff, Douglas Bale, Noel Davies, John Morgans and Dafydd Owen) were invited to discuss this plan with Peter Walker MP and with the leader of the opposition, Neil Kinnock MP. The plan was totally rejected by Peter Walker for the same reason as before. According to a spokesman for the leaders, Noel Davies: 'there was no encouragement at all for the kind of proposals we have made so far . . . Mr. Walker said that [our] plans . . . would only delay decisions that had to be faced now.'[7]

A week later, a representative group returned to London to meet with the Chairman of the National Coal Board and the following day with the Executive Committee of the National Union of Mineworkers. The response of the former – as might have been anticipated – was negative, while the latter welcomed the efforts. Nevertheless, there were grounds for believing that the churches could act as mediators between the parties, and in order to facilitate this task, a 'basis for negotiations' was drawn up in the light of these meetings, which was made public on 1 February. It was accepted by the Union but not by the Board. However, despite these best efforts, negotiations did not re-commence and at the beginning of March the miners started going back to work. They did this with sadness but also with honour, even though they and the churches in Wales realized, in the words of John Davies, that 'Despite the suffering and solidarity, the strike furthered the very process it was intended to avert.'[8]

Enormous energy was given to sustaining the constant efforts of the churches over a period of four months, not only among the national leaders but also in local communities throughout the coalfield. It was a painful experience for all those involved to see that efforts to secure justice and the future of the coal-mining communities did not win the day, and that the omens were pessimistic for many of these communities. Twenty years later, these prophecies have been largely fulfilled and the coal industry in south Wales has been largely decimated.

## CHURCHES AND DISPUTE IN THE COAL-MINING INDUSTRY

When the significance of what happened was examined in the spring meeting of the Council on 25 April 1985, the suggestion was made that the future of the coal industry in Wales should be reviewed in the wider context of an energy policy for these nations, as recommended by the Council throughout this dispute. Six months later, in the Annual Meeting of the Council on 2 November 1985, the following resolution was agreed:

> That a review body be set up to examine the future of the coal industry and the coal-mining communities in Wales, which would concentrate on the needs of the neighbourhoods and the positive response of the churches to the crisis in these areas; [that] a review body should invite varied evidence over a period of about a week; and that a report, which would include general recommendations as well as recommendations to the churches, should be published as soon as possible.[9]

It was also agreed that not more than £2,000 should be spent on this review.

When the meeting of the Executive Committee on 2 December 1985 considered how to put the resolution into practice, decisions concerning the future of the industry and the communities had already been made. The task for the churches would be to come to terms with these changes. This was a call to mission. It was agreed to concentrate on analysing the crisis, examining the theological implications and preparing a programme for the churches' response in mission and witness. The Council stressed that this should be a programme priority for the Council and that the churches should be challenged to release resources to enable the Council to do the work with all speed. Alas, in the next meeting of the Council on 10 March 1985, it was reported that no further steps had been taken, and there is no further reference to this proposal.

In attempting to evaluate this response, the fundamental question remains: what was its significance in terms of Christian witness? A number of very important lessons became clear.

First, the churches acted in the belief that responsible stewardship of the resources of creation is an essential aspect of our Christian obedience. This was the basis of the resolution of the

Council of Churches for Wales on 12 October 1984: 'The debate should be not only about profit, but about our stewardship of God's natural gifts for the benefit of all.' This is why the need for an energy policy became so important. Stewardship of creation calls for a just balance in the use of resources, for ensuring that sufficient energy resources are available for the future, and for rejecting the economic logic which enforces increasing dependence on nuclear power without caring too much about the human price of such a policy in the future. It is interesting to note that twenty years later, when the supply and environmental cost of coal is being increasingly questioned, the issue of the potential and danger of nuclear power as a source of essential energy is being debated once again and a new commitment to nuclear power for energy production is likely.

The WCC's *Justice, Peace and the Integrity of Creation* process (initiated at the Vancouver Assembly in 1983) reminded the churches anew that the faith of the Church is in God the Creator, a God who is set on rescuing a creation which is being trampled by human sin and selfishness. A responsible attitude towards energy resources is essential to our obedience to the purpose of God, 'namely, that the universe, everything in heaven and on earth, might be brought into a unity in Christ' (Ephesians 1:10).

Secondly, the campaign threw new light on the nature of economic decisions within our society. It was central to the dispute – indeed, in one sense this was the heart of the debate – that economic decisions were being seen in isolation from their effects on individuals, families and communities and, indeed, on the future of Wales itself. The title of the Council's resolution was significant in this context, 'The Future of the Coal Industry in the Context of the Future of Wales'. In the churches' discussion and reflection, defining the terms 'economic' and 'uneconomic' became extremely important. For instance, the idea of 'the total cost', that is, not only the financial cost but personal, community and national costs, became central – an idea which reflected the analysis made by the Industrial Committee years previously. There was a complete failure to get the authorities to recognize this understanding. The question is: why this failure? The answer was suggested in the paper on *Dangerous Trends in British Society*:

... the disproportionate increase in long-term unemployment, in poverty, in divided families and communities, in conflict between allies and colleagues, in the erosion of hope, in the feeling of powerlessness and despair and ... an increase in most measures of social and personal disturbances ...

The Government ... has exercised a covert influence on the dispute ... by a shrewd assessment of how people and groups are likely to react when their own interests are set against the interests of others, when the immediate benefits are set against the long term and when private and personal considerations are set against those of the group.[10]

In the succeeding years, these divisions did not diminish. Indeed, it could be argued that they have intensified. Certainly, in the years since then, the challenge which faced Christians during this dispute, namely, to try to discover a vision of human society which reflected the foundations and ideals of the Kingdom of God, in justice and interdependence, where those who are rejected become instruments of God's world-transforming judgement, so that all yield their own economic claims to each other, has remained as powerful as ever.

Thirdly, and more practically, new partnerships were created through this dispute. In many areas, the churches cooperated with other movements within the community to meet the material needs of the miners' families and to express their solidarity with their stand. Many feared that these would be lost when the dispute came to an end, and that is what happened in most of the areas. But, as has already been seen, the partnership between the denominations, and especially their chief officers and leaders, was a key factor in the churches' engagement in the dispute. One leader said that this cooperation 'has done more for ecumenism than anything else'.

At the end of the dispute, the Council recognized it was necessary to build on this partnership by developing the fullest cooperation possible between the denominations in matters of social responsibility, by sharing resources in experience, workers and finance with each other. But it also became evident – not least through the failure of the Council to put into practice the recommendation that a thorough review of the implications of the changes in the coal-mining communities for the mission of the churches be conducted with all haste in 1986 – that this could not be done effectively without appointing someone to promote this cooperation. The sadness was that the resources devoted by the denominations were (and are) so scarce in this field in Wales – it is still the case that only the Church in Wales has made a full-time appointment – so that the pressure of other issues has meant that the close partnership which was possible during the strike did not develop as it should have done. This continues to be a clear challenge to the member denominations and churches of Cytûn. There is no doubt that it is in partnership with each other that the churches will be effective in their national and local witness, and that this cooperation demands considerable commitment of time, energy and money, if it is to be effective. The key task is to find ways of promoting this partnership in fields where there is considerable agreement between the denominations, and of seeking greater mutual understanding in those fields where there is considerable disagreement on fundamental principles. The appointment of Cytûn's National Assembly Liaison Officer has been a notable example of significant collaboration in a key area of Christian witness in the social sphere within Wales and augurs well for the future.

Throughout the 1980s, the percentage of unemployed people had been increasing gradually from 8.4 per cent in 1980 to 14.6 per cent in 1985, a percentage which was about 3 per cent higher than the corresponding figure for the United Kingdom during the same period.[11] There were 173,000 out of work in Wales in 1985 compared with 78,000 in 1980.[12] In response to this, a statement on unemployment was issued on St David's Day 1986 by a group of eighteen prominent people in Wales, with some from the churches among them. The core of this statement was that this scale of unemployment was unacceptable:

> ... the economic and social losses from unemployment at its present scale [make] it intolerable; [we call] for a more active policy to expand the economy and create opportunities for the unemployed to do useful work.[13]

On St David's Day 1987, a further statement was issued on behalf of the Council of Churches for Wales and those who signed the St David's Day 1986 Declaration. It sought to offer ways ahead based on some of the conclusions of a conference convened in October 1986 for industrial leaders, representatives of agencies and voluntary bodies as well as the churches. The aim of this national conference was to examine unemployment in Wales and to seek practical responses. It offered guidelines on policy changes in fields such as investment, training in industrial expertise, regional policy and local initiatives, social security and tax, and the Community Programme. But alongside these changes, which demanded political responses, there would need to be changes in behaviour: 'Something more will be needed than the changes in economic policy; changes in attitude are essential too. Such changes would contribute not only to a reduction in unemployment but to the creation of a united, socially healthier and even happier nation.'[14]

The final paragraphs of the statement issued following the October 1986 conference, summarize not only the discussions of the eighties with regard to industry but the whole approach and perspective of the Industrial Committee and of industrial mission over a twenty-five-year period in Wales:

> ... our greatest need is for hope, and for the confidence that unemployment on the present scale is not inevitable ... It was, in part, to challenge pessimism and its consequent apathy, that the 1986 St David's Day Declaration was issued and the conference was convened last year.
>
> The sense of hopelessness which so often characterises talk about unemployment and industrial decline derives in part from the heresy that 'Mammon Rules'. There clearly are economic constraints. But it is wrong that, in the name of those constraints, standards of social provision which are essential to a fair and responsible society are denied. The Bible insists that it is 'righteousness' (which here means social justice, not just being good) that makes a nation great, and that social justice is a necessary part of real prosperity.
>
> The Church has its part to play in seeking to change those attitudes which unnecessarily prolong the agony of unemployment. But the Church's voice is not the only voice that is being heard demanding effective measures to create jobs and reduce unemployment ... [The subject of this paper] is the lives of men and women, their families,

and their communities, and indeed the wealth and well-being of our country as a whole . . . the need for action is now.[15]

This is why so many people put such energy, enthusiasm and commitment into work which, throughout the period in question, was breaking new ground in the story of the churches' witness in Wales. The need persists for the churches and denominations to learn the lessons of this involvement, not only in order to strengthen their ability to set aside sufficient resources for the specialist mission in industry and commerce but also in order to strengthen the witness and service of the local churches in areas across Wales (at a time of changed economic realities) where economic pressures can still cause suffering to individuals and their families in rural as much as in urban communities.

Twenty years after the end of the dispute in the coal industry, it has become increasingly clear that the churches, at a time of increasing entrenchment, are giving ever decreasing priority to this key aspect of their contemporary witness and ministry. To such an extent that many of the Industrial Missions which played such a key role in the story told in this chapter are struggling for their very existence. In the long term, the churches could pay a heavy price for such short-sightedness and lack of vision.

# ~ 9 ~
# Wales and racism in southern Africa

In 1948, in an election amongst the white minority, the National Party was elected to form a government in South Africa. It fought the election on the platform of apartheid (i.e. separatism) as a basis for defending the power and privileges of the whites. Although this was the first time that this term was used, the social principle can be traced back to 1913 at least, when the Government agreed upon a Land Act to be a basis for separating the black majority (80 per cent of the population) from the white minority (13 per cent of the population). There were theological beginnings to apartheid as far back as 1829, when the Synod of one of the Dutch Reformed Churches in South Africa decided that coloured people should be prevented from taking communion together with whites. From the very beginning, a theological 'foundation' had been laid to the policy of apartheid, and churches across the world, and inter-church bodies in particular, were deeply concerned at the injustice of this separatism, and there was a commitment to oppose it.

It did not get onto the agenda of the Welsh Council of Churches until 1970, when concern was expressed, in the resolution on the occasion of the twenty-fifth anniversary of the United Nations, that there were reports of a recommencement of the arms trade to South Africa. The telegram sent to the British Government expressed the belief that this was 'contrary to the United Nations resolutions' and added, 'we suggest that such a policy can only weaken the authority of the UN in that area and thereby be a serious threat to peace'.

When the Council's Department of Church and Society was set up in 1973, it was believed that it should give priority, among other matters, to campaigning for 'a just political and social order in states',[1] and South Africa and Rhodesia were referred to as examples. Worldwide developments influenced its work.

In 1968, on the basis of the Church and Society Conference of Geneva (1968), the Uppsala Assembly – a few weeks after the assassination of Martin Luther King Jnr, who had been invited to speak – presented an analytical framework for abolishing racism, pressing the churches to undertake a vigorous campaign against it. Racism was defined as:

> ... ethnocentric pride in one's own racial group and preference for the distinctive characteristics of that group ... strong negative feelings towards other groups who do not share these characteristics, coupled with the thrust to discriminate against and exclude the outgroup from full participation in the life of the community.[2]

Particular attention was given to white racism which was at the root of their domination and their privileges. This was the basis of the decision of the Central Committee of the World Council of Churches in 1969 to establish a *Programme to Combat Racism*, 'during a heated debate', according to the minute. It would give priority to racism among whites ('by far the most dangerous form of present conflicts')[3] and would give attention to institutional racism in structures that use racism to intensify their power. Redistribution of power from the powerful to the powerless would also be a priority. The programme and special fund were launched for an experimental period of five years, initially, and it was renewed in the WCC Central Committee in 1974.

An article in *The Guardian* on 12 March 1973 asserted that 97 of the 100 companies that were active in South Africa mistreated their black workers. In presenting its report, the Department of Church and Society reminded the churches that these figures 'relate to human suffering and raise deep religious questions'.[4] A memorandum expressed the Department's concern about apartheid and drew attention to the Programme to Combat Racism as a means of campaigning against it:

> ... white racism is the open and officially acknowledged foundation of (South Africa's) social, political and economic life and ... we in Britain are not distant observers of the system but deeply involved in its maintenance.[5]

And the churches were implicated in this unjust system through a variety of financial and commercial links. Faced with a situation like this, the churches had a responsibility to ensure:

> ... that their worship of God is not in fact substantially financed by the exploitation of the defenceless ... [The facts] preclude any self-righteous condemnation [by the churches] of secular bodies ... This is such a blatant denial of God's purpose, and a source of such human suffering for others, and material benefits for ourselves, that we in Britain dare not acquiesce in it any longer.[6]

This demanded a review of their investments in South Africa. Two actions were believed to be possible. The first choice was to sell their investments. That was the policy of the World Council of Churches, because investment strengthened the white minority. The other choice was to use the investments to bring pressure to bear on the companies to improve the working conditions of black people, and the British Council of Churches was considering coordinating the efforts of the churches in this direction.

The memorandum also examined the nature and aims of the Programme to Combat Racism of the World Council of Churches. Despite considerable doubts among some of its members, the Department recommended that the Council of Churches for Wales should commend the Programme to the attention of the denominations of Wales, urging them to contribute to the Fund. The Council accepted both recommendations at its annual meeting on 11–12 October 1973, making only one amendment, namely, that the denominations should be urged 'to consider contributing to the Fund' rather than 'to contribute to the Fund'![7] The significance of this worldwide fund cannot be underestimated. In the opinion of one observer: 'The World Council of Churches would never be the same again; it had taken sides with the racially oppressed ... Concrete action against racism had severely tested the ecumenical fellowship, but it was not broken.'[8] But in Wales this was only a beginning!

By January 1975, although not all the denominations had responded to the recommendations of the Council, the Chairman of the Department, Bishop B. N. Y. Vaughan,[9] was able to write to Pauline Webb, at the time one of the vice-moderators of the Central Committee of the World Council of Churches:

> ... we know that not all – if any – accept the policy of the WCC to withdraw all investment from South Africa. For this reason it would be advisable to let you know that you should not presume that unanimous support will be forthcoming from the churches in Wales for a policy of total withdrawal. However, I think you can presume that a policy to exercise stockholder pressure on companies and governments in the interest of justice will be fully supported by the churches of Wales.[10]

In September 1975, a further Memorandum on southern Africa (and not South Africa alone) was issued as part of the Department's consideration of the theme of the Fifth Assembly of the World Council of Churches (Nairobi, 23 November to 10 December 1975), 'Jesus Christ Frees and Unites'. Opposition to apartheid was restated, which, in the words of the South African Council of Churches, was a false faith, a new gospel, in contrast to the Gospel of Jesus Christ.[11] It also emphasized the fact that Britain invested more than any other country in the dominating structure of apartheid. In 1970, £1,728 million from a total investment of £2,984 million had come from Britain.[12]

Concern was expressed about the future of the Christian Institute of South Africa – which was founded in 1963, as a direct result of the Cottesloe consultation, to try to make Christianity a more powerful influence in society – and about the safety of its director, Dr Beyers Naudé.[13] He had refused to testify in secret before a sub-committee of the Le Grange Commission, set up 'to inquire into certain organisations', as a result of which he was arrested and brought to trial[14] (which had been attended by the Archbishop of Wales, G. O. Williams, on behalf of the British Council of Churches). The memorandum quoted the British Council of Churches' statement in response to the original court sentence: 'The actions of the South African Government are ... reprehensible since it claims to be motivated by Christian principles. We urge Churches and Christians in the U. K. to express their support for the Christian Institute and their opposition to the attempt by the S. A. Government to stifle religious freedom of conscience'[15] – a position that was supported by the Department and the Council.

The Programme to Combat Racism continued to raise questions for the churches. What kind of support should the churches give to the Programme? How did pacifist principles and the need to stand against injustice and oppression hold together? It was claimed that it was valid to distinguish between military and humanitarian support, as did the Programme itself. Although this may have seemed naive to opponents of the Programme, nevertheless it concluded that it was reasonable for the World Council of Churches to offer aid to freedom movements on condition that it would be used for humanitarian purposes, but without seeking a guarantee of this. Recommendations passed by the Council in 1975 continued to express support for the Programme.

Within two years, on 19 October 1977, the Government of South Africa announced that the Christian Institute along with seventeen black movements had been declared illegal and their officials were either banned or imprisoned without trial. Among them were Beyers Naudé and Brian Brown, a Methodist minister, who later returned to the United Kingdom and became Africa Secretary to the British Council of Churches. When this news broke, Council of Churches for Wales's officers issued a strong statement expressing opposition to this repressive action:

> Such repressive actions cannot but exacerbate the situation of the black population in South Africa. The voice of black consciousness and hopes has been stifled; but their determination to struggle for justice and for basic human rights for their people must be strengthened through this action.
>
> We particularly deplore the banning of the Christian Institute of Southern [sic] Africa, and of its director, Dr Beyers Naudé ... The Institute ... has stood beside and spoken for those opposed to apartheid and who are committed to a peaceful struggle for justice and equality in South Africa ... [W]e share with the Institute ... in the Christian struggle of bringing about the equality and justice which is the goal and reality of our vision of society, both in our own country and in all countries, where human rights are denied and injustice reigns.[16]

While the response from the Labour government was positive ('We believe that a society like ours is morally bound to oppose apartheid and to bring about change in South Africa by peaceful means . . . If this does not take place we fear that the prospect may be one of increasing violence in South Africa'[17]), the response of the South African Ambassador in London was very different. It was maintained that the violence among the black people of South Africa was the product of the efforts of a small number of 'political activists' who were trying to create 'a revolutionary climate which could be exploited when conditions were right'. [18] It was only after careful consideration, in the words of the Ambassador, that the Government decided to ban these movements and individuals in order to safeguard law and order. He claimed that: 'the people under [the Government's] jurisdiction were not subjected to intimidation, and their fundamental rights were not encroached upon by subversive methods and actions.' An incredible assertion in view of what the Government had done to undermine the fundamental rights of the black and coloured people of the country since 1948.

The year 1978 was designated an Anti-Apartheid Year by the United Nations and on 21 January a seminar was held in Cardiff jointly between the Council of Churches for Wales and Christian Concern for Southern Africa 'to deepen understanding of the situation in South Africa and to discover how we, Christians in Wales, can play our part in the struggle for justice for the black people there'.[19] Recommendations emphasized the centrality of 'equality', the importance of effective information about the effects of *apartheid*, the continuing need to consider disinvestment and the need for an education and advocacy campaign.

In August 1977 the Executive Committee of the World Council of Churches had set aside the sum of $85,000 from the Special Fund of the Programme to Combat Racism for the campaign for racial justice and self-government in Zimbabwe, authorizing the officers to release it to a suitable movement or movements when they thought it appropriate to do so. The money was transferred to the Patriotic Front in Zimbabwe in August 1978 to be used, in accordance with the conditions of the Programme, for humanitarian purposes. This caused a worldwide storm in the churches and the media, and the World Council of Churches was accused by its opponents of giving 'grants for guerrillas'.

Since one of the duties of the Council of Churches for Wales was to interpret, support and promote the World Council of Churches among churches and Christians of Wales, it was decided that the Council should issue a statement to express support for the grant, for the Programme to Combat Racism, and for the World Council of Churches. There was unanimous agreement on a suitable statement at the Annual Meeting of the Council in Newtown on 19 October 1978. It affirmed the Council's confidence in the World Council of Churches and called upon the member churches of the Council of Churches for Wales to do likewise. After expressing appreciation of the WCC's contribution to the mission and service of the churches in Wales and explaining the nature of the Programme and the special grant to Zimbabwe, the statement addressed the controversial issue of using violence in unjust situations. It took a firm position:

> While respecting those who take a genuine pacifist stand, nevertheless, the World Council of Churches cannot condemn those who, after exhausting every other reasonable means, are forced to use violence, with a good conscience, as a means of obtaining justice for those on whose behalf they are struggling. Despite this, the World Council of Churches has shared, and continues to share, in the condemnation of the atrocities committed by both sides in Zimbabwe.[20]

It continued:

> The complicated nature of the political situation in Zimbabwe means that it is very difficult to form a political judgement. Individual Christians can find themselves in complete disagreement with the judgement reached by the Council, but the World Council of Churches cannot avoid risking such a political judgement if it is to share in the campaign to combat racial oppression.[21]

This statement, which, as already noted, had the unanimous support of the Council, was more unambiguous in its support of the officers of the World Council of Churches and its Executive Committee than any other similar statement in Britain at the time. As might be imagined, the response was mixed. It was supported by the Synod of Wales of the Methodist Church that met in Llanrhaeadr-ym-Mochnant in April 1979. Already in its Annual Meeting in June 1978 in Caernarvon, the Union of Welsh Independents had passed a resolution supporting the Programme and agreeing to make a contribution of £50 towards the Special Fund (the only Welsh denomination to make a contribution to it). A more cautious response was received from the Provincial Council for Mission and Unity of the Church in Wales, expressing 'unease' not so much in connection with the grant itself but with the way the decision was made and announced. But support for the general work of the Council was reiterated.[22]

Reflecting a similar spirit, the Archbishop of Wales, G. O. Williams (the first person ever from Wales to serve on the Central Committee of the World Council of Churches), expressed the same desire to foster the Church's relationship with the Council. When a number were calling on the Church in Wales to pull out of the World Council of Churches, Dr Williams's response in the Governing Body was: 'When my church does something with which I disagree, I do not withdraw my membership.'

The only local reaction came form the Llandudno Council of Churches, which was a response to the World Council of Churches grant rather than the position of the Council of Churches for Wales. In his reply, the General Secretary of the Council, Noel Davies, explained that:

> Christian Aid and the Commission on Inter Church Aid and World Refugee Service (of the World Council of Churches) do play a vital role in caring for victims of racial violence and oppression in Rhodesia but . . . there are many refugees both inside and outside Rhodesia to whom the Patriotic Front has access which conventional aid agencies can reach only with difficulty. The humanitarian purpose of this grant is vital but it is a caring which aims also at combatting racism. No such purpose can be achieved without some political judgement and political involvement. Para. (8) . . . seeks to express the agonising conflict for any Christian as he seeks to stand against racism.[23]

It seems that neither the response to the Programme nor to this special grant was as fierce in Wales as it was among many of the churches in other Western countries, not least in England. One reason for this may have been the radical tradition of many of the denominations in Wales, particularly the nonconformist denominations. But it is likely that apathy and ignorance with respect to the World Council of Churches and its activity were also contributory factors.

At any rate, within another year, in October 1979, the British Council of Churches published its report, *Political Change in Southern Africa: Britain's Responsibility*, and the Department of Church and Society of the Council of Churches for Wales prepared a report aimed at helping Welsh churches to consider the BCC document. As a background to their work, the Department asked Professor Ieuan G. John[24] to prepare a paper on South Africa's position in international politics. This paper made a detailed analysis of the strengths and weaknesses of the country from an economic and political standpoint, outlining the changes in its strategic position within the southern region of Africa and suggesting what might happen there in the future. Having studied the two reports, the Department proposed the text of a statement. It aimed to answer a number of key questions.

In explaining why the Churches should make statements on political matters, it quoted the BCC report:

> With responsibility before God, Creator of heaven and earth, with love for Christ, who referred particularly to the poor, the needy and sinners, and also in the hope of the coming of the Kingdom of God, when perfect peace will hold sway, the Church has no option but to dedicate its message and its whole life to trying to ensure here and now as much human dignity, justice, peace and freedom as possible.[25]

It came to the conclusion that swift action was necessary if the situation was to be changed. The churches were urged 'to listen carefully to black leaders . . . who speak for the oppressed' and 'to pray and work to secure majority rule within a democratic order of government within a united South Africa'. It was also believed that the Government should be pressed 'to stem the inward flow to the country of the capital, technology and professional technological instruction which enable it to withstand the international pressure to change its apartheid system'.[26]

When this report was discussed at the Council meeting, doubts were expressed. Would it really represent the voice of Welsh churches? Some (including the Chairman of the Department, Bishop B. N. Y. Vaughan) felt that the denominations would not support economic sanctions and that it would be wiser not to pass a resolution but to ask the Department to study the matter further. This is an example of the Council's difficulty in such matters: how could it point a way forward for the churches while at the same time seek to express the churches' views on controversial issues. The question of economic sanctions was subsequently raised many times by the Council and every time it was agreed to commend it to the consideration of the denominations. But there was always a question of whether Council statements and recommendations were ever taken seriously by the churches. In an ecumenical situation where the Council did not have – and rightly so – any authority over the denominations, it depended solely on effective influence. On a contentious matter like this, it is likely that the climate within the Council itself (where all the denominations had their representatives) was very different from that within the denominational courts and committees. If this was true, it raises a fundamental question about the nature of the ecumenical partnership in Wales at this time and the influence of Council resolutions on the decisions and policies of the denominations.

Be that as it may, Jim Wilkie[27] responded to the Council debate by emphasizing that what was needed was a general change of attitude. He said: 'keeping on talking is not enough ... greater energy is necessary. Urgency is increasing daily. Education is more important than pompous statements.'[28] Erastus Jones's comment was characteristic: 'Caution must be set alongside urgency.'

At the end of the discussion the two resolutions in the report were passed, namely, that the Council 'heartily commends the report of the British Council of Churches for study' and 'supports a policy of economic sanctions against South Africa in order to ensure that the majority of the people have an effective voice in national decisions'.[29] This resolution was a backward step compared with some of the previous resolutions of the Council, but perhaps more representative of denominational positions on this contentious matter!

During the same period, for the first time, the difficult question of sport, and in this particular case, rugby, was raised. A South African rugby team was about to visit Wales at the invitation of the Welsh Rugby Union to play two games, one in Newport and the other in Llanelli, the first to be shown on television by the BBC. As a result of the Council's general debate about South Africa, three resolutions were agreed unanimously condemning the WRU, the two clubs and the BCC. In a letter which accompanied the resolutions, the General Secretary explained:

> ... the multiracial nature of this present team does not reflect the true state of rugby playing in South Africa itself, but rather, in our judgement, serves to generate sympathy for the present unjust apartheid system.[30]

In his response, Owen Edwards, on behalf of the BBC, noted that it was not appropriate for them to make decisions on matters like this for political reasons but solely on an editorial basis.

The Gleneagles agreement on apartheid in sport had been accepted by the British Government in 1977 and had also been accepted unanimously by all Commonwealth leaders. It stated that it was:

> ... the urgent duty of each of their governments vigorously to combat the evil of *apartheid* by withdrawing any form of support for, and by taking every practical step to discourage contact or competition by their nationals with, sporting organisations, teams or sportsmen from South Africa or from any other country where sports are organised on the basis of race, colour or ethnic origin.[31]

In a comprehensive paper prepared at the request of the Chairman of the Department Church and Society in January 1981, Brian Brown[32] emphasized that the black people of South Africa believed that holding international sports events in South Africa or against teams from there undermined the struggle against apartheid by giving support to the white minority, creating the impression that they could practise apartheid and continue to enjoy international acceptance. International sporting events also contributed to the international image of apartheid in the media, which ignored the facts as far as the life and leisure of the black and coloured people were concerned, and above all, it encouraged the belief of the whites that cosmetic changes would be sufficient to gain the support of the international community.

Thus, when a further resolution on South Africa was passed in a meeting of the Council on 5 May 1983, the British Government was called upon 'to continue to adhere firmly to the Gleneagles agreement which regulates the relationship with the Republic of South Africa in the field of sport'.[33] In the same resolution (passed unanimously), the churches were also called 'to follow a policy of economic disengagement, and to urge their members to pull investments out of South Africa'. Thus, after a period of three years, the principle that had previously been rejected was accepted.

In the meantime, a new threat was facing the churches in South Africa, and the South African Council of Churches in particular. In 1981, the Eloff Commission was appointed to look into the administration and financial position of the South African Council of Churches. At least, that was the official reason. It soon became obvious, however, that the Commission had been authorized by the Government to inquire into 'the inception, development, objectives, history and activity of the Council as well as the organisation and people connected with the financial support or assets of the South African Council of Churches'.[34] The chief of police had applauded the fact that the Council was considered 'an affected organization'. The effect of this, among other things, would be that it could not receive any financial contributions from outside the country. Since the Council relied on such funding for 96 per cent of the revenue necessary to maintain its structures and aid programmes – much too high a percentage, incidentally, for the good of its own work and for the churches' partnership through the Council – such a decision would have undermined its whole existence.

On 1 September 1982, the General Secretary of the Council, Bishop Desmond Tutu, was called before the Commission, and in his testimony he stressed that it was not the Council's revenue nor its activities that were in the balance: 'It is the Christian faith, it is the Christian churches who are members of the South African Council of Churches, who are on trial.'[35]

The dispute between the Council and the government was a theological one. 'The South African authorities are trying to dictate to the SACC what the nature of Christian ministry should be. No one can understand why we exist as a Council and why we do and say the things we do unless they understand our theological, biblical justification for doing so', said the Bishop.[36]

While the Commission was still sitting, the Council of Churches for Wales sent a letter of support and greetings to Bishop Tutu and the South African Council of Churches based on the May 1983 resolution. In his reply, Bishop Tutu set out the theological premise of his and the Council's stance:

> ... we have no doubt that the great Liberator God, the God of the Exodus, will lead us all, black and white, in South Africa to true freedom for all because, whilst one section is still unfree, no one can be truly free. We belong to a wonderful fellowship which transcends time, space, race, culture, wherein we are members one of another because we are members of the body of Christ ... We know that those for us are many times those against us.[37]

The report of the Eloff Commission was published on 15 February 1984 and it pronounced this verdict on the South African Council of Churches: 'It is revolutionary, destabilizing, secretive and confrontational.'[38] It is condemned for not restricting itself 'to spiritual work and [for] advocating a radical transformation of society ... It is inappropriate for a church ... body to make pronouncements on political or economic policies (such as the promotion of disinvestment).'

In view of this verdict, another resolution on South Africa was passed at the meeting of the Council of Churches for Wales in May 1984, drawing the attention of the churches in Wales to Bishop Tutu's words, in reply to the Commission's report, that '[The South African Council of Churches] is compelled by the Gospel of Jesus Christ to condemn apartheid because it is wicked and immoral in an absolute sense'.[39] In view of some changes made by the Government in its attitude towards neighbouring countries and towards Asians within the country, the resolution went on to affirm that 'no changes in South Africa which leave the apartheid system unchanged can justify support for South Africa' and expressed support for the South

African Council of Churches and its Secretary in its opposition to apartheid.

The year 1985 was historic for the Christians of South Africa. First, this was the year of publication of the Kairos Document,[40] which offered a theological reflection on the country's political crisis by a number of theologians and others in South Africa. This document had an incredible influence. According to the Foreword to the Second Edition:

> Responses ... were overwhelming ... [It] generated more discussions and debate than any other theological document in South Africa. [There was] overwhelming excitement about it in the Black townships. It reinforced the people's faith and hope for a new and just society in South Africa ... It was welcomed as a statement of what it means to be truly Christian in a violent apartheid society.[41]

> The starting point was that the *kairos* [the critical time, the moment of crisis] had arrived in South Africa. The moment of truth has arrived. South Africa has been plunged into a crisis which is shaking the foundations and there is every indication that the crisis has only just begun ... It is the moment of truth not only for apartheid but also for the Church.[42]

It called for a prophetic theology based on the Bible, a theology that was capable of reading the signs of the times, was a call to action, and was therefore always on the attack ('It confronts the evils of the time and speaks out against them ... ').[43] Such a theology should be spiritual ('infused with the spirit of fearlessness and courage, a spirit of love and understanding, a spirit of joy and hope, a spirit of strength and determination'), and pastoral ('It will denounce sin and announce salvation'). But the greatest need was hope: 'As the crisis deepens day by day, what the oppressor and the oppressed can legitimately demand of the churches is a message of hope.'[44] The way to this sure hope would be hard and painful. This was now inevitable since the oppressor was so stubborn. Now is the time to act. There was a challenge to action. It would have to mean siding with the oppressed, participating in the struggle for justice, transforming church activities, special campaigns, civil disobedience and offering moral leadership.

This revolutionary document received very little attention in Wales, nor did it have much influence on the thought and action of the Council of Churches for Wales. This could have been a failure of communication by the Council and the denominations in Wales, or another example of missional and theological apathy. Those who did pay attention to the document raised important questions, not only about the situation in South Africa, but also about our theological and practical response, as Christians and churches in Wales, to the growing crisis here. But these did not result in any significant theological reflection or prophetic action.

In December 1985, the World Council of Churches called an international conference in Harare, twenty-five years after the first international conference convened by the Council in Cottesloe in 1960. It called for a number of steps to be taken immediately: end the state of emergency; withdraw the military from the black townships; free Nelson Mandela and every political prisoner; create the circumstances to allow refugees to return; free everyone who was in prison without trial; lift the ban on all banned movements; begin negotiations with genuine leaders of the people with a view to handing over power to the people. The main recommendation of the conference was that there should be continued pressure for economic sanctions:

> It is the strategy of economic sanctions that emerged for us most powerfully and touched us most deeply ... We recognised the consistent demand from South Africa for powerful economic sanctions as the strategy of the hour in the defeat of apartheid.[45]

This was the basis of another resolution on South Africa passed at the Council meeting on 1 May 1986. Whilst welcoming some changes, for instance in the pass laws, it reiterated calls for targeted economic sanctions, enactment of the Gleneagles agreement and urged Welsh Christians 'to join in the Day of Prayer and Fasting for putting an end to the unjust Government in South Africa [on 16 June] and to join in lobbying the House of Commons on economic sanctions [on 17 June]'.

In fact, South Africa received more attention in the Council of Churches for Wales during 1986 than at any other time before or since. In February, the General Secretary, Noel Davies, visited South Africa as an observer on behalf of the British Council of Churches at two treason trials in Delmas and

Pietermaritzburg. In both cases, prominent Christians were on trial, and a continuous presence from among the worldwide ecumenical family was maintained in the courts. In his report to the Council of Churches for Wales, the General Secretary spoke of three key issues which the majority of those he met believed would be central to solving South Africa's crisis. First, free Nelson Mandela. Secondly, secure equal education for all. Finally, when he asked people what the Christians of Britain could do, the answer, almost without exception, was, 'Support economic sanctions'. In the words of Beyers Naudé: 'This is perhaps the last chance for peaceful change in South Africa.'[46]

But undoubtedly the climax of the involvement of the Council of Churches for Wales (and perhaps all the churches and denominations of Wales) with the situation in South Africa was the visit of Bishop Tutu to Wales for the God's Family Festival on 24 May 1986. He spent three days in Wales meeting leaders and officers of the denominations, receiving the freedom of the Borough of Merthyr Tydfil, giving endless interviews, speaking and preaching in the Festival itself and preaching in a special service in Gellimanwydd Congregational Church, Ammanford, on Sunday, 25 May. He had an incredible effect. According to the authorities of the Royal Welsh Show, where the festival was held, between 15,000 and 20,000 people, including national and religious press, not only from Wales but from across Britain, attended. The climax of the Festival was Bishop Tutu's sermon in the final service on a text from Genesis, 'It is not good for the man to be alone . . .' (Genesis 2 verse 18). The theme of his sermon was that we have been made for community: 'we are made for fellowship, for community, for partnership, for independence; made for family.'[47] He quoted an African proverb: 'A person is a person through other people.' He believed this was fundamental to humankind: 'at a time of nuclear disasters and economic imbalances no one can lay claim to absolute self-sufficiency that can enable them to ignore others with gay abandon.'[48] Jesus came, he said, into the centre of a divided society, and a miracle was seen opening up before them. Slaves and masters, rich and poor, men and women, Jews and Gentiles were treating each other not just as equals but as brothers and sisters. And when people are brothers and sisters, they are brothers and sisters, whatever happens: 'He can be more awkward, can be an utterly uncongenial and unlovely creature, it makes not an iota of difference . . . he is your brother.'[49] The implications of this for the situation in South Africa were obvious:

> P. W. Botha [President of South Africa at the time] and I are brothers by virtue of our baptism. I may not like the evil policies of his government but I can't consign him to hell. I am my brother's brother. I am consigned by my faith . . . to be concerned for the welfare of white South Africans. I must understand their fears and anxieties . . . I must long for the very best for them . . . I must announce with fervour that God loves them and that this love is unconditional and unchanging . . . Nothing to do with achievement.[50]

Most particularly, the church was a community of prayer. He spoke of a letter which he received from an anchorite nun living in a wooden hut in a forest in California assuring him that she prayed for him by name every day: 'I was being prayed for by name in the woods of California at 2 a.m. every day. What chance does the South African Government stand?' In such a community we are called to share pain also, and he quoted another African proverb, 'When a thorn enters the foot, the whole body has to bend to remove it!' At the end of his sermon, the whole congregation, amid the rain, was clapping and he had to raise his voice above the noise:

> God says, 'Help me to change the evil . . . in this world so that they become the compassion and the caring, the love and the joy and the sharing of my kingdom' so that the kingdoms of this world will become the kingdom of our God and of his Christ; and he shall reign for ever and ever. Amen.[51]

It was an inspiration, an encouragement and a challenge, and the Festival itself was a means, through him, of bringing the situation in South Africa to the forefront of people's minds. And over the following years, those who attended continued to speak of the Bishop's influence on them, on their faith and on their understanding of the crisis and opportunity of South Africa.

On 12 February 1990, another conference was held – the last in the history of the Council of Churches for Wales – jointly convened by the Council and Christian Aid in Wales. About 60 people attended the conference held at the Guildhall, Swansea. A more dramatically appropriate day could never have been chosen. On 11 February, what the oppressed peoples of South Africa, and many millions of people in the worldwide community had been longing for, happened: Nelson Mandela was freed! Naturally, this created an excited atmosphere in the conference; here was a sure sign that changes were possible which could revolutionize the country. However, the strong belief of the representatives from the trades unions, sports associations, development agencies, the Wales Anti-Apartheid Movement, as well as the churches, was that the struggle should not now end but that the international pressure on South Africa should continue. And therefore the chief recommendation of the conference was that pressure on the government should be maintained 'until there were fundamental changes in laws (such as the Land Act, the Population Registration Act, Education Acts) which uphold apartheid as an oppressive system'.[52] In particular, the recommendation asked for 'the continuing of sanctions . . . [and the exerting] of pressure on the banks not to agree new loans to South Africa . . . since [we] believe that the voice of those who were oppressed for these 40 years should be heeded as the true voice of peace with justice in South Africa'.[53] There was also pressure to continue to operate the Gleneagles Agreement. Greetings were conveyed to the Christian Council of Namibia on the occasion of the country's independence on 21 March 1990.

The Council of Churches for Wales had ceased to exist before the fruit of this continuing support for the costly struggles and campaigns of our brothers and sisters in South Africa could be fully evaluated. On 27 April 1994, a general election for the whole population was held, when Nelson Mandela, imprisoned for twenty-seven years, was elected President of the country, to preside over the process of creating a united, democratic, equal and non-racist country. The task for the churches in South Africa now – and for Christians in Wales who wished to support them – was to move away from a ministry of witnessing against and opposing apartheid and move towards a ministry of service and partnership in order to build a new nation and society. This would not be an easy task.

## Conclusions

Looking back over more than twenty years of statements and actions by the Council with respect to South Africa, a number of conclusions may be suggested. What strikes us, first of all, is the consistency of the engagement of the Council, and the denominations which were members of it, with the situation, and the unanimity of their opposition to apartheid. Through statements, activities and prayers and, from time to time, through visits, Christian concern for the situation was expressed and there was deep solidarity with the black and coloured people who were being oppressed. There was also agreement within the Council and among the denominations that it was entirely appropriate to focus on South Africa, not only because Christians should campaign on behalf of those who suffer oppression wherever they are, but also because of the historical, political and economic connections that existed between the two countries. Their histories have been interwoven, and the British Government and the Christians of Britain had a particular responsibility to seek to secure a just and free future for our brothers and sisters there in a united and non-racist country. But throughout the period under consideration, it was agreed that South Africa should not be the sole focus of concern. The churches also had a responsibility to stand up for freedom and justice for the peoples of neighbouring countries, in particular Namibia and Zimbabwe (Rhodesia).

Secondly, the Council took its lead, theologically and practically, mainly from the World Council of Churches (and to some extent also the British Council of Churches). The timing of statements and their contents reflected the constant activity of that Council, which had been tireless in its opposition from the year (1948) when the National Party came to power in South Africa and the World Council of Churches was established. Indeed, such was the Council's commitment to this struggle that it was accused more than once of being tunnel-visioned and blind to other crises. This is an unfair criticism, but no one can deny the single-mindedness of the World Council of Churches in its stand and its anti-apartheid efforts. All this heavily influenced the work of the Council of Churches for Wales.

Thirdly, there was no thorough theological study either in respect of racism in general or apartheid in particular. From time to time, however, there were hints of theological themes that can be summarized as follows:

(a) We were all created by God in the image God and to be children of God and thus brothers and sisters to one another. In the words of Desmond Tutu in the God's Family Festival, we were created for community.

(b) The will of God is justice and freedom for all in a world that reflects God's will. Therefore, every injustice, every oppression and every power that separates people from one another on the basis of race or colour or nationality or culture, is contrary to the will of God. The essence of apartheid is to discriminate between people on a racial basis. Therefore, apartheid is contrary to the will of God and it must be uncompromisingly condemned.

(c) The Gospel offers reconciliation to all, through the cross of Christ. Therefore, the Church cannot respond to the call to share in the ministry of reconciliation without facing the reality of human sin and without opposition to the consequences of that sin in oppression, cruelty and suffering, nor without the confidence that God reconciles the world through the cross of Christ in order to create a new society.

(d) If this ministry in society and nation is to gain credibility, this reconciliation must be at work in the life of the Church itself. There the primary task is to 'break down ... the barrier that separated them and kept them enemies'[54] and build a new society where 'there is neither Jew nor Greek, there is neither slave nor free, there is neither male nor female; for you are all one in Christ Jesus.'[55] Thus there must be condemnation of apartheid or racial injustice within the Church as well as within society.

(e) This ministry calls us to practise a prophetic theology (such as is outlined in the *Kairos* document) that urges us to recognise that the Gospel has to do with all of life and the whole world and not only with 'spiritual' life; that we are called to proclaim God's will to the oppressor and the oppressed; that this, from time to time, compels us to venture to challenge governments and authorities which, through their actions, deny the will of God; and that we have a Christian duty to stand with the oppressed and to pray for oppressed and oppressor alike.

Fourthly, there was fairly general agreement that the Programme to Combat Racism and its Special Fund offered an acceptable understanding of the nature of the struggle against racism, a suitable framework for sharing in that struggle and an effective means of helping those suffering as a result of racist policies. In particular, despite the opposition of some in the churches in Wales, the Council applauded the fact that the denominations of Wales were supporting the activity of the Programme in Southern Africa (even though only one denomination, as was seen, made a contribution – and a comparatively small one at that – to the Special Fund).

Lastly, it was agreed from the beginning that there were at least five aspects to the efforts made by the Council and the denominations in Wales against apartheid and they recurred constantly in inter-church and denominational statements and resolutions. The anti-apartheid policy of the Council included a call for general or specific economic sanctions, disengagement by withdrawing investments in the country, the isolation of South Africa – its teams and individuals – in the field of international sport (an element which attracted more attention in Wales than in the other countries of Britain), educating Christians (and others) in Wales about the injustice of apartheid and its effects, and constant prayer for justice and freedom for all in the country.

Over the years, as has been seen, there was disagreement on some of these matters, but on the whole, in this field more than in relation to any other national and international issue, there was considerable agreement not only on issues of principle but also on ways of engaging in the Christian witness against apartheid in South Africa. But two painful questions remain. First, the Council paid considerable attention to racism in South Africa but precious little attention to racism here in

Wales and in Britain generally. The Council may be criticized for this. Justice is one. Therefore, the battle against racism should also be one. Secondly, throughout the years the public statements by the Council and the denominations were clear enough, but to what extent were conference or council resolutions translated into effective measures against apartheid (for example, through economic sanctions and disengaging investments) by the Council, its member churches or individuals? It is one thing to agree on a principle, but it is a completely different matter to put it effectively into practice.

In one respect, Wales made only a small contribution to this worldwide struggle. The black and coloured people of South Africa and their white friends who bravely stood with them, struggled most and paid the highest price, but by standing beside them the Council did make its contribution, enabling a better understanding of God's call to the churches in Wales to struggle against all injustice everywhere.

## ~ 10 ~
## *War and peace: nuclear disarmament*

The Council's first reference to war and peace was at the conference on 'The Church and Society' in Carmarthen in 1970. Section III on 'Economic Priorities and Political Decisions in the context of Poverty and World Peace' examined the morality of war and, according to the report, there was considerable diversity of views:

> Nevertheless, all were agreed in condemning nuclear war and even the stockpiling of missiles employed in such strategy. Few adopted the pacifist attitude and some agreed that there were occasions when a war with conventional weapons could be justified. On the positive side, the groups considered that the Church should be deeply concerned in finding the causes of war and of ensuring that these were eradicated.[1]

Bearing in mind the horror of the Second World War, its cost in lives and suffering in Wales and worldwide (15,000 Welsh soldiers were killed, and a total of 30,000,000 people worldwide), and the strong and courageous stance adopted by so many (according to John Davies, there were proportionately more conscientious objectors from Wales than from the other countries of the British Isles),[2] it is surprising that the Council took so long to express any opinion at all on the question of war. It is even more surprising in view of the strong pacifist tradition of many of the churches and the influence of some of the leaders of the pacifist movement.

Certainly, the ecumenical movement in general was not silent on the question of peace. When the First Assembly of the World Council of Churches met in Amsterdam, it made a strong statement on the issue:

> War as a method of settling disputes is incompatible with the teaching and example of our Lord Jesus Christ. The part that war

plays in our present international life is a sin against God and a degradation of man.³

Nevertheless, there was disagreement among members of the Section of the Assembly which discussed this central question: can war any longer be a just act? Agreement was not possible and the only alternative had been to present the various attitudes towards war among Christians. The Section Chairman's report to the Assembly concluded that, faced with these differences: 'there is a deep consciousness that the ecumenical movement had come for just such a day as this – perhaps just in time for the churches to face their task.'⁴

Given that the beginnings of the Council of Churches for Wales had been so heavily influenced by Amsterdam and the wider ecumenical movement, why did the question of war and peace not receive more attention during the early years?

There were probably two main reasons. First, the main priority at this time was promoting a deeper unity between the denominations in Wales and encouraging more cooperation and unity at a local level. Indeed, this was the main impetus for forming the Council. This concern became the focus not only of the life and work of the Council itself, but also in the various essays and articles published in denominational journals in Wales in the late 1940s and early 1950s. Secondly, the Council felt a special responsibility to encourage the denominations to speak with one voice on public affairs to do with Wales and its people, such as, land in Wales, broadcasting and unemployment. Considerable energy was expended by a small body, which had no paid staff, on these two priorities, and only gradually did it become possible to give some attention to wider matters. One example of this was the growing commitment to the work of Inter-Church Aid (later to become Christian Aid), which was trying to meet the needs of refugees in Europe and worldwide, many of them suffering as a result of the persecution which took place after the Second World War.

It was natural enough, therefore, to concentrate on matters of faith and order in the beginning – the Carmarthen conference in 1963 and the Nottingham Conference in 1964 – and only after devoting time to implementing some of the main recommendations of these conferences (not least the discussions concerning

## WAR AND PEACE: NUCLEAR DISARMAMENT

the Covenant towards Unity in Wales which began in 1965) did the Council begin to consider how best to act on public and international affairs.

As has already been seen, one of the main influences was the Church and Society Conference of the World Council of Churches in Geneva in 1966 which considered the need for revolutionary changes in worldwide social, political and economic patterns in the face of increasing injustice. It is no surprise, therefore, that the Carmarthen conference, which was so heavily influenced by the Geneva conference, combined – for the first time in the life of the Council of Churches for Wales – the concern for worldwide peace and justice with justice and reconciliation in Wales.

Therefore, when the Council's Church and Society Department was established in 1973, it was agreed that it should include among its priorities the 'search for world peace'. But nothing was done about this until the eighties, when there was a series of resolutions on nuclear disarmament in 1981, 1982, 1983 and 1986.[5] In one sense, these represent the formed view of the Council on nuclear disarmament during this period, a view which was heavily influenced by some leaders of the Council (including Huw Wynne Griffith, who was secretary to the Department during this period) and some experts in the field. In 1984, the educational pack on nuclear disarmament *Swords into Ploughshares* was published. According to the foreword: 'The pack was prepared to help the churches to study the complex matters which arise, and to find ways of sharing in action to secure nuclear disarmament'[6] in the awareness that there was a growing concern about 'threats to peace and to the continued existence of mankind connected with the possession and use of nuclear arms'.

In 1986, a report on the churches' positions (chiefly as expressed through the Council) on peace issues was prepared by the secretary of the Committee on National and International Affairs (John Holdsworth). In March 1987, a Peace Council was convened by the Council of Churches for Wales, which focussed attention on nuclear disarmament but also considered other peace related issues.

Throughout this period, the national and international debate was very lively. These were the years of strength for movements such as CND. CND Wales was formed and the Council received an invitation to join. No agreement was reached on this invitation because, as has been seen, there was considerable difference of views among the churches and the denominations in Wales. On the other hand, the Council agreed in 1981 to recommend membership of the World Disarmament Campaign,[7] which did not recommend unilateral disarmament as the only way ahead but accepted multilateral disarmament as an important step towards total nuclear disarmament. There was also considerable pressure in support of the Campaign for a Nuclear Freeze. It received attention in the 1987 Peace Council and the support of a number of denominational leaders, but it did not become official Council policy.

The Council's position on these complex issues may be analysed under four headings: the theological foundations, interpreting and analysing the situation, messages to the Government, and guidance to the churches.

### Nuclear disarmament: the theological foundations

Two fundamental questions arise when considering the theological foundations of the Council's statements and publications, namely, first, what were their doctrinal foundations, and secondly, could nuclear war and nuclear deterrence be 'just' in the traditional meaning of this term? According to Mark Ellingsen[8] with reference to churches worldwide: 'more church statements call for peace by appealing to doctrinal themes not associated with the doctrine of creation than those that appeal to that doctrine.'

He went on to support this assertion with evidence of statements from various churches across the world. This was not true of the Council's statements. In these, the doctrine of God the Creator and the doctrine of the person and work of Christ are as influential as each other. For example, in April 1981 the Council stated:

> Since we believe that the earth and all that is in it belongs to God and that God has revealed the Kingdom of his love in the Lord Jesus Christ; and that God has entrusted to man decisions of life and death,

we are urged, in all humility, carefully to consider the crisis which faces the human race as a result of the discovery of nuclear energy.[9]

Similarly, in May 1983, the Council:

> ... stated [its] belief that the stewardship of God's creation is the responsibility of all the people of Christ, understands that God's loving purposes for his creation were revealed in Christ, and perceives that a threat to [the] creation and ... God's loving purposes for humankind is posed by the possession and spread of nuclear weapons.[10]

In these two examples are combined the doctrine of God the Creator (and human responsibility as stewards of creation) and the Christian doctrine that God has revealed his saving love towards humankind in Jesus Christ and that we are called to submit to his loving purposes: the destruction of the human race was seen to be in the balance.

When, in *Swords into Ploughshares*, the relationship between nuclear weapons and the divine purpose was discussed,[11] it was maintained that possessing or using nuclear weapons 'raises fundamental questions with respect to the meaning of life and the hope of the human race'. Indeed, this was primarily a matter of faith and provided an opportunity to witness to faith in the risen Christ:

> Such a crisis provides a special opportunity for the churches to proclaim the faith that 'the earth is the Lord's and the fullness thereof', and that he intends to complete his work, not by destroying enemies but by loving them ... Christians should reject the bomb in the full confidence of faith that God has a better way of accomplishing his purposes; even though that could mean that we ourselves suffer rather than causing suffering to others.[12]

The final chapter of *Swords into Ploughshares* dealt with the question of war and the vengeance of God, and challenged the claim that war is proof of a vengeful God. How can the God who revealed himself in Jesus, the one who 'did not argue to defend himself' before his accusers and those who crucified him, suffer the slaughter of millions? Many who saw the terrible suffering and killing in the wars of the twentieth century, find it difficult to reject the belief in a vengeful God. It is often easier for them to see God's vengeance than God's saving grace. Probably the key is not so much in the doctrine of the wrath of God but in a true understanding of the enormity of humankind's suffering in the light of faith in a God whose purpose is to save the world in Jesus Christ. *Swords into Ploughshares* did not deal directly with this, but it hinted at an answer when it referred to 'the hope of salvation in the life and death of Christ' and the realization 'of man's innate sinfulness'. It argued that the basis of hope for humankind, even in the face of a nuclear threat, was that the God who governs history has 'the will to create a new world'. The future is 'the purpose of God' and God can 'surprise us afresh',[13] through the one who was crucified and raised again, in whom everything co-exists. If we are to face the future hopefully on the basis of this certainty, we are forced to consider the practical implications of 'acting in hope'. A number of key issues for further consideration by the churches were noted.[14] It would be necessary to discover a way of exercising political authority 'justly, without violence or threat' and of solving clashes 'without using force of arms'. It was suggested that there was a need to consider the significance of 'forgiveness in politics' and how to 'channel technological nuclear knowledge towards peaceful ends'.

> Our world is God's world. Nothing, not even discouragement and rank despair, can release us from our responsibility to protect it. But awareness of the reality must affect our hopes, and our actions must bring them to realisation.[15]

In a sermon (based on Psalm 120, verse 6) to the Anglican Peace Society in 1987, the former Archbishop of York, John Habgood, came to similar conclusions:

> We need more than prophecy and policy. Without prophetic vision there is no fire, no drive, no sense of ultimate goals. Without careful policy-making there is no effectiveness. The bridge (between prophecy and policy) is the process by which God teaches us through history . . . we have to reflect on and learn from human experience – on history as the arena for the Spirit's action . . . It is on the plane of historical events that Christ meets us.[16]

Another important element of *Swords into Ploughshares'* theological exploration was the relationship between disarmament and world development. The theological starting point for this discussion was the understanding of *Shalom* (*peace with justice*) in the Bible. The assertion of this chapter was that the Biblical vision of *Shalom* had been fulfilled in Jesus. This was illustrated in terms of 'establishing the Kingdom', bringing 'mankind and creation into wholeness', 'living in solidarity with those on the margins of society', 'a repentance which would include . . . a complete reassessment of the economic priorities of the life of individuals and society' and 'living a love which destroys self-centred fear'.[17]

In the Peace Council in March 1987, Siân ap Gwynfor, who had been invited to present the pacifist standpoint, came to a similar conclusion, namely, that human beings had a responsibility to protect God's creation and to offer hope:

> Scripture teaches us that we cannot say we love and respect God if we do not love and respect God's creation. And at the moment his creation is being destroyed . . . In this hopeless situation there is an opportunity for the Church to present the hope of the Gospel of Jesus Christ . . . [and] become a positive force, relevant to the needs of the world today. Both believing and acting are important.[18]

So there were strong theological foundations for the Council's position on disarmament. The starting point was the doctrine of God the Creator, who called his people to protect the creation which was given to them as a gift, and God the Saviour, who fulfilled in Christ the Kingdom of his love and his loving intentions towards the creation and humankind. There is no place for destructive force in this Kingdom; one of his gifts is *shalom*, peace with justice, through his death and resurrection for all. In Christ, humanity is called to repentance, to set new priorities, the priorities of God's Kingdom, and to lay aside weapons of destruction. In the face of terrible threats, we are called to offer the hope of the Gospel, namely, that it is the purpose of God to renew the world through the risen Christ.

The discussion of the question of 'a just war' was a difficult one for the Council, not only with respect to nuclear war but also with respect to war of every kind. *Swords into Ploughshares* summarized the traditional guidelines for a just war. It is necessary to secure 'a proper and constitutional authority'. It is necessary for the cause to be just and for 'every means of avoiding war to have failed'. Establishing 'permanent peace' is the only intention which justifies war, and that by means of proportionate aims and military force. Lastly, 'the war should not affect non-combatants and non-military targets should not be attacked'.[19] '[S]erious difficulties arise under each of these headings.' In his analysis of traditional attitudes to war, Robin Gill concludes that the history of theological approaches to war argues that the doctrine of a just war is essential for churches who want to take the state and its welfare seriously.[20] Only a sect can adopt a pacifist attitude! But he also recognizes that such a theory has enormous difficulties. Among them he lists the difficulty of reconciling the answers of the Old Testament to war with those of the New Testament, of defining a 'legitimate authority' in a world of unjust governments, and of applying the theory to modern warfare which uses such horrifying armed force. But he pays particular attention to nuclear war in this connection and comes to the conclusion that even possessing nuclear arms could go beyond the bounds of the doctrine of a just war:

> Nuclear warfare ... may exceed the bounds of any Christian just-war theory ... exacerbated by the connection that is becoming increasingly apparent between nuclear weapons and nuclear power, by the proliferation of nuclear knowledge beyond the Western countries, by the possibility of nuclear terrorism or by strategical discussions of limited nuclear war.[21]

After a thorough consideration of traditional and contemporary Christian beliefs, Gill's view is: 'if modern warfare is to be justifiable at all, it is only to be justified with extreme reluctance and as a very last resort. Even the possession of a nuclear deterrent is a concession to an evil world.'[22]

In the 1987 Peace Council, the Dean of St Asaph, Raymond Renowden, was asked to argue the case for the just war doctrine. In his view, such a justification presupposed 'a social and political order', 'that human nature was fallible', and that it was a 'moral responsibility to oppose those wishing to threaten the (social and political) order'.[23] On this basis, he concluded that just war principles 'remain relevant despite the destructive force of nuclear weapons – through an appeal to principles of understanding and proportion'. He went on to discuss the moral distinction between 'use' and 'deterrence' and concluded:

> Despite all the serious doubts with regard to the morality of *use*, deterrence is morally acceptable under specific circumstances, particularly since this *should not* be seen as *an intention in itself* but as a step towards a system of controlling arms and of *progressive disarmament* ... Whatever are the moral weaknesses of a policy of deterrence, they need to be weighed against the moral weaknesses of the other choices we have.[24]

This reflected the statement of Pope John Paul II in his address to the Second Special Session of the United Nations on Disarmament in 1982: 'In current conditions "deterrence" based on balance, certainly not as an end in itself, but as a step towards progressive disarmament, may still be judged morally acceptable.'[25]

But this position was never adopted as the official position of the Council. Indeed, the conclusion was reached in *Swords into Ploughshares* that there was 'an innate contradiction between the concept of deterrence and the doctrine of a just war; the more disproportionate the threat, the more effective it is'.[26] And although some in the churches and denominations, including some of their representatives on the Council, argued that the doctrine of 'a just war' was acceptable with regard to possession, if not use of nuclear weapons, the Council adhered in each of its statements to the view that was clearly expressed by the British Council of Churches in its statement in November 1979, namely, that 'nuclear arms are offensive to God and a denial of his purpose for man'[27] and that therefore possessing them as well as using them would be inconsistent with the moral requirements of a just war. We shall have to return to these arguments.

### Nuclear disarmament: analysing and interpreting

The Council never doubted that the terrible effects of nuclear weapons were repugnant. It noted, for example,[28] that 60,000 were killed in Hiroshima around 6 August 1945 and that a total of 200,000 had been killed by the early 1980s, and that the nuclear powers had enough bombs to destroy each other twenty or thirty times over. According to the American association 'Doctors for Social Responsibility':

> Medical planning is senseless. There will be no possibility of a medical response ... The majority of hospitals would have been destroyed and the majority of medical staff would have been killed or injured ... the majority of the survivors of the initial catastrophe would die ... The basics of human life would have been destroyed in the U.S., Russia and a large part of the world. The radioactive dust from the bombs would have contaminated much of the earth and atmospheric effects would damage all living creatures.[29]

As well as the medical effects, there would be terrible economic consequences. A paper by the Swedish Royal Academy was quoted which maintained that up to a billion people would die in the countries of the South because of the destruction of the basis of trade and economic markets. The Council echoed the conclusions of the Pugwash[30] conference in 1980 that it would be a mistake to think that it would be possible to survive a nuclear war, that civil defence would be able to secure the continuation of society, and that it would be necessary for the two sides to have equal arms in order to prevent an attack.

Since the political threat was bound up with the economic injustice of the present order, the question was asked: 'is it possible that creating a just and compassionate world order is a condition of solving the nuclear threat?'[31]

J. E. Williams,[32] at the start of his lecture on 'International Society and the Search for Peace' in the Wrexham Peace Council, called on the churches to face this situation realistically: 'There are no quick fixes ... Our fallible leaders must deal with impossible situations with insufficient knowledge and imperfect understanding.'[33]

In its analysis of the international situation, the Council recognized both the horror of the nuclear threat and this political reality. A number of related aspects of the nuclear threat became the focus of the Council's analysis over the years. First, in 1981 and again in 1983, the fear was expressed that the nuclear crisis was intensifying the political divisions in the world 'according to a political ideology, as if this division were synonymous with the difference between good and evil'.[34] This, it was claimed, was the result of the hypocritical propaganda of the two 'sides': 'a study of propaganda is a study of self-justification and demonizing of the enemy – as Christians we strongly oppose these tendencies.'[35] Indeed, J. E. Williams asked whether the policy necessitated such propaganda: 'perhaps it was necessary for governments to paint the world in bald moral terms in order to persuade people to accept a policy which presumed a readiness to commit national suicide.'[36]

Secondly, particular attention was paid to the relationship between disarmament and development. The Brandt Report was quoted (in Welsh):

> The increase in arms in large parts of the Third World ... is causing increasing instability and is undermining development. A new understanding of defence and security is vital ... More weapons are not making mankind safer, but poorer.

The view of the Palme Report (1982) was accepted, that there is no hope for general security without economic recovery: 'we are more and more dependent on one another ... We are facing dangers which are common to all of us, therefore it has to be with one another that we foster our security.'[37]

There was greater disagreement on the third matter discussed, namely, deterrence. According to J. E. Williams, the basis of deterrence 'is the belief that whoever is making decisions is influenced by the threat of punishment, especially if that punishment cannot be avoided at all', and that what causes anxiety 'is the way in which this simple idea has been used to justify the building of a monstrous war machine'.[38] On the other hand, he recognized that 'the deterrent force of nuclear arms is more effective than any previous system of arms since the revenge was greater and more certain, because, so far there was not an effective defence against missiles'.[39] Nevertheless, he concluded that:

> ... the peace lobby is right to condemn nuclear deterrence as something morally irresponsible. A strategy which purposely sets out to kill millions of innocent people is mad and wicked ... At the same time, it must be recognized that some of the aims of these two military alliances have a very high moral value – peace, independence and freedom.[40]

On the other hand, Raymond Renowden was able to justify a policy of deterrence:

> ... while it would be immoral to use nuclear weapons, keeping them for purposes of deterrence is the less evil path which is open to us at the moment ... The only purpose (nuclear weapons) have is to prevent waging a nuclear war. What is needed is the least deterrence.[41]

So he concluded that deterrence was:

> morally acceptable under specific circumstances, especially since this should not be seen as an intention in itself but as a step towards a system of controlling arms and of progressive disarmament ... for Wales. However, in May 1986, the Council did ... Whatever are the moral weaknesses of a policy of deterrence, they must be weighed against the moral weaknesses of the other choices we have.[42]

Fourthly, an attempt was made to evaluate some of the disarmament and defence programmes which were suggested, such as the campaign for a freeze and the SDI. The Campaign for a Nuclear Freeze was very influential during the eighties and received the support of a number of the denominations in Wales and their leaders. The aim of this international campaign was to put a stop to modernizing and proliferating nuclear weapons as a first step towards disarmament, and this necessarily by means of multilateral steps. During a short presentation on this campaign in the Peace Council in 1987, Roberta Owen, one of the organizers of the campaign in Wales, argued 'that this was the most effective way ahead'.[43] But though she suggested a number of ways which could be adopted by the Council to promote the campaign, they were not acted upon and the Campaign for a Nuclear Freeze did not become official policy of the Council of Churches for Wales, although (in May 1986) the Council did commend the Campaign to Christians in Wales.

John Holdsworth[44] argued that a cynical person could maintain that the main achievement of the campaign was to encourage President Reagan to recommend his 'anti-freeze political initiative' in March 1983 by suggesting a Strategic Defence Initiative with these words:

... let me share with you a vision which offers hope ... What if free people could live in the knowledge that their security did not rest upon the threat of instant US retaliation ... We could intercept ... strategic ballistic missiles before they reached our own soil and that of our allies ... I call upon the scientific community to turn their great talents to the cause of mankind and world peace.[45]

In summarizing the Council's response to this vision, John Holdsworth expressed the international community's doubt that such a plan was possible and would be economically effective. 'Why not concentrate only on reducing offensive weapons, which could be done quickly, cheaply and without the distabilization [sic] that a 20 or 30 year development programme would bring.'[46]

On this basis, a resolution was adopted at the meeting of the Council in May 1986 which welcomed the paper's analysis of the Strategic Defence Initiative, 'shared the doubts' of the Government about it and asserted that a reduction in nuclear arms would 'accomplish the aims of the Plan more effectively'.[47]

Fifthly, there was an attempt to evaluate the effectiveness of a policy of unilateral disarmament compared with a policy of multilateral disarmament. *Swords into Ploughshares* offered a number of arguments in favour of unilateral disarmament on the part of Britain. It would put a brake on:

> ... the headlong rush to the precipice ... It could remove one of the obstacles hindering the unilateral negotiations so far ... It would strengthen Britain from a moral and economic standpoint. It would enable Britain to contribute more effectively to the task of sharing the earth's resources more fairly for the Third World. It would strengthen the hands of those in the East as well as the West who realize the madness of the arms race which has no end in view but destruction.[48]

But in the last chapter, *Swords into Ploughshares* concluded that 'opposing unilateral and multilateral disarmament (is not) helpful'[49] and it suggested to the British Government, as a first step, that it should not renew Polaris nor set up the Trident system. This, it was believed, would ease the obstacles which could not be removed by diplomatic negotiations only, and in a way that would not threaten international stability. It was noted that other groups that came to the same conclusion had been accused of wanting to leave Britain 'naked and defenceless'.[50] According to the authors, 'this is an emotional and misleading response', and they went on to argue strongly in favour of the kind of unilateral/multilateral disarmament which was commended, despite a number of powerful arguments in favour of this standpoint. It 'recognises the reality of the situation, . . . allows room for God's intervention and hopes for it, . . . reduces international tension and helps the cause of multilateral disarmament'.[51] This position was seen as a combination of applying the principles of a just war to the nuclear situation with a realistic calculation of the likely consequences of separate actions. In the same way, J. E. Williams argued for a combination of arms control and responsible unilateral action, as well as seeking agreements to reject first use of nuclear weapons and to create nuclear-free zones.

This analysis shows that the Council succeeded in gathering together a considerable technological and political expertise in analysing and interpreting these complex matters. The Council could hardly be accused of naivety (although many did so), and it reached its decisions responsibly and intelligently. It made an important contribution, too, especially in *Swords into Ploughshares* and the 1987 Peace Council, to communicating this analysis and sharing it with the churches and denominations, as well as with Christians in local churches. However, despite the quality of the documents and reports themselves, publicity was ineffective – a criticism which can be fairly made with respect to other aspects of the Council's social responsibility work. The Council also managed to avoid the polarization which was an obvious danger in a body that was acting as a bridge between denominations in Wales that held such a diversity of views on issues that aroused such strong passions during these years. As a result, it succeeded in offering a responsible middle way which was, on the whole, acceptable to both 'sides' in this debate.

## Messages to the Government

On the basis of the theological discussions and the careful analysis, a number of messages were conveyed to the

## WAR AND PEACE: NUCLEAR DISARMAMENT

Government. One example was the resolution of the Council on 29 April 1982, 'condemning the recent decision of Her Majesty's Government to purchase *super-trident* weapons' and urging the Government:

> ... to participate in the Special Session of the United Nations on Disarmament with fresh commitment and urgency and to use all its influence to secure agreement on substantial measures towards nuclear disarmament in order to slow down the arms race and in order to ensure that the Special Session makes a substantial contribution to world peace.[52]

In May 1983, partly on the basis of the conclusions of *Swords into Ploughshares*, pressure was put on the Government to devote itself to a programme of disarmament to abolish Britain's independent nuclear deterrent and to remove nuclear arms from British soil.[53]

In his lecture to the Peace Council, J. E. Williams suggested a number of appeals which could be made to the Government, including a call:

> ... to reconsider the threat from the East [which here meant Eastern Europe and the Soviet Union in particular], ... to give up painting worst-case scenarios ... to promote policies which will encourage interdependence in trade ... and to ensure that a search for a worldwide common good takes the place of a Gaullite pride.[54]

In the meeting of the Council on 29 April 1982, there was also discussion on the decision of every County Council in Wales (with the exception of Powys County Council, at the time) to be a 'nuclear-free zone'. These decisions were noted 'with approval' and the Council expressed the 'sincere hope that these symbolic actions will be first effective steps towards general nuclear disarmament'. In a brief presentation to the Peace Council, Mervyn Phillips, chief executive of Clwyd County Council, explained the significance of these county decisions:

> It stands alongside the election to the House of Commons in 1923 by the University of Wales of George Davies as Member of Parliament, who was a Christian pacifist, the Message of Goodwill of the children of Wales, the naming of the Temple of Peace in Cardiff, and the decision in 1947 to establish the Llangollen International Eisteddfod, as a general statement by the people of Wales in the cause of peace.[55]

There was probably some overstatement in this assertion, but there is no denying that they were significant decisions in forming public opinion in Wales with respect to nuclear arms. The Report of the Peace Council published the response of the Government to the decision of Clwyd County Council. It summarized the Government's position on disarmament:

> The Government believes that nuclear weapons are an essential part of the defence policy of maintaining adequate defence forces, both conventional and nuclear, sufficient to deter attack by a potential aggressor. The first responsibility of any government must be the security of the nation . . . Our main objective is not to win a war but to prevent one from happening in the first place . . . this strategy is intended to maintain peace between East and West in Europe, as it has done for over 30 years . . . NATO countries do not believe that nuclear weapons could be used to achieve military victory in any meaningful sense and have no desire to fight a limited nuclear war . . . Unilateral disarmament by the United Kingdom – and a nuclear free zone in Europe would be, for us, the same as unilateral disarmament – would do nothing to reduce the dangers of war. Indeed . . . such a move might make war more rather than less likely.[56]

This response revealed the extent of the gap between the Government and the fairly moderate position of the Council on the issue of nuclear disarmament. It is no wonder that so many in the churches (and beyond, of course) felt anger and frustration that their voices, again and again, fell on the deaf ears of the Government. Yet the Council and its member denominations insisted on continuing to call for nuclear disarmament as an essential contribution to worldwide peace and justice in an age when the nuclear threat was alarming and real.

### Guidance to the churches

From one point of view, everything which the Council did in this field, as in every other field, was aimed primarily at offering a lead to the churches, to enable them to act more effectively – together, whenever possible. In this particular context, the main desire of the Council was to foster understanding and commitment among the Christians of Wales with regard to nuclear disarmament, and this was the aim of the majority of the resolutions already referred to. It was the sole purpose of *Swords into Ploughshares*, but it is questionable whether it had the desired publicity or influence.

The Peace Council identified the urgent need for material which would help the churches to 'consider the implications of a gospel of peace in all aspects of church life . . . especially in worship'.[57] It also believed that there was an enormous gap between the person in the pew and the decisions the churches and the denominations make as institutional bodies, and that there was a need to discover ways to encourage 'ordinary members to take small steps in making peace'. One reason, at least, for this failure was the difficulty many Christians felt about politics – a difficulty which sprang, according to the report, from the tension between the institutional and individual understanding of Christianity.

### *Nuclear disarmament: conclusion*

By the time the Council of Churches for Wales ceased to exist in 1990, the worldwide political picture had changed enormously. The Berlin Wall had fallen, a sign of incredible changes in the ideology and politics of the countries of Eastern and Central Europe which had been part of the Alliance with the Soviet Union. Indeed, soon afterwards the Soviet Union itself was dismantled, and the campaigning and struggling for independence for those countries which had been a part of that Union speeded up. In the same way, the social and political changes in the countries of Eastern and Central Europe were far-reaching and expensive and Europe, even today, continues to try to cope with these fundamental changes, in a now expanded European family.

But one consequence was very clear. It was no longer possible to think of the countries of Eastern Europe as enemies and they no longer had either the desire or the ability to go to war against other European Countries and America. The nuclear threat receded, destruction began of weapons that created such dread and ways of promoting political and economic partnerships with these countries were sought. Now there are other threats, such as the perceived terrorist threat and the response in terms of the so-called 'War on Terror' following the events of 9/11. But with the fall of the Berlin Wall and its incredible consequences, an important chapter in the history of the churches' efforts for peace had come to an end, at least for the time being. But as this volume goes to press, the debate has begun from within the British Government about the need to replace the Trident missiles. The churches may well have to re-visit the position they so firmly held in the 1980s.

# ~ 11 ~
# War and peace: the Malvinas war

On 2 April 1982 the Malvinas Islands (or the Falkland Islands) in the South Atlantic were invaded by Argentinian forces. At the time, the majority of us had to go to look for these Islands on a map of the world, but overnight they became the main news story of the day. The Islands had been invaded and inhabited by Britain in 1833. However, Argentina did not accept the legality of this situation. In their view, this was Argentinian soil, historically and geographically. The inhabitants of the Islands regarded themselves as British and there was a British Government appointed governor. The ownership of the Malvinas had been a matter of diplomatic negotiations between the governments of the two countries for fifteen years, but very little had come of these discussions. In 1982 many experts believed that the British Government had been lukewarm in its efforts to secure a solution to the dispute which would be acceptable to the inhabitants. But now it was an international crisis.

There was no doubt among the churches in Britain in general, nor here in Wales, that Argentina had acted unlawfully and immorally. The response of the Welsh Assembly of Christian Youth (in a letter dated 26 April 1982) was typical: '[The] Assembly regrets ... that Argentina decided to take possession of the Falkland Islands by violating human rights with the use of military force.' Similarly, a resolution of the Council of Churches for Wales 'regretted that there was such a long delay before coming to an agreement on the future of the Islands despite fifteen years of negotiations [and] condemned the Military Government of Argentina for taking military control of the Islands contrary to international law and the wish of the islanders.[1] But what was the appropriate response to this unlawful military takeover? The Government sent the military task force on 5 April 1982, much to the anxiety of many in the Welsh churches. Foreseeing that a military dispute was now inevitable, the president of the Security Council of the United Nations had (on 1 April 1982) called upon the governments of Britain and Argentina not to threaten or use military force in the region of the Malvinas Islands. On 3 April, the Security Council agreed Resolution 502, which called for an end to the fighting, for all the Argentinian soldiers to leave the Islands, and for the two governments to try a diplomatic response and to respect the principles of the United Nations Charter.[2]

With his usual perceptiveness, Huw Wynne Griffith, Secretary of the Council's Department of Church and Society, warned against simple responses either on pacifist grounds or on the basis of a just war. Rather, he believed that this crisis revealed a new situation for humankind. He claimed that the alleged claims of both governments were based on force and the ability of people to move around the world was clouding the definition of 'a nation' and the concept of national sovereignty. National sovereignty was subordinate to worldwide powers, he believed, and the focus was shifting from sovereign states to the United Nations.[3] He therefore urged: 'Negatively, the issue must not be one of sovereignty . . . Positively, the aim (should be) to build up the United Nations as an effective organ for valid world interests . . . Practically, it should urge the Government to pursue agreement through negotiations under UN auspices.'

On the same day, the British Council of Churches published a statement which was a basis for elements of the Council of Churches for Wales' statement (see above), calling for UN Resolution 502 to be implemented with all speed and, should the diplomatic negotiations on the basis of this resolution fail, pressing the British Government 'not to launch an armed attack until all remedies available in the UN have been explored'.

In the meantime, the World Council of Churches distributed an inter-church statement from Argentina:

> In the name of Jesus Christ, Prince of Peace, we fervently urge the Governments of Argentina and Great Britain to refrain from all military action which would endanger precious human lives and

world peace. Our churches will pray and work without ceasing for a peaceful, just and permanent solution to the dispute, confident in the help of God, our Lord.[4]

This position was supported by the World Council of Churches, adding: 'Violence runs the risk of escalating into a major conflagration, further exacerbating world tensions and the security of all peoples.'

Nevertheless, the British task force went ahead and the Island of Georgia was re-taken on 25 April. When the Council of Churches for Wales met on 29 April, Huw Wynne Griffith and the General Secretary (Noel Davies) presented a paper which referred to statements agreed by other bodies, a draft of a resolution to be presented to the Council and questions concerning national sovereignty in a changing world, with the suggestion that they should be borne in mind by member churches during any discussions of the crisis. The questions were: was there a danger 'in connecting sovereignty with military force'? Was the idea of 'colonial sovereignty' any longer acceptable? It was suggested that it was necessary 'to try to understand the sovereignty of a nation in terms of an international partnership rather [than] an undeniable right' and that there was now a need to think in terms of the United Nations as the focus for international relationships rather than maintaining the claims of 'sovereign states' as the focus of power and international authority.[5]

The paper also proposed that there were Christian and moral principles which were fundamental to the life of every nation, including 'respecting the fundamental rights of every person as created in the image of God, the freedom of peoples to choose their own government and to expect them to act in their name'.

The discussion was long and difficult, with considerable tension between those who were able to accept the war as a 'just war' and others who felt that there was no such thing as a just war and that both sides should be condemned equally. This tension was (and is) characteristic of differences of opinion both within and between the denominations in Wales on the question of the morality of war. In one respect, the draft resolution was strengthened by adding the following paragraph:

> The Council of Churches for Wales is very concerned about the jingoistic and militaristic spirit among the people of Britain and their leaders demonstrated in their response to the invasion of the Islands by Argentina, since it believes that this response is contrary to the Christian witness to the way of peace.[6]

On the other hand, the clause 'condemning the use of military force to regain sovereignty over the Islands' was altered to read 'opposing the further use of military force', in order to tone down the condemnation of the British Government and to reflect the view of some members that what had already been done to try to regain the Islands came within the terms of a just war.

The resolution continued:

> [The Council of Churches for Wales . . . ]

> . . . opposes the further use of military force to regain sovereignty over the islands, especially since every possible diplomatic path towards a peaceful and just response to the crisis has not yet been pursued to the utmost, and expresses grave concern that such militarism, on both sides, endangers the peace and security of humanity;

> welcomes the first response of the United Nations through the Security Council's resolution 502 . . . and calls upon the governments of Britain and Argentina to use all the resources of the United Nations to seek a peaceful, just and permanent response to the crisis, and to encourage the countries of the world to make the United Nations a more effective and recognised international instrument to respond to situations such as this;

> and calls upon our fellow-Christians to pray for a response to the crisis which will not be dependent on military force and which will give the Islands a peaceful and secure future.[7]

At the time, this resolution was seen as one of the clearest amongst those of inter-church bodies in the United Kingdom in its criticism of the jingoistic and militaristic attitude which characterized the Governments and the public in both countries. Its emphasis on continuing diplomatic efforts rather than military campaigns, and its call to give primacy to the United Nations were typical of the resolutions of other denominations and ecumenical bodies.

One of the most radical resolutions was that of the Fellowship of Reconciliation in Wales, agreed at its meeting on 1 May. It expressed:

> ... disappointment and horror at the response of the British Government ... and our sadness in realising how easy it is to stir a section of the British population to support war ... The present situation is a direct result of having a militarist policy. One inevitable consequence of an arms policy is an increase in warlike attitudes ... We proclaim with sadness that the Church [i.e. the denominations of Wales] has not faced up to its responsibility and we call upon it to wake up and to act in the name of Jesus Christ.[8]

The FoR Wales asked the Council of Churches for Wales to call a national public meeting 'which would be an opportunity for the voice of the Christian Church to be expressed'. (But such a conference was never held, even though the Council convened a small group to consider the implications of the war for churches' Christian witness in Wales.) When the Council of Churches for Wales's resolution was sent to the Prime Minister, the General Secretary believed:

> ... that it expresses the deep concern of our fellow Christians in Wales that the present military action is inconsistent with a Christian spirit and places the islanders and the whole of humanity in great danger. We believe that other means towards a negotiated agreement, particularly through the United Nations, should be pursued urgently before any further military action is undertaken.[9]

In her reply, the Prime Minister asserted:

> It has always been our wish, and it is still our wish, to settle this dispute by negotiation ... Military achievements have been in support of our overall strategy; they have not been and will not become a substitute for it ... Our immediate concern is to implement the resolution passed by the UN Security Council ... But so far the Argentinians have shown no inclination to implement the resolution. Until they do, we will continue to exercise our rights of self-defence, including the use of force under Article 51 of the UN Charter, if this proves necessary.[10]

The response of the Foreign Office was along the same lines, emphasizing the rights of the islanders to determine their own future and that the Government was determined 'that the

Argentines should not achieve by force what they have failed to achieve in the negotiations'.[11]

In the same Council meeting, it was agreed to send greetings to the Consultative Council of the Churches of Argentina (which included Protestant denominations as well as the Roman Catholic Church). They were sent on 12 May and were seen as a contribution to maintaining 'with bonds of peace the unity which the Spirit gives' (Ephesians 4: 3, REV):

> The Council asserts that Christians should not be primarily concerned with sovereignty over islands ... but with the Kingdom of God and his righteousness ... It realises that control over the Falkland Islands (Islas Malvinas) has in the past rested on military power and regrets that the Governments of Argentina and of Britain have sought and are seeking to establish control of the islands for the future in the same way, by the use of force ... It judges that the Governments of Argentina and Britain should obey the resolution of the Security Council and, if necessary, refer the further settlement of their dispute to the UN.

The letter ended by expressing the desire to see the Christians of Wales and Argentina discover a deeper fellowship with each other after the war is over.

On 28 July (after the end of the war), the Consultative Council of the Churches of Argentina sent a copy of a general response which was drawn up for fellow Christians across the world who had sent them greetings during the period of the war. Bishop Federico Pagura (President of the Council, Bishop of the Evangelical Methodist Church of Argentina, and one of the prominent leaders of the ecumenical movement in Latin America and worldwide) attached a message on a visiting card in his own handwriting:

> Thank you for the Declaration of the Council of Churches for Wales with reference to the recent war. It has been very much appreciated in the Welsh congregations in the Patagonian Region of our Church. We are glad to send you the last document of our Consultative Council of Churches, hoping it will help you to understand something of our feelings and hopes.

During the days following the meeting of the Council, the situation worsened. On 1 May, British aircraft bombed Stanley airfield; on 3 May, one of the Argentine warships, the General

## WAR AND PEACE: THE MALVINAS WAR

Belgrano, was sunk, and the following day the British ship HMS Sheffield was sunk. Many lives were lost.

Pope John Paul II was to visit Britain during May and June and there were doubts about the visit right up to the day of his arrival, 28 May. In a powerful address in Coventry on 30 May, which was chosen because of the destruction there during the Second World War, he called for the building of peace, as the Cathedral in Coventry was built, patiently, with unshakeable faith: 'the cathedral of peace is again destroyed. Today, the scale and horror of modern warfare – whether nuclear or not – makes it totally unacceptable as a means of settling differences between nations. War should belong to the tragic past, to history; it should find no place on humanity's agenda for the future.'[12]

The fighting lasted for the whole of May and on 8 June the Prime Minister announced that she would not return to the United Nations. It was obvious to the churches that it would not be possible to influence the political process any further, since the Government was determined to secure a military victory. On 12 June, the final attack on Port Stanley began and on 15 June the document which conceded victory to Britain was signed.

### Questions to Christians

A number of important questions to Christians were raised by this war which were discussed widely among the denominations and their leaders.

*Interference in politics*

First, the involvement of the churches and denominations in political issues remained a bone of contention both within and outside the churches. On the one hand, for instance, a very critical article was written by Clifford Longley in *The Times* on 3 May condemning 'the major religious institutions of Britain' for expressing on behalf of the Church 'judgements which are quite beyond their competence to make'. He quoted the British Council of Churches, the Methodist Church, and the Baptist

Union of Great Britain as examples of this: 'The bodies holding these opinions are made up of mere newspaper readers . . . It is a pervasive and peculiar conceit that persuades executives and assemblies and councils that they have something to say on the detail of political and diplomatic processes.' He argued that only in relation to moral and theological matters did the churches have the right to interfere and, therefore, they should not interfere in diplomatic and political affairs. Unfortunately, the dividing line between moral and political aspects of a situation such as the Malvinas war is never as clear as Longley imagined. On the other hand, Christian organizations and church leaders themselves believed strongly that the churches had a Christian duty to express informed and responsible views on matters which had to do with the life of the nation. Bishop John Robinson, for example, asked, 'Has the voice of prophecy really departed from the land? Is there no troubler in Israel prepared to confront the statements of each side . . . especially since they both claim to lead Christian countries?'[13] As has been seen, the unease would surface in the discussions of the Peace Council of 1987, and it arose mainly from the tension between an understanding of Christianity which is chiefly institutional and one which is largely individual. Various traditions within the Council held differing views on this tension and this was partly responsible for the hesitation on the part of some (chiefly the Roman Catholic Church, at the time) with regard to statements on public affairs, most particularly by ecumenical bodies. The theological challenge of this tension has still not gone away.

*The morality of the war*

Secondly, there was considerable discussion concerning the morality of this war. Some believed it was a just war. In a statement on 28 April, Cardinal Hume, the Archbishop of Westminster, quoted the report of the Second Vatican Council on 'The Church in the Modern World': 'As long as the danger of war persists and there is no international authority with the necessary competence and power, governments cannot be denied the right to lawful self-defence, once all peaceful efforts have failed.'[14]

On the basis of traditional principles of a just war, he concluded that this war meets the requirements: 'Unilateral annexation [of the Falkland Islands] by armed invasion breaches international law and ignores the rights and ... wishes of the inhabitants ... Such action is unacceptable both legally and morally ... Faced with aggression it is not morally wrong to resist or to reassert rights with a measured degree of force.'[15]

But he also insisted that it was not sufficient for Christians to rest on such an argument: 'We should be active in such areas as educational programmes for peace, in work for the abolition of the arms trade and in extending between countries a greater flow of cultural exchanges particularly between young people.'

The Archbishop of Canterbury expressed a similar position in a statement on 2 May: 'within the complexities of an imperfect world, self-defence and the use of armed force in the defence of clear principles can sometimes be justified.' Nevertheless, the Lambeth Conference of Anglican Bishops in 1948, 1958, 1968 and 1978 had stated: 'War as a method of settling international disputes is incompatible with the teaching of our Lord Jesus Christ' – a verbatim quotation from the first Assembly of the World Council of Churches. In such a moral crisis, John Habgood, Archbishop of York, had a timely word: 'Christian people may sometimes find themselves regretfully drawn into war and accept it as part of the penalty of living in a sinful world ... But we must be careful not to glorify the fighting itself, or see it as anything other than evidence of human failure.'[16]

In a paper presented to the Assembly of the British Council of Churches in November 1982, Roger Williamson, one of the secretaries of its Division of International Affairs, offered an analysis of the moral justification of the war in the light of the traditional 'just war' principles. Some of the principles may have been fulfilled (such as the authority of the governments, an official declaration of war, a fair certainty of success, an avoidance of injuring or killing the civilian population and, perhaps, that the methods were commensurate with the cause). Nevertheless, he judged that it was much more difficult to reach a decision on matters such as a just cause, going to war after having exhausted every other possibility, and the proportion of the evil and destruction of the war compared with the injustice that caused it. A number of representatives of the denominations in Wales who were content to accept the moral principle of a 'just war' shared these doubts with respect to the Malvinas war but tended to think that the action of the British Government could, on the whole, be justified, while maintaining the belief that war is an indication of human failure.

At the same time, of course, many of the denominations, most particularly the Welsh-language Nonconformist denominations, took a pacifist standpoint on this war as on all war, as their resolutions show. Although representatives of this tradition tended to be in the majority on the Council, the tension between the two positions was a difficult and painful one. Little was done during the following years to reach a consensus on the matter. The first meeting of the Council of Cytûn: Churches Together in Wales, in November 1990, had to come to a judgement on the Gulf War which was being fought at the time, with British forces at the heart of the conflict. A draft resolution was presented to the Council, after considerable consultation with the denominations and their leaders, which steered a moral path similar to the one accepted on 29 April. But it was not approved. The main reason for this was that the number of those in favour of the moral principle of a just war had grown in the new body. The consequence was a weak and generalized compromise. Cytûn was severely criticized by some for such an ineffective stand and some judged that Cytûn could never be prophetic in such public matters if it insisted on being fair to the standpoint of all its member denominations and churches. The truth, however, is that there is a difference of view between the various denominations and churches on the subject of war and peace. Indeed, there is room to believe that there is just as much difference of opinion on these matters within the denominations themselves. As the Peace Council of 1987 noted, there is at times a considerable gap between the official view of a denomination – even of a denomination with a pacifist standpoint – and members in local congregations. There is a need for theological reflection and teaching both within and between the denominations before there can be unanimity on the morality of war.

## International challenges

Thirdly, there was a perceived need to give special attention to a number of international matters which came to the fore as a result of this war. When the Council's Committee on National and International Affairs met on 26 July 1982 to consider the request for a national conference (which in the end was not held), it was agreed that the central topic was Securing World Peace, and that issues to be considered should include the effectiveness of the United Nations in view of its failure during the Malvinas war, sovereignty in a nuclear world, and the need for reconciliation between Britain and Argentina.[17] When a group met to discuss some of these issues, it was noted that one of the key questions – not least in Wales – was the appropriate relationship between love of nation and relationships between nations, and the relationships between the nations of Britain and Ireland. The British Council of Churches saw the need for a fresh consideration of the arms trade (in view of the supposed ambiguity of the policy of the British Government, which had sold arms to Argentina) and the implications of a willingness to go to war over the right of the inhabitants of the Malvinas to decide their fate for themselves, in relation to the Governments' attitude to the inhabitants of other territories (such as Hong Kong) which were also seeking their political rights at that time.

## Wales and Argentina

Fourthly, while continuing to condemn Argentina for taking possession of the Islands by military means, the war did lead to a deeper understanding of the views of the people of Argentina, including fellow Christians. The reply sent by the Consultative Council of the Churches of Argentina on 28 July was an especially revealing one. It was very critical of the country's government and society. Democratic institutions were destroyed by a series of *de facto* military governments. Human rights were denied. Now it was necessary to review and rebuild. 'In this process Christians of all confessional families must participate without reserve as a sign of our fidelity to Jesus Christ and our love for the people to which we belong.'[18]

Despite this, they were totally supportive of Argentina's claim on the Malvinas: 'we shall continue supporting our present or future leaders in their efforts to achieve the recovery of the territory which belongs to us historically and geographically.' This deep-seated feeling was confirmed by Professor Jose Miguez Bonino, one of the presidents of the World Council of Churches and a prominent Methodist theologian in Argentina, when he visited Britain between 29 May and 1 June 1982. He believed that part of Argentina's self-awareness was tied up with the Islands: 'This is an old, deeply felt claim. They are part of the integrity of Argentina.'[19] Furthermore, suspicions were expressed that the Western and Christian alliance (*their words*) which had fought in the South Atlantic was a sign of the deep crisis of the countries of the West, 'which conserves very little Christianity and very much of a materialistic and imperialistic spirit . . . [and betrays] a much deeper crisis of values'. They also became aware of the solidarity of the peoples of Latin America with Argentina, which caused the people of Argentina to rediscover their identity. Christians were called upon to join in this great cause, 'which may mark the beginning of a fuller and more genuine independence for our peoples and justice for their oppressed classes'. To many Welsh-speaking Christians of Wales, these lessons were comparatively easy to learn. The founding of the Welsh colony in Patagonia had created a very close relationship between Wales and Argentina. A number of people who were now in Wales had either lived in Patagonia or had family or friends there. The religious and cultural links had been very close. All this created considerable sympathy, especially among the Welsh-speaking Nonconformist denominations. The message of Bishop Pagura has already been mentioned, which informed the Council that the Welsh congregations in Patagonia had appreciated the message which was sent to the Consultative Council of the Churches of Argentina.

There was a wish to build on this foundation of sympathy and deeper understanding by trying to foster a new relationship between the churches of the two countries. This had already been expressed in the message which was sent to the Consultative Council at the beginning of May. When the Central Committee of the World Council of Churches met in Geneva in July 1982, an informal meeting was held between representatives from Argentina, Britain and Ireland, and the Secretary of the Council of Churches for Wales (Noel Davies) shared in the meeting. It was recognized that there had been a failure to use the ecumenical relationship 'to counsel together to help avoid the present conflict and to promote a deeper understanding of the issues involved'.[20] It was believed to be of the utmost importance that discussions between the Christians of Britain and Argentina should continue, since they could help reconciliation between the two countries and contribute to discovering a just and peaceful answer to the situation. The message published by the Consultative Council of the Churches of Argentina on 6 July expressed its appreciation that channels of prayer and communication had remained open throughout the crisis. The question was asked whether the time had come 'for our confession of faith as disciples of Jesus Christ to include the rejection of the contemporary idols (of the arms race and the monster of war) which threaten humanity with destruction'.[21] The same desire was expressed in Christmas greetings received by the Council of Churches for Wales, as well as other Councils and denominations in Britain: 'Now, we cannot but ask you in love for us to continue to be in contact with those who have the right to make decisions, and trying to influence them so that, with God's help, it will be possible to settle the differences that are between our nations in a just and honourable way.'[22]

In July 1985, Noel Davies, General Secretary of the Council, visited Buenos Aires as a member of a three-person delegation from the British Council of Churches. There was an opportunity to visit leaders of the Protestant denominations and the Roman Catholic Church, as well as the Inter-Church Theological College and human rights movements in the capital, with the specific intention of discussing how best to build a relationship between the churches and denominations of Britain and Argentina.

These steps were the fruit of the worldwide ecumenical movement, but they were probably not as effective as they should have been. In the words of Roger Williamson: 'How can the ecumenical fellowship be maintained and improved so that we are not restricted to exchanges of points of view in wartime, but are able through the ecumenical movement tomake a genuine contribution to peace, conflict prevention and resolution?'[23]

## WAR AND PEACE: THE MALVINAS WAR

*Perils of rejoicing in victory*

Finally, there was a consciousness of the dangers of rejoicing in the 'victory' of the British forces and the political exploitation which followed. John Habgood was one of the first church leaders to warn against this danger: 'The danger is . . . that the scent of victory distorts perceptions. A subtle process begins whereby putting the "Great" back into Britain becomes an unacknowledged war aim.'[24] In his memoirs, Denis Healey, as perhaps might be expected, made a similar point:

> Mrs Thatcher exploited the victory of our forces in the Falklands to create the feeling, both at home and abroad, that Britain was great again. We have ceased to be a nation in retreat . . . We have instead a new-found confidence – born in the economic battles at home and tested and found true eight thousand miles away.[25]

It became more obvious during the preparations for the service in Saint Paul's Cathedral to remember the end of the war. The Dean of St Paul's Cathedral and the Archbishop of Canterbury refused to agree to the Prime Minister's request to 'rejoice' in the victory. This stand was a cause of considerable criticism. At one time, there was a suggestion from those that were planning the service that the Lord's Prayer should be said in Spanish (as well as English) during the service, as a token of reconciliation. When it was decided not to do this, a report appeared in *The Sun*: 'The disgraceful plan for the Lord's Prayer to be said in Spanish was, thankfully, dumped.' Nevertheless, there were prayers for the families of those killed from Britain and Argentina, and for soldiers of the two countries who were wounded. In his sermon, the Archbishop of Canterbury, Robert Runcie, underlined this point: 'In our prayers we shall quite rightly remember those who are bereaved in our own country and the relations of the young Argentinian soldiers who were killed. Common sorrow could do something to reunite those who were engaged in this struggle. A shared anguish can be a bridge of reconciliation. Our neighbours are indeed like us.'[26] He went on to say: '[God] is able to deepen and enlarge our compassion and to purify our thanksgiving . . . talk of peace and reconciliation is just fanciful and theoretical unless we are prepared to undergo such a revolution.'[27] This standpoint was admired by many in Welsh churches at the time, at a period when rejoicing in victory was in danger of closing our eyes to the horror of war and its price in lives for both sides.

## *War and peace: conclusion*

This survey of the Council's engagement with the question of nuclear disarmament and the Malvinas Islands war enables us to come to some general conclusions.

First, while, in relation to the issue of nuclear disarmament, there was an attempt to set a theological foundation for the Council's position, on the whole the response to the Malvinas war was pragmatic. As has been seen, the heart of the theological approach was the doctrine of creation and the doctrine concerning Christ. Little attempt was made to consider the biblical testimony in relation to these matters. Perhaps the ambiguity in that testimony contributes to this failure, although there is a strong case for arguing that there is no ambiguity in Jesus's own teaching. It is also true to say that, whereas there was considerable discussion concerning the relevance of the doctrine of a just war, no detailed consideration was given to the expression of this doctrine by Thomas Aquinas and others – at least, if documentary evidence is to be accepted. On the whole, the discussion was based on secondary sources. Neither was there unanimity on the relevance of the doctrine of a just war either to a conventional war (such as the Malvinas war) or to nuclear war. Those who believed that the doctrine continued to be relevant would find it easier to argue that case with respect to a conventional war but were likely to recognize that there was always the danger in the contemporary situation that such a war would develop into a nuclear war, and that one could not apply the doctrine to justify the use of the powerful forces which would be unleashed in such a situation. Of course, this discussion is entirely theoretical and frustrating to those – perhaps the majority among the representatives of the Welsh denominations on the Council – who profess a pacifist standpoint on the basis of Jesus's teachings. They can find no justification for war under any circumstances. There is room to believe that this voice is stronger among the churches of Wales than it is in the other countries of Britain and Ireland. But so far there has been no obvious success in coming to theological and moral unanimity on the question of war. A case could be argued that the strong criticism of the recent war against Iraq and the continuing violence that has followed has increased the urgency of this debate and has raised the key issues in relation to just war principles much more sharply in the public mind. 9/11 has changed the dimensions of this debate. However, this continues to be one of the few subjects in the field of church and society where a consensus has not been developed through the growing ecumenical partnership over the last half century. There is a need for further theological reflection, and that in the context of a new worldwide political map. Such theological reflection would need to consider the relevance of old theological doctrines to a new situation and would need to seek to apply Gospel imperatives to the threats of the twenty-first century.

Secondly, the main contribution of the Council in this field was to promote the study of the subject of war and peace and to agree statements which aimed at expressing the views of the denominations in Wales. It did not seek to be a campaigning movement. As was seen, it succeeded in bringing together a number of experts in these fields, mainly from the University, and *Swords into Ploughshares*, most particularly, represented the fruit of this labour. The sad thing is that these studies did not – any more than studies in other fields – have the desired impact. However, these studies were the Council's strength. Many wished the Council to be a campaigning movement, giving a lead to the churches, most particularly at the local level, with respect to war, peace and disarmament. In one way, *Swords into Ploughshares* and the Peace Council of 1987 were intended as resources in this essential task. In both, the Council offered valuable resources to enable churches and individual Christians better to understand these issues and to act together more effectively. But the Council did not wish, and certainly was not able, with its scarce financial and personal resources, to campaign in this field. This caused considerable frustration to a number within the Council and to leaders of other movements who sought the Council's cooperation in special campaigns. It could do no more than offer only general support for such requests.

Thirdly, in this field, as in other fields, Wales depended heavily on its partnership with other ecumenical bodies, most particularly the British Council of Churches and the World Council of Churches. Those two Councils had full-time experts concentrating on international affairs and extensive use was made of their work. The Council of Churches for Wales could avoid such dependence only by a substantial increase in the resources at its disposal. It can be argued whether this dependence was an advantage or a disadvantage. But in this particular field, where the relationship of countries and governments with each other is such an important element, there is no doubt that the churches of Wales have gained considerable benefit from being a part of the wider partnership. Time and again, the horizons of our understanding and our prayer were widened through the relationship that was built up between us and Christians in other countries. The ecumenical movement is at its best when the relationship of countries with each other is under threat. Roger Williamson's question remains remarkably relevant when we deal with international matters as significant as war and peace: How can our ecumenical fellowship with each other be maintained and deepened so that we can, through the ecumenical movement, make a real contribution to world peace and resolve discord between countries? The strong pacifist tradition of a number of Welsh denominations could make an important contribution to this ecumenical partnership.

# Concluding reflections

This account of the history of the Council of Churches for Wales has concentrated on two streams in its life and work, namely, first, fostering ecumenical relationships and Christian unity and, secondly, Christian witness in Wales and worldwide. The story of these two streams shows that the ecumenical movement in Wales – as it was worldwide – was more than the endeavour for Christian unity and more than a framework for cooperating in Christian witness. Basically, the heart of the ecumenical movement is in the relationship of the two streams to each other. Joint witness can strengthen unity and deepening unity can facilitate the witness. The Council was a catalyst for this process in Wales. But one of the chief contributions of the Council, as a small instrument in the wider ecumenical movement, was also to enable Welsh Christians to discover the challenge of the worldwide Church. Thus, in evaluating the history of the Council, we must do this from a Welsh and a world perspective.

The focus of this study has been on the period 1956–90. Much has happened ecumenically since that time, especially with the formation of Cytûn: Churches Together in Wales (and the other Churches Together bodies) but the details of these developments are beyond the scope of this volume. Suffice it to say that it has become clear during the years since 1990 that these new partnerships have added a new dimension to ecumenical relationships which have made the search for unity and for more effective united Christian witness both more promising and more challenging.

### The Council and the churches

This account shows that the attitude of the denominations towards the Council varied greatly from denomination to denomination and from topic to topic. For example, the discussions on covenanting towards unity were instigated by the Council itself, as a result of the Nottingham Conference on Faith and Order in 1964, but the churches came to own this activity and they were more than ready to entrust responsibility for promoting the discussions to the Council. Likewise, the Council facilitated the partnership of the churches and the denominations during the coal dispute. Their partnership through the Council was, without any doubt, the main factor in the effectiveness of that campaign. In situations such as these, the Council could be seen as a body that was truly representative of the denominations.

On the other hand, in fields such as independence for Wales and campaigning against apartheid in South Africa, the Council represented the position of some of the denominations but its stand was unacceptable to others. To some extent, therefore, the Council was a pioneer, offering a lead to the churches and, by means of study programmes, activities and worship materials, seeking to persuade the denominations and the local churches to adopt the Council's view.

The response of the denominations depended to an extent on the 'status' and responsibility of the denominational representatives on the Council. Some denominations ensured that their chief officers were among the representatives every time and they were able to ensure that the Council's view was taken into consideration when particular matters were discussed by the denomination. On other occasions, representatives were appointed who had a particular interest in the ecumenical movement but had neither 'status' nor special responsibility within their denomination. In both cases, there was a danger of representatives failing to recognize that they had as much responsibility as the Council itself for ensuring effective communication and responsible debate in their denominations of issues that had been given priority within the Council.

The Council was also the primary facilitator of the mutual understanding and cooperation which have grown to be such natural elements in denominational life and within local congregations. From time to time, it was inevitable that differences of opinion created tension, but seldom did they divide denominations and churches from each other. The Council had a key role in this process of fostering natural friendship and trust among the Christians of Wales.

Another factor in the relationship of the Council and the churches was communication. From time to time, of course, there was very effective communication. The classic example was the coal dispute, when the churches' views were reported and evaluated daily. There were numerous reasons for this. First, the Council and its member denominations were expressing a Christian view on matters that were of the utmost importance and interest to the public. Secondly, all the denominations, mainly through their chief officers, were fully engaged and – from time to time – published joint statements. Thirdly, the effectiveness of this particular campaign depended on the readiness of the Council's officers (and others) to devote the majority of their time during this period to organizing action and promoting communication.

However, during most of its history, the Council did not have sufficient resources to give such priority to communication. There were other reasons, too, for this failure to communicate effectively. Frequently, good work was done in a particular field without asking how best to publicize the work most effectively. Neither were the denominations always effective channels for promoting information about the Council's work among their local churches; information reached the head offices without being distributed further.

The Council faced financial difficulties throughout the years. From the very beginning, many who were in leadership within the Council were keen to secure a salaried officer to promote ecumenical developments in Wales, but lack of financial resources meant that this did not happen until 1977, twenty-one years after the Council's foundation.

These financial difficulties can be attributed to a number of factors. First, the readiness to contribute financially to an inter-church body is a measure of the ecumenical commitment of a church or denomination. Only with a deeper commitment would more adequate funding be secured. The new commitment of the denominations to each other through Cytûn was a turning point for the ecumenical movement in Wales. Time will tell whether that early commitment will lead to a real transformation in ecumenical partnership and fuller unity,

## CONCLUDING REFLECTIONS

but progress in this regard over the last eighteen years has been slow.

The second reason for the financial difficulties was the tension between the understanding of the Council as a challenging and radical movement, and the Council as an ecclesiastical and national institution. In the early years, the Council was a challenging and radical body, depending on the vision, commitment and energy of some of its leaders and pioneering servants. The denominations were contributing to the work, but the financial demands were not heavy, and the churches were not willing (and sometimes not able) to increase their ecumenical contributions.

It was the appointment of a full-time secretary, with an office in Swansea and secretarial help, that changed the nature of the Council. It became an ecclesiastical institution. The issues that had been given priority by the Council became priorities for the denominations as well, and more and more of the time and resources of the denominations was devoted to ecumenical matters. This process had been at work before 1977, but the 1977 appointment was the key turning-point. From this time onward, the denominations had the specific responsibility for maintaining an ecumenical institution (which represented their ecumenical commitment and partnership) with its salaried staff and its office. From time to time, this was a strain, but there was no escaping the commitment.

Another financial factor, of course, was that the Council of Churches for Wales was not the only inter-church body that was asking for support. Some of the denominations belonged also to the British Council of Churches, the Conference of European Churches and the World Council of Churches, as well as worldwide denominational bodies, each asking for financial support through annual contributions and regular attendance at meetings. There was a price to pay for the change which took place in the ecumenical movement, in Wales and worldwide, from being marginal to the life and work of the denominations to being central to them, and it was no easy matter finding the financial resources to pay that price.

## CONCLUDING REFLECTIONS

### The Council and Christian unity

The foremost priority of the pioneers who were chiefly responsible for setting up the Council was to secure an instrument which would be able to promote a 'reuniting' of the churches. In the 1950s and 1960s the denominational and ecumenical journals regularly contained articles urging movements towards Christian unity and considering its appropriateness. These pioneers were confident that God was calling his people to unity and that the Council was an instrument for promoting unity in Wales.

The Council was very effective in the early years, concentrating attention and energy on the goal of unity, most particularly in the wake of the Carmarthen and Nottingham conferences. The Covenant for Visible Unity in Wales was the fruit of this activity. During the same period there were the 'Towards Union' discussions between the four Welsh-language denominations and the talks between the Church in Wales and the Methodist Church. Throughout the period under discussion, the efforts to promote the Covenant continued – not least through the Council itself. The Commission of the Covenanted Churches, set up in 1975 and renamed 'Enfys' (Rainbow) in 1990, carried the main responsibility for this task. Publications such as *Principles of Visible Unity in Wales*,[1] *The Holy Communion*,[2] *Ministry in a Uniting Church*[3] and *Baptism*[4] played a significant role in enabling the churches to explore the challenge and opportunity of the covenant But even the most optimistic commentators have not been able to avoid the conclusion that despite the best efforts of many there have been no real steps towards visible unity in Wales at a denominational level (except for the union that led to the United Reformed Church in 1972).

During the period since 1990, a number of new initiatives have been taken. In 1997 new talks were inaugurated between the Nonconformist Churches in Wales with a view to forming a United Free Church for Wales. However, in 2000 denominational decisions meant that this plan had to be abandoned. In 2004, thirty years after the original covenant agreement, the Covenanted Churches were invited to reflect carefully on their commitment to the original vision of the covenant and to come

## CONCLUDING REFLECTIONS

to a mind on whether they were able to reaffirm this commitment. All the covenanted churches agreed that they remained committed to one another through this covenant, especially at local level. Now the Commission of the Covenanted Churches (Enfys) has been brought to an end and the work of the Covenant has become part of the responsibility and structure of Cytûn: Churches Together in Wales. This has placed the search for unity among the covenanted churches at the heart of the ecumenical agenda again.

One response to these developments was the inauguration of the 'Companions for a Change' programme within Cytûn. This aimed at exploring some of the fundamental issues raised by the challenge of deeper partnerships in mission and ministry between the churches and denominations in Wales, especially locally, at the beginning of the twenty-first century. Through local study groups and a national conference the churches were encouraged to shape, through theological reflection, shared worship and practical planning, a new understanding of 'ministry for mission' for the coming years.

So after a period when Christian unity was not high on the agenda of the denominations, it has become a key issue, especially in terms of local unity. Certainly, the inter-church climate is very different at the beginning of the twenty-first century compared with the 1950s and 1960s. But probably the aim has also changed. The majority of the denominations no longer think in terms of one visible ecclesiastical body but in terms of a pattern of partnership and collaboration that would enable churches to recognize each other and recognize and exchange ministers and members, and by this means, rather than by forming one visible church, live in unity whilst retaining aspects of their independence. Unity in diversity and diversity in unity have become increasingly central to the search for Christian unity. And although this is a very different vision from that of the early pioneers, the Council, in striving for fuller unity, made an important contribution to keeping the vision of Christian unity before the churches, to promoting debate about the difficult issues which had to be faced and, perhaps more than anything, to fostering ecumenical faithfulness.

The deeper partnership with the Roman Catholic Church – particularly during the last decade of the Council – was an important factor in this change. This partnership was a subject of joy to the majority who had been involved in the Council of Churches for Wales. On the one hand, it gave a new edge to the search for Christian unity, which was, and continues to be, very high in the priorities of the Roman Catholic Church. On the other hand, this new partnership has raised new and fundamental questions about the nature of the Church and its ministry, and about the content of the faith. It is also fair to note that the Roman Catholic Church has urged other denominations to take steps towards fuller union with each other that it could not itself take. However, without doubt, the presence of the Roman Catholic Church in the partnership of Churches Together has made a fundamental difference. It could almost be said that the search for unity has had to be on a totally different level and that it has been necessarily slower and more difficult. The Council played a key role in promoting and developing this partnership in the years after the Second Vatican Council but was less effective in promoting theological reflection on some crucial questions that were raised in the wake of Vatican II.

At the beginning of the twenty-first century there is a need for a wider vision of Christian unity than was cherished in Wales in recent times, a vision which combines the search for the unity of the churches and the struggle for unity, reconciliation and justice for persons, society, nation and humanity. According to Michael Taylor: 'here . . . lies the real genius of the ecumenical movement . . . to unite a divided church, to make one a divided world, to make the many into a whole, to draw together into communities what is separate and apart.'[5] It may be that it is through developing an understanding of Christian unity rooted in this holistic vision that the challenge and opportunity of the ecumenical call to Welsh Christians of the twenty-first century is to be found.

## The Council and public life

The history of the Council reveals a tension between institutional Christianity and individual Christianity. Most often, this tension, within the churches and in the media, was in the form

CONCLUDING REFLECTIONS

of a question: What right have the churches to interfere in politics? Much of the criticism of the Council arose from people who disagreed with its particular standpoint, mostly with regard to public life in Wales or worldwide. The history of the Council's involvement with South Africa, for instance, and its backing for the Programme to Combat Racism, revealed this tension in a dramatic way. Throughout its history, the Council for Churches in Wales had a commitment to stand for justice in Wales and across the world. Indeed, its stand for these contentious issues gave credibility to the churches in the view of many people outside the churches. The Council believed that Christian witness in public affairs was central to Christian mission. That commitment has continued in Cytûn's work in relation to the Welsh Assembly Government established in 1998. The appointment of a Churches Assembly Liaison Officer within Cytûn was a sign of this commitment and placed Cytûn and its member churches at the heart of debate about public and national affairs in Wales.

*The Council and theological engagement in Wales*

Another question is suggested by this historical overview: To what extent did the Council succeed in promoting interdenominational theologizing in Wales? Notable examples become apparent in the history of the Council. There was an obvious place for ecclesiology in the discussions in relation to covenanting for union in Wales. The essays on the nature of the Church, the ministry, the priesthood, and the sacraments made an important contribution to a mutual understanding of the traditions of the churches.[6] Likewise, the invitation to respond to the report of the World Council of Churches, *Baptism, Eucharist and Ministry*,[7] was a unique opportunity to engage in theological reflection in relation to some of the fundamental doctrines of the Christian faith.

In a completely different field, as we have seen, the Council's Industrial Committee made a notable contribution in offering theological reflection on the world of industry and the critical changes to persons and communities during the period under consideration. *Towards a Contemporary Theology of Work*[8]

## CONCLUDING REFLECTIONS

was a unique contribution in Wales in this field and it was the product of activity within the Council of Churches for Wales. In the same way, *Swords into Ploughshares* and the Wrexham Peace Council in 1987 were attempts at theological reflection on one of the key areas of concern during the latter half of the twentieth century.

Some argue that neither individual Christians nor the denominations of twentieth century Wales took theology seriously, particularly compared with the fierce theological debates of the past. This could be responsible for any failure on the part of the Council to promote interdenominational theological reflection in Wales (although the Theological Consultative Group made a notable contribution from time to time in the life of the Council). A number of factors could have been at work in such a process: indifference towards theology as such, or (worse) indifference towards the nature and content of the Christian faith, or a lack of theological discussion among Christian leaders in Wales. One of the contributions of the contemporary ecumenical movement has been to promote consideration of the way in which Christian action, contemporary theology and Welsh and worldwide developments challenge tradition, cast new light on it and urge us to rejuvenate the tradition for a new era. The raw material for this process is already available to the churches. The challenge now is to tackle this task.

There is a further question: to what extent did the Council succeed in promoting discussions on contentious theological issues which have divided the denominations? Some of these issues have already been mentioned. The essays on the Covenant and the responses to *Baptism, Eucharist and Ministry* examined questions such as the nature of the Church, the nature and recognition of ministry, the meaning of the sacraments and joint communion. The acceptance of the Covenant by some denominations in 1974 was a sign that they had grown closer to each other with respect to these contentious topics. However, as we have seen, there were no substantial discussions on some of the other fundamental issues that divide Christians, such as the relationship of the Bible and tradition as sources of authority in the Church, the place of Mary, the mother of Jesus, in the scheme of salvation, and the meaning of justification by faith.

## CONCLUDING REFLECTIONS

### The influence of the Council

The basic question remains: What influence did the Council have? Some of the main influences were very remarkable. The publication (in 1988) of Y Beibl Cymraeg Newydd (the New Welsh Bible), which was inagurated and, initially, coordinated through the Council of Churches for Wales, was one of the historic events of the twentieth century.[9] The formation of Inter-Church Aid and Service to Refugees (which was to become Christian Aid) and its development during the first sixty years of its history was one of the key ecumenical influences in Wales. As we have seen, working together for Christian Aid was the beginning of local ecumenism in many areas of Wales and it has continued to be one of the most effective instruments for fostering the churches' partnership.

It is likely that some developments would not have happened at all had it not been for the vision of some early pioneers on the Council. Two noteworthy examples of this were the conferences which were held in Carmarthen in 1963 and 1970. From the one stemmed the discussions that led to the Covenant towards Union, ecumenical studies of worship and liturgy, and local ecumenical initiatives, including local ecumenical partnerships. From the other conference came the increasing cooperation in the field of social responsibility in Wales, specifically by establishing the Church and Society Department, which gave to the Welsh denominations for the first time a forum for study and action in this field.

One important aspect of this activity, which long preceded the development of the Department, was witness in industry. Throughout the years, the Council fostered and encouraged its creative and progressive work by raising awareness of these issues among Welsh Christians and supporting industrial chaplaincies. This experience was a key factor in the Council's conciliatory efforts during the coal dispute.

The Council also had an influence on the relationships between Welsh-speaking and English-speaking Christians within the denominations. In the early years, chiefly because of lack of resources, English was the main medium of administration and meetings. When the Welsh language developed a higher profile in Welsh life during the 1960s, the use of Welsh in the

CONCLUDING REFLECTIONS

Council increased. By the 1970s, all the main publications of the Council, such as minutes and reports (including all the covenanting for union publications) were bilingual. By the 1980s, the meetings of the Council itself were held bilingually with simultaneous interpretation. These developments fostered sympathy and trust between Welsh-speaking and English-speaking representatives on the Council. This in turn was a contribution towards engendering support for the Welsh language and its development among all the churches and denominations of Wales.

*The Council and the worldwide ecumenical movement*

We have already seen that the inauguration of the World Council of Churches in Amsterdam in 1948 was one of the main stimuli – indeed, perhaps the main stimulus – for establishing the Council of Churches for Wales in 1956. This first Assembly was a signal, three years after the Second World War, that reconciliation between Christians was possible, even after such a terrible massacre in Europe and worldwide.

Over the years of its history – and during the early years most especially – worldwide conferences had a pervasive influence on ecumenical events in Wales. We need do little more than name these conferences: The Second Assembly of the World Council of Churches, Evanston, 1954; the Third Assembly in New Delhi, 1961; the Montreal Faith and Order Conference, 1963 (which led to the Welsh Faith and Order conference in Carmarthen,1963, and British conference in Nottingham, 1964); the Church and Society Conference, Geneva, 1966 (which was the basis of the Carmarthen Conference four years later); the Fourth Assembly in Uppsala, 1968 (which was seen as an opportunity to renew the ecumenical vision and commitment in Wales on the basis of the booklet, *Uppsala and Wales*). Representatives from Wales were present at the majority of these conferences and in subsequent conferences and assemblies.

But these would not have had the influence that they did had early Welsh ecumenical pioneers not shared the vision of these conferences and devoted themselves to rooting their

## CONCLUDING REFLECTIONS

challenging, worldwide vision in the soil of Wales, its culture, its social condition and its Christian life. It could be argued that the vision of these pioneers was the key that succeeded in unlocking the ecumenical developments which became a natural part of the life of the churches and denominations in the last years of the Council.

When the Council of Churches for Wales became an Associate Council of the World Council of Churches in 1982, it was seen as an expression of the Council's commitment to the worldwide movement through a direct relationship and not through the British Council of Churches as in the past.

One must recognize, of course, that the British Council of Churches had an important place in the ecumenical history of Wales. Three of the indigenous Welsh denominations of Wales, namely, the Church in Wales, the Presbyterian Church of Wales and the Union of Welsh Independents were members of the British Council of Churches from the early years of its existence. The British denominations that had churches in Wales were also members, of course. Consequently, it was a means of promoting ecumenical awareness in Wales in the years between 1942 (when the British Council of Churches was established) and 1956. But, negatively speaking, one reason for establishing the Council of Churches for Wales was the feeling among many that the British Council of Churches was not able to represent the interests of Wales effectively (for example, in relation to promoting local ecumenism and fostering awareness of the wider ecumenical movement, most particularly through the Welsh language). As national awareness grew in Wales, the desire also increased to strengthen the Council of Churches for Wales as a national ecumenical body that was administratively independent of the British Council of Churches but that also continued to cooperate on common issues, with the support of general secretaries such as Harry O. Morton and Philip Morgan (who himself was of Welsh extraction and had been a minister in Wales). On the positive side, it must be recognized that the Council of Churches for Wales would not have been so effective in many fields without the ready and professional help of some of the specialist officers of the British Council of Churches who provided support with matters such as promoting local ecumenism and the Council's response to international issues.

Over the years, there was considerable international coming and going. For example, Philip Potter and Emilio Castro paid a visit to Wales on behalf of the World Council of Churches. The membership of G. O. Williams (1968–75), Meirion Lloyd Davies (1975–83) and Carol Abel (1983–91) of the Central Committee of the World Council of Churches was a very important connection. Delegations were received from the Soviet Union, Argentina and China, as well as visits by individuals from other countries, such as Desmond Tutu (1986). During his time as general secretary, Noel Davies visited India and Sri Lanka (1981), China and Hong Kong (1983), Argentina (1985), and South Africa and Lesotho (1986), as well as attending a number of the major meetings of the World Council of Churches. These exchanges enabled a deeper awareness of the churches' partnership with each other within the one worldwide ecumenical movement.

## *Future prospects*

As we turn from evaluating past trends and look towards the future, a number of themes suggest themselves.

First, as has been noted, there will need to be a re-evaluation of the search for Christian unity and union in Wales. The failure of the proposals for a United Free Church in Wales, and the recent process of reaffirming the churches' commitment to the covenant for union have raised with some urgency the issue of how we understand the search for unity and union. There are those who believe that a death knell has been sounding in Wales. Others believe that the nature of Christian unity and union needs to be redefined (not least in view of partnership agreements between the Church in Wales and the Methodist Church, the Methodist Church and the United Reformed Church and the United Reformed Church and the Presbyterian Church of Wales, and the recently promulgated Church in Wales Ecumenical Canons). Can there be an organic or structural vision of unity or must it be defined in relational and more local terms?

Secondly, there needs to be a re-affirmation of the ecumenical task as political engagement. In a Wales which has had limited self-government through the National Assembly Government and which has grown in self-confidence, despite a high degree of political apathy within Welsh communities, what are the priorities for the churches? Cytûn's Assembly Liaison Officer[10] has contributed in very significant ways to the two-way communication between the Assembly and the churches. How should this involvement be developed for the future? Should the churches' collaboration in relation to the Assembly as such be extended to include broader engagement with issues raised locally, regionally and nationally (and internationally?). What is the nature of the churches' 'prophetic' task in contemporary Wales, and how do ecumenical instruments forge partnerships that will contribute to this task within Wales but also more widely in the nations of Britain and Ireland and within the enlarged European community?

Thirdly, there are challenges around identity and unity. These two issues converge around the WCC Faith and Order programme, Ethnic Identity, National Identity and the Unity of the Church, which has held two of its key consultations in Wales (the inaugural consultation in Hawarden in 1997 and a consultation for biblical scholars in Bangor in 2003). How do issues of identity – culture, language, tradition, political and socio-economic relationships, moral/ethical principles etc. – affect the understanding of our unity? How can diversity and unity be understood, not only in ecclesiological terms but also in social and communal terms? There are key issues here that need to be addressed from a Welsh perspective, within our contemporary multilingual, multiethnic and multifaith society.

Fourthly, there is a need to redefine ecumenism in a global and pluralist environment. In his address to the inaugural meeting of the Welsh National Centre for Ecumenical Studies,[11] Professor Michael Taylor highlighted the need to explore the nature and understanding of the ecumenical vision in the light of growing globalization and the increasingly plural nature of Western society. The current world situation (especially after '9/11', events in the United Kingdom and the effects of 'the War on Terror') presses this need upon us with greater urgency. The recently established Inter-Faith Forum for Wales, initiated by the Welsh Assembly Government, will be an important catalyst in this process.

Finally, there has been a fundamental change in the nature of the ecumenical partnership that is bound to have an effect on ecumenism in the coming years. The setting up of Cytûn: Churches Together in Wales, as a successor to the Council of Churches for Wales, in 1990, following the Inter-Church Process on 'the nature and mission of the Church in the light of its calling in and for the world' symbolized this change. At the heart of this new commitment is the role of Cytûn not so much in undertaking the ecumenical task on behalf of its member churches (which was often how the Council was understood), but as an enabler of the churches' engagement as partners in the ecumenical enterprise. Cytûn facilitates this commitment, but the nature and pace of this task is firmly rooted within the churches themselves. Unless the churches and denominations have a common will to foster and resource this enterprise in the future, the ecumenical process will falter.

### Building the ecumenical house

In a powerful meditation on Biblical images of the house (*oikos*) and the earth or whole of humanity (*oikoumene*), Philip Potter said:

> It is this image and understanding of the living house which has motivated the ecumenical movement . . . (It is) the means by which the churches which form the house, the *oikos* of God, are seeking so to live and witness before all the peoples that the whole *oikoumene* may become the *oikos* of God.[12]

We have seen that there has been a tendency in Wales to think of the ecumenical movement in terms of church unity alone, and to judge it on the basis of different attitudes towards that unity. The images that are behind the word 'ecumenical' demonstrate that this is too narrow an understanding. The search for Christian unity and the witness of the churches to reconciliation, justice and peace are not two separate aspects but rather elements of the same ecumenical endeavour. The Council of Churches for Wales was an instrument for building this house in Wales. Over the years it has been necessary to extend and adapt it. By 1990 it was felt necessary to rebuild it.

## CONCLUDING REFLECTIONS

But the intention throughout this period was to make ecumenical instruments in Wales more effective tools for the building of this 'house' for the Christian family in Wales and more effective signs of the reconciliation, unity and renewal which are possible for the people and nation of Wales through the Gospel.

This book has been an attempt to chronicle the history of this house, its successes and its failures. The story has been told in the belief that the Council of Churches for Wales was a vehicle of renewal, through the Holy Spirit, not only in the churches but, at its best, in local communities and in the nation, a renewal which has been, in the words of the basis of the Council, 'to the glory of God, Father, Son and Holy Spirit'.

# Appendix I
## Officers of the Council of Churches for Wales, 1956–90

| | | |
|---|---|---|
| 1956–8: | President: | The Bishop of St. David's |
| | Vice-Presidents: | E. Whitford Roberts |
| | | J. R. Evans |
| | Joint Secretaries: | E. Curig Davies |
| | | W. R. Williams |
| 1958–60: | President: | J. R. Evans |

(There is no record of names of Vice-Presidents)
The two secretaries remained for a second term of two years.

| | | |
|---|---|---|
| 1960–2: | President: | W. R. Williams |
| | Vice-Presidents: | Eryl S. Thomas |
| | | Whitford Roberts |
| | Joint Secretaries: | W. Ungoed Jacob |
| | | E. Curig Davies |
| 1962–4: | President: | W. R. Williams (for a second term) |
| | Vice-Presidents: | Whitford Roberts |
| | | E. Curig Davies |

Note: Principal W. R. Williams died during his second term and Whitford Roberts was elected President for the rest of the term and G. O. Williams Vice-President.

| | | |
|---|---|---|
| | Joint Secretaries: | W. Ungoed Jacob |
| | | M. J. Williams |
| 1964–6: | President: | G. O. Williams |

## OFFICERS OF THE COUNCIL OF CHURCHES FOR WALES, 1956–90

|  |  |  |
|---|---|---|
|  | Vice-Presidents: | E. Curig Davies |
|  |  | W. J. Roberts |
|  | Joint Secretaries: | M. J. Williams |
|  |  | Gwilym H. Jones |
| 1966–8: | President: | G. O. Williams (for a second term) |
|  | Vice-Presidents: | Huw Wynne Griffith |
|  |  | M. J. Williams |
|  | Secretary: | Dafydd H. Owen (for one year) |
|  |  | Erastus Jones (from 1967, for five years) |

Note: From now on one vice-president was appointed annually to serve for terms of two years, in order to ensure continuity among the officers.

| 1968–70: | President: | Huw Wynne Griffith |
|---|---|---|
|  | Vice-Presidents: | M. J. Williams (for another year) |
|  |  | W. Ungoed Jacob |
| 1970–2: | President: | Huw Wynne Griffith |
|  | Vice-Presidents: | W. Ungoed Jacob (for another year) |
|  |  | Alun Francis |
| 1971: | President: | W. Ungoed Jacob |
|  | Vice-Presidents: | Alun Francis (for another year) |
|  |  | Emrys Jones |

Note: During 1972 Meirion Lloyd Davies was appointed General Secretary for a term of five years.

| 1973: | President: | W. Ungoed Jacob |
|---|---|---|
|  | Vice-Presidents: | W. George Evans |
|  |  | Emrys Jones (for another year) |
| 1974: | Vice-President: | Glyn Parry Jones |

OFFICERS OF THE COUNCIL OF CHURCHES FOR WALES, 1956–90

| 1975: | President: | W. Ungoed Jacob (for another year) |
|---|---|---|
| | Vice-Presidents: | W. George Evans (re-elected) |
| | | Glyn Parry Jones (re-elected) |
| 1976: | President: | W. George Evans |
| | Vice-Presidents: | Glyn Parry Jones |
| | | B. N. Y. Vaughan |

Note: In 1977 Noel A. Davies was appointed Secretary of the Council of Churches for Wales and the Commission of the Covenanting Churches for a term of seven years, which was extended in 1984 for a further term of five years and further extended in 1989 until 1990, when the Council would be disbanded and Cytûn set up as its successor.

| 1978: | President: | Glyn Parry Jones |
|---|---|---|
| | Vice-Presidents: | B. N. Y. Vaughan |
| | | Iorwerth Jones |

Note: Glyn Parry Jones resigned in April 1980 on the grounds of ill health (he died in 1983) and B. N. Y. Vaughan was appointed President for the rest of the term; Iorwerth Jones would remain Vice-President for another year and Hugh Rowlands was appointed Vice-President for a term of two years.

| 1982: | President: | Iorwerth Jones |
|---|---|---|
| | Vice-Presidents: | Meirion Lloyd Davies |
| | | Iorwerth Thomas |
| 1984: | President: | Mervyn Woodman |
| | Vice-Presidents: | Iorwerth Thomas |
| | | W. O. Thomas |
| 1986: | President: | John I. Morgans |
| | Vice-Presidents: | Erastus Jones |
| | | Irene Williams |

OFFICERS OF THE COUNCIL OF CHURCHES FOR WALES, 1956–90

1988: President: John I. Morgans (re-elected)
Vice-Presidents: Irene Williams
Dafydd H. Owen

# Appendix II
## Summary of the work of the Liturgical Study Group

The group was founded in 1965 as a direct outcome of the Faith and Order conference of the British Council of Churches, Nottingham 1964. Every denomination which was a full member of the Council was invited to appoint three representatives. In addition, the Roman Catholic Church and the Religious Society of Friends were invited to appoint representatives – an especially important step so soon after the Second Vatican Council. At the first meeting, W. Ungoed Jacob was appointed Chairman and remained until December 1976, when Noel A. Davies was appointed Chairman. He remained in office until the Group was succeeded by the Unity in Prayer Group in 1981. E. Stanley John was the secretary during the early formative stage. From the start, the group saw that its main purpose was to study the liturgical principles and patterns of the denominations and churches of Wales. Its main activities may be summarized under three headings.

First, during the first few years, the group focused on the general principles of worship. In 1971, a series of papers was published in a very important book, 'Thine is the glory'. According to the chairman of the group, this represented 'years of pioneering work'. In addition to chapters on worship and liturgy, it contains an analysis of Sunday worship in the various traditions in Wales, a study of the elements of worship, and chapters on The Lord's Supper, Baptism, The Church Year, and Worship in Wales Tomorrow. In Wales as it was at the end of the sixties, this was a progressive and important publication.

The second element of the working programme was special studies on the sacraments, focusing on the two main sacraments of baptism and the eucharist. Papers were prepared on particular aspects of these topics and these were edited by

## SUMMARY OF THE WORK OF THE LITURGICAL STUDY GROUP

members of the group with a view to publishing another booklet. But that did not happen. Rather, it was adapted by producing a statement on the two sacraments, with an introduction on the meaning of sacrament in worship. The group considered the possibility of publishing a discussion document on the sacraments to demonstrate the growth in mutual understanding there had been between the churches and the denominations. But neither the document nor the statements were published. This was regrettable, since they represented core work. Nevertheless, this activity contributed to the mutual understanding of the churches in other ways. This work was used as a basis of the attempt by the Commission of the Covenanting Churches in Wales to summarize the meaning and pattern of the sacraments and to produce an order for holy communion. There are traces of this mutual understanding in the responses of the denominations to *Baptism, Eucharist and Ministry*.

Finally, the group completed a number of varied tasks on behalf of the Council, such as devising an order of service for local united services. The group undertook a study of the World Council of Churches' document *Towards One Baptism, One Eucharist and a Mutually Recognised Ministry*, one of the forerunners of *Baptism, Eucharist and Ministry*. The important statement of the Bench of Bishops of the Church in Wales (1975) on intercommunion was considered, and discussions were begun on the principles of family worship, experimental patterns of worship, and ministry to the sick.

Space has not permitted a thorough consideration of these matters. Hopefully this summary shows that this group made a key contribution to the process of building on the positive but rather general statements of the Nottingham conference, and opened the way to the increasing convergence which developed during the last quarter of the century in relation to theology and patterns of worship.

# Notes

## Preface

1   WCC Faith and Order Paper, No. 111, Geneva, 1982.
2   The Revd Dr R. Tudur Jones (1921–98) was Emeritus Professor of Church History at the University of Wales, Bangor and former Principal of Coleg Bala-Bangor (the College of the Welsh Independents). He supervised the doctoral research upon which this volume is based.

## Introduction

1   However, Edinburgh 1910 itself was the product of a number of significant developments during the latter years of the nineteenth century, such as the Lambeth Conference call to unity in 1888, the work of the YMCA/YWCA and the World Student Christian Federation and the recognition by many missionary societies which had gathered for previous world missionary conferences that the call to unity was integral to Christian witness and evangelism. It should be recognized also that although 'western' missionary societies were the dominant influence in Edinburgh 1910, many leaders in the churches of Asia, Africa, Latin America, the Caribbean and the Pacific were also calling for greater unity, such as V. S. Azariah of India, who gave one of the key addresses at Edinburgh.
2   A. Hastings, *A History of English Christianity, 1920–1985* (London, 1987), p. 87.
3   See Appendix II.
4   R. Tudur Jones, *Teyrnas Crist a'r Tywyllwch yng Nghymru* (The Kingdom of Christ and the Darkness in Wales) (Aberystwyth, 1994), p. 6.
5   K. O. Morgan, *Rebirth of a Nation: Wales 1880–1980* (Cardiff, 1981), p. 412.
6   Ibid., p. 409.
7   Ibid., p. 419.

NOTES

## 1. The search for Christian unity in Wales: the beginnings

1. There is considerable ambiguity within the documentation concerning the use of the words 'union' and 'unity'. Whilst the quotations in this chapter reflect this ambiguity and inconsistency, in general 'unity' is used to denote the attempt to foster cooperation, interrelationship and partnership between Christians in all aspects of their life together, and 'union' is used to denote the search for organic, institutional unity between churches and denominations.
2. The First Assembly of the World Council of Churches, *The Official Report* (Geneva, 1949), p. 57. Many of the quotations in this volume appeared originally in English but were translated into Welsh for the Welsh-language publication that is the basis for the present text. In these cases, the English version that appears in this volume is a re-translation into English by the present author.
3. A Presbyterian Minister in Aberystwyth who was formative in the early years of the formation of the Council as well as throughout most of its history.
4. *Yr Efrydydd*, 5(2) (1957), 73.
5. A Methodist minister who was at one time Secretary of the Wales for Christ committee.
6. *Yr Eurgrawn* (a Welsh Methodist periodical) (1957), 92.
7. A Welsh Congregational minister who became Professor of Christian Doctrine at Coleg Bala-Bangor, Bangor.
8. *Y Dysgedydd* (Welsh Congregational periodical), 134(11) (1954) 274ff.
9. A Congregational minister who was one of the pioneers of the ecumenical movement in Wales, attended the inaugural Assembly of the World Council of Churches, and served as the General Secretary of the Council of Churches for Wales.
10. A Congregational minister.
11. *Y Dysgedydd*, 135(2) (1955), 26ff.
12. Council Minutes, 24 May 1956.
13. A Presbyterian minister in Pwllheli and a former general secretary of the Council.
14. O. E. Evans (ed.), *Gwarchod y Gair* (Denbigh, 1993), p. 185.
15. Ibid., p. 186.
16. H. E. Fay and S. Neill, *A History of the Ecumenical Movement, vol. II, 1948–1968* (Geneva, 1986) p. 43.
17. Carmarthen Faith and Order Conference, Message to the Churches, p. 2.
18. Hastings, *A History of English Christianity*, p. 541.
19. *Unity Begins at Home, A Report of the British Faith and Order Conference* (London, 1964), p. 17.
20. Ibid., p. 18.
21. Ibid., p. 34.

## NOTES

22 Principal of New College, London – a Congregational college – and the first General Secretary of the United Reformed Church.
23 *Unity Begins at Home*, p. 39.
24 Ibid., p. 41.
25 A Congregationalist who was one of the pioneers of the ecumenical movement in the UK and worldwide.
26 *Unity Begins at Home*, p. 45.
27 Ibid., p. 43.
28 Lossky et al. (eds), *Dictionary of the Ecumenical Movement* (Geneva, 1991), p. 633.
29 *Unity Begins at Home*, p. 79.
30 A Welsh Congregational minister, who has ministered in Treorci, Tanygrisiau, Swansea and Machynlleth and has played a pioneering role, especially in promoting local ecumenical relationships.
31 *Y Dysgedydd* (1964).
32 Ibid., 219.
33 A Congregational minister who was General Secretary of the Union of Welsh Independents.
34 *Y Dysgedydd* (1964), 222.
35 A Congregational minister who became General Secretary of the Union of Welsh Independents.
36 *Y Dysgedydd* (1964), 172.
37 *Unity Begins at Home*, p. 76.
38 Council of Churches for Wales, Report to the Executive Committee, 20 October 1964.
39 Minutes of the Council, 29–30 October 1964.

## 2. The beginnings of the Covenant in Wales

1 *The Call to Covenant* (Bangor, 1965), p. 2.
2 Ibid., p. 8.
3 Ibid., p. 8.
4 *Covenanting towards Union in Wales, Part I* (Bangor, 1971), p. 12f.
5 Ibid., p. 34.
6 Ibid., p. 36f.
7 Ibid., p. 24ff.
8 The Covenant.
9 Ibid.
10 *Why Covenant?* (Bangor, 1972), p. 22.
11 *Yr Haul* (spring 1975), 4.
12 At the time Sub-Warden of St Michael's (Church in Wales) College, Llandaff, Cardiff and later Bishop of St Davids.
13 A Baptist minister who returned to Wales following a period as Ecumenical Officer in Milton Keynes.
14 A minister of the United Reformed Church, who had served a period as Warden of the Presbyterian Coleg Trefeca.

## NOTES

15  Evans, *Gwarchod y Gair*, p. 192.
16  A minister of the Disciples of Christ (USA) who has been a key figure in the ecumenical movement (and especially in the field of faith and order) in his own church, in the USA and within the World Council of Churches.
17  Lossky et al., *Dictionary of the Ecumenical Movement*, p. 244.
18  Formerly Secretary of the Division of Ecumenical Affairs of the British Council of Churches and latterly President of the Selly Oak Colleges.
19  Martin Conway, *Unity – Why not yet?* (London, 1981), p. 13.

## 3. Fostering local ecumenism in Wales

1  Message to the churches, Sixth Assembly of the World Council of Churches, Evanston 1954, quoted in *Yr Efrydydd*, 4(3) (1954).
2  *Yr Efrydydd*, 5(1) (1955).
3  Ibid., p. 3
4  A minister of the Presbyterian Church of Wales.
5  Friends of the Council of Churches for Wales Newsletter (ed. M. Islwyn Lake), Issue 1, November 1965.
6  Minutes of the Executive Committee, the Council of Churches for Wales, 25–6 January 1965.
7  A lay Anglican from Erwood in Powys.
8  Minutes of the Department of Ecumenical Action, 25 September 1965.
9  Letter to the *Western Mail*, 28 October 1966, following a meeting of the Council, 20–1 October.
10  *Pobl Drws Nesaf*, Council of Churches for Wales, 1967.
11  Ibid., Introduction.
12  See Chapter 1 above.
13  Minutes of the Council, Pwllheli, 12–13 October 1972.
14  Consultative Committee for Local Ecumenical Projects in England, *Guidelines for Local Ecumenical Projects* (London, 1975), pp. 6–7.
15  For an excellent account of these developments, see R. Howells, *A Tale of Two Grandmothers* (Swansea, 1994), p. 48ff.
16  Noel A. Davies, in *Views from the Pews*, BCC/CTS (1986), p. 80.
17  Ibid., p. 80.
18  See Chapter 9 for an account of Desmond Tutu's address and sermon.

## 4. Relationships with the Roman Catholic Church

1  For an account of the Roman Catholic Church in Wales up to 1962, see Trystan O. Hughes, *Winds of Change: The Roman Catholic Church and Society in Wales, 1916–1962* (Cardiff, 1999).
2  Quoted by R. Tudur Jones in an article on 'Anglican Claims in Wales' in *Y Dysgedydd* (1960), 138.

## NOTES

3   *Y Dysgedydd*, (1961), 57.
4   Catholic Truth Society, 1967.
5   *The Directory for the Application of the Decisions of the Second Council of the Vatican Concerning Ecumenical Matters* (London, 1967), p. 4ff.
6   Dr J. P. Brown was a Catholic layman, he lived in Llangollen and devoted his life to encouraging and promoting the ecumenical involvement of the Roman Catholic Church in Wales and fostering friendship amongst the denominations. During recent decades he was solely responsible for 'Cylch Translations' which summarized, in English, key articles, reviews etc. from the Welsh-language denominational and ecumenical press. He died early in 2008.
7   From a letter by Dr J. P. Brown, 2 January 1968.
8   Letter dated 8 January 1968.
9   Letter dated 14 January 1968.
10  Letter dated 14 January 1968.
11  A minister of the Cymru Synod of the Methodist Church.
12  General Secretary of the Baptist Union of Wales.
13  A Catholic layman who was a Consultant Psychiatrist and is a well-known author and broadcaster.
14  Minutes of the first meeting of the Working Group, 24 May 1968.
15  Ibid.
16  Joint Statement by Bishop Langton Fox and the General Secretary of the Council, 28 November 1968.
17  Ibid.
18  The results of the Working Group's work were published in two publications, namely, *Towards Christian Unity: A Symposium* (London, 1968) and *Implications of Possible Membership of the British Council of Churches* (London, 1971).
19  *Implications of Possible Membership of the British Council of Churches* (London, 1971).
20  Ibid., p. 7.
21  Ibid., p. 8.
22  *Congress Contact* (1980), p. 1.
23  Ibid., para. 24, p. 15.
24  *The Easter People* (London, 1980).
25  Ibid., para. 70, p. 27.
26  Archbishop of Canterbury and President of the British Council of Churches.
27  Ibid., para. 74, p. 29.
28  Ibid., para. 79, p. 29.
29  Minutes of the CCW Executive Committee, 12 June 1980, confirmed by the Council, 16 October 1980.
30  See R. Howells, *A Tale of Two Grandmothers* (Swansea, 1994), p. 117.
31  A Presbyterian minister in Pwllheli and formerly General Secretary of the Council of Churches for Wales.
32  A Methodist minister, who was on the staff of the Department of Theology and Religious Studies at the University of Wales, Bangor,

## NOTES

Director of the New Welsh Bible, and convenor of the Council's Theological Consultative Group.
33 At the time an Auxiliary Bishop in the Archdiocese of Cardiff and later to become the first Bishop of the newly formed Diocese of Menevia.
34 A Catholic layman from Swansea who played a pioneering role locally and nationally in fostering the ecumenical commitment and partnership of the Roman Catholic community.
35 Ron Howells in his report to the Commissions, 16 May 1981, Appendix A.
36 Catholic Bishop of East Anglia and Chairman of the Ecumenical Commission of the Bishops' Conference of England and Wales.
37 *Implications of Roman Catholic Membership of the BCC* (1971).
38 See paper presented to the Working Group, 10 November 1981, p. 3.
39 Working Group minutes, 19 April 1983.
40 Minutes of the Council, 20 October 1983.
41 Originally a Churches of Christ (Disciples) minister and subsequently a minister and Moderator of the United Reformed Church, whose ministry began in the Merthyr Tydfil area of south Wales, became General Secretary of the Churches of Christ in Great Britain and General Secretary of the British Council of Churches.
42 Letter dated 4 September 1980.
43 *The Pope Teaches: The Pope in Britain – The Complete Texts* (London, 1982), p. 219.
44 Ibid., p. 223.
45 Ibid., p. 223.
46 *Prospects for Wales* (London, 1983), p. 42.
47 *Faith and Order Paper No. 111* (Geneva, 1981).
48 See, for example, *The Catechism of the Catholic Church*, Chapman (1994), pp. 305f, esp. para. 1376.
49 See, for example, the ARCIC report, *Mary: Grace and Hope in Christ* (London, 2005).
50 V. Nicholls (ed.), *Reflections* (Geneva, 1986), p. 66.

## 5. The churches and society: beginnings and foundations

1 P. Abrecht, in Fey (ed.), *A History of the Ecumenical Movement*, vol. II, p. 235.
2 Ibid., pp. 241–2.
3 Minutes of the Joint Committee, 7 October 1955.
4 Report of the Commission on Mid-Wales, The Council of Churches for Wales, p. 4.
5 Ibid., p. 4 ff.
6 Ibid., p. 14.
7 Minutes of the Council, 25 May 1959.
8 Davies, *A History of Wales* (London, 1990), p. 635.
9 Minutes of the Council of Churches for Wales, 26 October 1959.

10 Annual Report of the Council for 1960–1, p. 1.
11 Minutes of the Executive Committee of the Council of Churches for Wales, 25–6 January 1965.
12 Minutes of the Council of Churches for Wales, 19–20 October 1960.
13 Minutes of the Council of Churches for Wales, 21–2 September 1961.
14 See K. O. Morgan, *Rebirth of a Nation, Wales 1880–1990*, p. 355.
15 See Davies, *A History of Wales*, p. 642.
16 Morgan, *Rebirth of a Nation*, pp. 355–6.
17 Letter from Erastus Jones, General Secretary of the Council, 27 December 1967.
18 Director of the Sub-Unit of the World Council of Churches on Church and Society, 1948–83.
19 Fey, *A History of the Ecumenical Movement*, vol. II, pp. 250ff.
20 In Uppsala, Sweden, in 1968.
21 Fey, *A History of the Ecumenical Movement*, vol. II, p. 253.
22 See Lossky et al., *Dictionary of the Ecumenical Movement*, pp. 1056ff.
23 See Chapter 12.
24 Fey, *A History of the Ecumenical Movement*, vol. II, p. 259.
25 Minutes of the Council of Churches for Wales, 5 March 1969.
26 Memorandum presented to the Council 5 March 1969.
27 Report to the Churches, 8 April 1969.
28 Ibid.
29 From the draft paper on the third topic, 'Nationality and the Unity of Mankind'.
30 Ibid.
31 Report of the Conference on the Church and Society, the Council of Churches for Wales, Carmarthen 1970, p. 9.
32 Ibid., p. 7.
33 Ibid., p. 10.
34 Geneva World Conference, *Conference Declarations and Actions*, July 1970.
35 Memorandum to the Department, 12 March 1973.
36 See Chapter 6.
37 See Chapters 7–8.
38 See Chapter 9.
39 See Chapters 10–11.

## 6. The churches and self-government in Wales

1 R. Tudur Jones, 'Christian Nationalism', in Collegiate Centre for Theology, *This Land and People* (Cardiff, 1979), p. 74, which contains a series of valuable and diverse articles on Christian and Welsh national identity.
2 Ibid., p. 91.
3 Gwynfor Evans, quoted by R. Tudur Jones, ibid., p. 89.
4 G. O. Williams, in W. J. Morgan (ed.), *The Welsh Dilemma* (Llandybïe, 1973), p. 58.

## NOTES

5   D. Jenkins, 'A British Welsh Reaction', in P. Ballard, *This Land and People* (Cardiff, 1979), p. 113.
6   J. E. Daniel, '*Y Genedl a'r Wladwriaeth*', in *Y Ddraig Goch* (September/November 1939); and in D. D. Morgan (ed.), *Torri'r Seiliau Cedyrn* (Llandysul, 1993), p. 143.
7   Morgan, *Torri'r Seiliau Cedyrn*, p. 53.
8   Ibid., p. 54.
9   Ibid., p. 58.
10  Ibid., p. 63.
11  A. B. Phillips, *The Welsh Question: Nationalism in Welsh Politics, 1945–1970* (Cardiff, 1975), p. 328.
12  Saunders Lewis, Radio Lecture, 'Tynged yr Iaith', 13 February 1962.
13  Report of the Conference of the Council of Churches for Wales on Church and Society, July 1970, p. 6.
14  Quoted in 'Christians and Nationalism in Modern Wales', by J. P. Brown, in *This Land and People* (Cardiff, 1979), p. 51.
15  A response that was presented in 1970 and published in *Yr Haul* (winter 1971).
16  K. O. Morgan, *Rebirth of a Nation 1880–1980*, p. 394.
17  J. Davies, *A History of Wales* (London, 1990), pp. 673–4.
18  Report of the Council of Churches for Wales Group on the Kilbrandon Report, spring 1974, p. 1.
19  British Council of Churches, *Devolution and the British Churches* (London, 1977), p. 38.
20  Ibid., p. 53.
21  Ibid., p. iii.
22  Minutes of the Council of Churches for Wales, 13 October 1977.
23  Letter dated 28 December 1978.
24  Letter dated 23 January 1979.
25  Quoted by Davies, *A History of Wales*, p. 677.
26  The Right Reverend B. N. Y. Vaughan, Chairman of the Church and Society Department of the Council of Churches for Wales.
27  Minutes of the Council of Churches for Wales, 21–2 March 1979.
28  Letter to the Welsh denominations, 14 July 1992.
29  Ibid.
30  Statement published on St David's Day 1994.
31  For a fuller account of this process and its outcome, see R. Williams and N. A. Davies (eds), *Wales: A Moral Society?* (Llandysul, 1996).
32  Ibid., p. 60.
33  Ibid., p. 62.
34  Ibid., p. 64.
35  Ibid., p. 67.
36  Response to the National Assembly Consultative Group's Consultative Paper, May 1998, paras 1 and 2.
37  N. A. Davies, 'Democracy in Wales Today', paper to the Cytûn Conference, Wales: A New Society (April 1999), p. 2.
38  Ibid., p. 6.
39  Ibid., p. 68.

NOTES

## 7. The Christian witness in industrial society

1. Annual Meeting of the Council of Churches for Wales, 21 November 1958.
2. Minutes of the Council, 26 November 1959.
3. For a full report see 'Yr Eglwys a Diwydiant', M. Islwyn Lake in *Y Tyst* (12 July 1962), pp. 6, 7 and 10.
4. Professor of Economics, University College of South Wales and Monmouthshire, Cardiff.
5. Lake, *Y Tyst* (12 July 1962), p. 6.
6. Ibid., p. 6.
7. Ibid., p. 6.
8. Industrial chaplain in Birmingham.
9. Ibid., p. 7.
10. Ibid., p. 7.
11. Anglican Bishop of Llandaff.
12. Lake, *Y Tyst* (12 July 1962), p. 7.
13. Ibid., p. 10.
14. Principal of Coleg y Fro, who was chairman of the Organising Committee.
15. Minutes of the Industrial Committee, 13 June 1967.
16. Minutes of the Council, 29–30 October 1964.
17. See Chapter 1.
18. Minutes of the Executive Committee, 25–6 January 1965.
19. It was held in Port Talbot on 22 March 1965.
20. See the report of the Conference, 'The Churches' Industrial Work – A Pattern for Wales and other papers', October 1967.
21. For a Welsh view, see David Lee (ed.), *Structures for a Missionary Congregation*, First Report of the Commission on Church and Industry in regions of south-west Wales, in the papers of the Blaendulais Ecumenical Centre (autumn 1964).
22. L. Newbigin, in Fey (ed.), *A History of the Ecumenical Movement*, vol. II, p. 193.
23. Ibid., p. 194.
24. Report of the Mexico City Conference, 1963, p. 121; ibid., p. 194.
25. Report of the Rhoose Conference p. 4.
26. Ibid., p. 5.
27. Ibid., p. 13.
28. Minister of the Welsh Independent Church in Y Wern, Aberafan, at the time, later to become a minister of the Congregational Union of England of Wales and of the United Reformed Church.
29. Report of the Rhoose Conference p. 14.
30. Ibid., p. 14.
31. General Secretary of the Board of Mission of the Presbyterian Church of Wales.
32. A Presbyterian minister who would later become Warden of Coleg Trefeca.

## NOTES

33 Report of the Industrial Committee, 14 October 1971.
34 Report of the delegation, p. 2.
35 Ibid., p. 2.
36 Ibid., p. 5.
37 Ibid., p. 6.
38 *Western Mail*, 22 May 1972.
39 Report of the deputation, p. 7.
40 First Secretary of the Welsh TUC.
41 Report of the Industrial Committee to the Council, 29 March 1973.
42 Ibid.
43 Report to the Council, October 1975.
44 See the Report of the Conference, 19–21 October 1979, *Why Work?*, by R. Taylor.
45 *Contemporary Wales: An Annual Review of Economic and Social Research*, 1 (1987), 7.
46 *Contemporary Wales: An Annual Review of Economic and Social Research*, 3, (1989), 238.
47 *Why Work?*, Report of the Conference.
48 Minutes of the Industrial Committee, 10 January 1980.
49 Ibid.
50 Minutes of the Industrial Committee, 25 January 1980.
51 Ibid.
52 Report of the Industrial Committee, 24 April 1980.
53 One of the main themes of the World Council of Churches in the period between the fifth Nairobi Assembly (1975) and the sixth Vancouver Assembly (1983). It was this study which led the way to the process Justice, Peace, and the Integrity of Creation which was adopted by the WCC in Vancouver.
54 Annual Report of the Industrial Committee, 1980.
55 An Anglican priest who was director of the Centre for Development Education, University College, Swansea.
56 Professor of Social Geography at University College, Aberystwyth.
57 Report of the Conference, *Wales – Making a New Future*, I, by R. Taylor, November 1980, p. 2.
58 Ibid., p. 2–3.
59 Report of the Conference, *Wales – Making a New Future*, II, p. 1.
60 A minister with the Church of Scotland, who was Secretary for Community Affairs at the British Council of Churches.
61 Ibid., p. 3.
62 Ibid., p. 2.
63 Ibid., pp. 3 and 4.
64 Ibid., p. 3.
65 See *Why Work?*, report of the conference of the Industrial Committee, 1979.
66 P. H. Ballard, *Towards a Contemporary Theology of Work* (Cardiff, 1982), jointly with the Industrial Committee of the Council of Churches for Wales.

# NOTES

67 From the Department of Religious and Theological Studies, University College, Cardiff
68 Ibid., p. 1.
69 Ibid., p. 57.
70 Ibid., p. 41.
71 Ibid., p. 48.
72 Particularly the prophetic concept of *shalom* as peace with justice, as found, for example, in Micah 4: 1–7.
73 Ibid., p. 56.
74 Ibid., pp. 60–1.
75 Ibid., p. 62.
76 See Chapter 10.
77 In this meeting also, there was agreement on the resolution which provided the basis for the Welsh churches' involvement in the coal dispute.
78 *Western Mail*, 9 November 1984.
79 *Privatisation – A Dangerous Trend in British Society*, pp. 4–5.
80 Ibid., p. 11.

## 8. The churches and the dispute in the coal-mining industry

1 Minutes of the Council of Churches for Wales, 12 October 1984, p. 3.
2 D. Jenkins, *God, Politics and the Future* (London, 1988), p. 8.
3 Ibid., p. 9.
4 *Western Mail*, 8 January 1985. Mr McGregor was Chairman of the National Coal Board.
5 *Western Mail*, 10 January 1985.
6 *Western Mail*, 16 January 1985.
7 *Western Mail*, 24 January 1985.
8 Davies, *A History of Wales*, p. 685.
9 Minutes of the Council, 2 November 1985.
10 The Council of Churches for Wales, *Dangerous Trends in British Society?* (1985, unpublished).
11 *Contemporary Wales: An Annual Review of Economic and Social Research*, vol. 2 (Cardiff, 1988), 165.
12 Ibid., vol. 1, (Cardiff, 1987), 30.
13 *Unemployment: What Can Be Done? A Statement for St David's Day 1987*, p. 7.
14 Ibid., p. 21.
15 Ibid., pp. 22–4.

NOTES

## 9. Wales and racism in southern Africa

1. Memorandum submitted to the first meeting of the Department, 12 March 1973.
2. Quoted in Lossky et al., *Dictionary of the Ecumenical Movement*, p. 841.
3. Ibid., p. 825.
4. Memorandum to the Department of Church and Society, Council of Churches for Wales, September 1973, p. 1.
5. Ibid., p. 1.
6. Ibid., p. 2.
7. Minutes of the Council of Churches for Wales, 11–12 October 1973.
8. Baldwin Sjollema in Lossky et al., *Dictionary of the Ecumenical Movement*, p. 825.
9. Who had recently returned to Wales after a period as an Anglican Bishop in Central America, most recently in Belize, and who would become Bishop of Swansea and Brecon.
10. Letter dated 6 January 1975.
11. Memorandum of the Department Church and Society, September 1975, p. 2.
12. Ibid., p. 3.
13. An Afrikaans minister of the Dutch Reformed Church, who had taken his stand alongside the black and coloured community in South Africa and was consequently ostracized by his Church. He was later to become General Secretary of the South Africa Council of Churches.
14. For background, content and analysis of the trial, see International Commission of Jurists (ed.), *The Trial of Beyers Naudé: Christian Witness and the Rule of Law* (London, 1975).
15. Memorandum of the Department, September 1975, p. 4.
16. Statement published on 20 October 1977 and signed by the President, George Evans, the Chairman of the Department Church and Society, Bishop B. N. Y. Vaughan, and the General Secretary of the Council, Noel Davies.
17. Letter dated 28 October 1977.
18. Letter from the Ambassador, Mr Matthys I. Botha, dated 25 November 1977.
19. Letter to the churches following the Seminar, Passion Sunday 1978.
20. Statement of the Council of Churches for Wales, 19 October 1978, para. 5.
21. Ibid., para. 8.
22. In a letter from Roy T. Davies, Secretary of the Provincial Council, 27 January 1979.
23. Letter from Noel Davies dated 9 November 1978.
24. Professor of International Politics, University College of Wales, Aberystwyth.
25. Quoted in the Department's report from The British Council of Churches, *Political Change in Southern Africa: Britain's Responsibility* (London, 1979), p. 8.

## NOTES

26 Quotations from the report presented to the Council of Churches for Wales on 19 October 1979.
27 Formerly a Church of Scotland missionary in Malawi and at the time Africa Secretary of the British Council of Churches.
28 From the written notes of the discussion by the General Secretary, Noel Davies.
29 Minutes of the Council of Churches for Wales, 19 October 1979.
30 Letter dated 29 October 1979.
31 *Commonwealth Statement on Apartheid in Sport*, Gleneagles, 15 June 1977.
32 A Methodist minister from South Africa, who had by then succeeded Jim Wilkie as Africa Secretary of the BCC.
33 Minutes of the Council of Churches for Wales, 5 May 1983.
34 From a note from the Executive Committee of the World Council of Churches, 28 February 1984.
35 Ibid.
36 Ibid.
37 Letter from Desmond Tutu dated 30 June 1983.
38 Note on the World Council of Churches, p. 2.
39 Minutes of the Council of Churches for Wales, 5 May 1984.
40 *The Kairos Document: Challenge to the Church*, September 1985.
41 *The Kairos Document*, Second Revised Edition (1986).
42 Ibid., p. 1.
43 Ibid., p. 18.
44 Ibid., p. 26.
45 *Memorandum from Harare*, in *PCR Information*, No. 23, (Geneva, 1986), pp. 29ff.
46 Ibid.
47 From a recording of the service made by the company Llygad y Ffynnon, 1986.
48 Ibid.
49 Ibid.
50 Ibid.
51 Ibid.
52 Council of Churches for Wales, Statement, *Wales and South Africa: The Way Ahead*, February 1990.
53 Ibid.
54 Ephesians 2: 14 (GNB).
55 Galatians 3: 28 (RSV).

## 10. War and peace: nuclear disarmament

1 Report of the Conference on Church and Society, Carmarthen, 1970, p. 3.
2 Davies, *A History of Wales*, p. 599.
3 W. A. Visser 't Hooft (ed.), *The First Assembly of the World Council of Churches, The Official Report* (London, 1949), p. 89.

## NOTES

4 Ibid., p. 100.
5 All these appear in an addendum to the report of the Peace Council of the Council of Churches for Wales, Wrexham, 10 March 1987, pp. 48ff.
6 Ibid., p. 10.
7 See the Report of the Peace Council, 1987, p. 49.
8 *The Cutting Edge: How Churches Speak on Social Issues*, BCC, 1993, p. 58.
9 Minutes of the Council of Churches for Wales, 30 April 1981.
10 Minutes of the Council, 5 May 1983.
11 *Swords into Ploughshares*, January 1984, p. 4.
12 Ibid., p. 4.
13 Ibid., p. 13.
14 Ibid., p. 17.
15 Ibid., p. 16.
16 J. Habgood, *Confessions of a Conservative Liberal* (London, 1988), p. 173.
17 Ibid., p. 12.
18 Report of the Peace Council, Council of Churches for Wales, 1987, p. 23.
19 *Swords into Ploughshares*, p. 8.
20 R. Gill, *A Textbook of Christian Ethics* (Edinburgh, 1995), pp. 301ff.
21 Ibid., p. 302.
22 Ibid., p. 413.
23 Report of the Peace Council, 10 March 1987, p. 16.
24 Ibid., p. 20.
25 Roger Williamson, 'Disarmament', in Lossky et al., *Dictionary of the Ecumenical Movement*, p. 298.
26 *Swords into Ploughshares*, p. 10.
27 Minutes of the Council of Churches for Wales, 30 April 1981.
28 *Swords into Ploughshares*, p. 6.
29 Ibid., p. 6.
30 Pugwash was an association of scientists which focused on issues concerning nuclear weapons and nuclear power and their influences. Dr E. M. Job, Aberystwyth, who was central to the Council's work in this field, was a member of this association.
31 Ibid., p. 7.
32 A lecturer in International Politics in the Department of Continuing Education, University College, Swansea.
33 Report of the Peace Council, 10 March 1987, p. 4.
34 Minutes of the Council, 5 May 1983.
35 *Swords into Ploughshares*, p. 19.
36 Report of the Peace Council, p. 11.
37 Ibid., p. 12, quoting from the Palme Report (The Independent Commission on Matters of Disarmament and Security 1982).
38 Report of the Peace Council, p. 10.
39 Ibid., p. 9.
40 Ibid., p. 10.

# NOTES

41 Report of the Peace Council, p. 16.
42 Ibid., p. 20.
43 Report of the Peace Council, p. 30.
44 In his paper, *Peace Issues*, p. 4.
45 Ibid., p. 5.
46 Ibid., p. 6.
47 Minutes of the Council of Churches for Wales, 1 May 1986.
48 *Swords into Ploughshares*, p. 3.
49 Ibid., p. 17.
50 Ibid., p. 18.
51 Ibid., pp. 18ff.
52 Minutes of the Council, 29 April 1982.
53 Appendix to the Report of the Peace Council, March 1987, p. 51.
54 Report of the Peace Council, p. 13.
55 Ibid, p. 28.
56 Ibid., p. 54.
57 Ibid., p. 31.

## 11. War and peace: the Malvinas war

1 Minutes of the Council of Churches for Wales, 29 April 1982.
2 Included in a collection of documents by the Council of Churches for Wales.
3 Note to the General Secretary of the Council, 23 April 1982.
4 Telegram from the World Council of Churches, 21 April 1982.
5 Paper dated 27 April 1982 and presented to the Council 29 April 1982.
6 Minutes of the Council of Churches for Wales, 29 April 1982.
7 Minutes of the Council, 29 April 1982.
8 Letter to the Council of Churches for Wales, 6 May 1982.
9 Letter dated 30 April 1982.
10 Letter dated 6 May 1982.
11 Letter dated 19 May 1982.
12 *The Pope Teaches: The Pope in Britain – the Complete Texts* (London, 1982), p. 170.
13 Letter to *The Guardian*, 3 May 1982.
14 *The Church in the Modern World*, report of the Second Vatican Council, p. 79.
15 *Statement of Moral Issues in the Falklands Crisis*, 28 April 1982.
16 Letter to *The Times*, 30 April 1982.
17 Minutes of the Committee for National and International Affairs of the Council, 26 July 1982.
18 Statement by the Consultative Council of the Churches of Argentina, 6 July 1982.
19 *The Aftermath of the Falklands Crisis*, report to the Assembly of the British Council of Churches, November 1982, Appendix III.
20 Ibid., Appendix VIII.

## NOTES

21 Message of the Consultative Council of the Churches of Argentina, 6 July 1982, p. 3.
22 From the Welsh translation of the message, dated 8 December 1982.
23 *The Aftermath of the Falklands Crisis*, November 1982, p. 17.
24 Letter to *The Times*, 30 April 1982.
25 Denis Healey, *The Time of my Life* (London, 1990), p. 494.
26 Adrian Hastings, *Robert Runcie* (London, 1991), p. 185.
27 Ibid., p. 186.

## Concluding reflections

1 *The Principles of Visible Unity in Wales* (Bangor, 1980).
2 *The Holy Communion* (Swansea, 1981).
3 *Ministry in a Uniting Church* (Swansea, 1986).
4 *Baptism* (Penarth, 1990).
5 M. Taylor, *Not Angels but Agencies* (Geneva/London, 1995), p. 167.
6 *Covenant towards union in Wales,* Parts I and II (Bangor, 1971).
7 *Baptism, Eucharist and Ministry,* Faith and Order Paper No. 110 (Geneva, 1982).
8 Ballard, *Towards a Contemporary Theology of Work.*
9 The first translation, completed by Bishop William Morgan, was published in 1588. In 2004 a revised edition of *Y Beibl Cymraeg Newydd* was published which includes some textual revisions, not least to accommodate an element of inclusive language.
10 The Revd Aled Edwards, a priest of the Church in Wales, who became Chief Executive of Cytûn: Churches Together in Wales in 2006.
11 Set up in Trinity College, Carmarthen in January 2001 with Dr Trystan Owain Hughes as Director and the present author (who is currently its Director) as President.
12 D. Gill (ed.), *Gathered for Life: The Official Report of the Sixth Assembly of the World Council of Churches* (Geneva, 1983), p. 193.

# Selected bibliography

## 1. Books

Abrecht, Paul, *The Churches and Rapid Social Change* (New York, 1961).
Ariarajah, I. S. Wesley, *Gospel and Culture* (Geneva, 1994).
Ariarajah, I. S. Wesley, *Did I betray the Gospel?* (Geneva, 1996).
Autton, Norman, *Gweini i'r Rhai sy'n Marw* (Penarth, 1979).
Ballard, Paul H. and Jones, D. Huw (eds), *This Land and People* (Cardiff, 1979).
Ballard, Paul H. (ed.), *Towards a Contemporary Theology of Work* (Cardiff, 1982).
Barth, Karl, *The Church and the Churches* (London, 1936).
Bell, George, *Documents on Christian Unity, 1920–1930*, Four Volumes (Oxford, 1928–50).
Bell, George, *Christian Unity: The Anglican Position, Volumes I – III* (London, 1948).
Bell, George, *The Kingship of Christ: The Story of the World Council of Churches* (Geneva, 1954).
Best, Thomas F. (ed.), *Instruments of Unity. National Councils of Churches within the One Ecumenical Movement* (Geneva, 1988).
Best, Thomas F. (ed.), *Living Today Towards Visible Unity, Report of the Fifth Consultation for United and Uniting Churches* (Geneva, 1988).
Best, Thomas F. (ed.), *Beyond Unity-in-Tension* (Geneva, 1988).
Best, Thomas F. (ed.), *Built Together, Report of the Sixth Consultation for United and Uniting Churches* (Geneva, 1996).
Best, Thomas F. and Gassman, Günther (eds), *On the way to a fuller koinonia, Official Report, Fifth Conference Faith and Order 1993* (Geneva, 1994).
Best, Thomas F. and Granberg-Michaelson, Wesley (eds), *Costly Obedience: Koinonia and Justice, peace and the integrity of creation* (Geneva, 1993).
Best, Thomas F. and Robra, Martin (eds), *Costly Obedience* (Geneva, 1987).
Bethge, Eberhard, *Dietrich Bonhoeffer: A Biography* (London,1985).
Bethge, Eberhard, *Friendship and Resistance: Essays on Dietrich Bonhoeffer* (Geneva, 1995).
Bevan, R. J. W. (ed.), *The Churches and Christian Unity* (London, 1963).
Blatherwick, David, *Adventures in Unity* (London, 1974).
Boesak, Allan, *Black and Reformed: Apartheid, liberation and the Calvinist tradition* (Skotaville, 1984).

## SELECTED BIBLIOGRAPHY

Boesak, Allan, *Walking on thorns: The call to Christian obedience* (Geneva, 1984).
Bosch, David, *Transforming Mission* (New York, 1992).
Braaten, C. E., and Jenson, R. W. (eds), *The Ecumenical Future* (Grand Rapids, 2004).
Bria, Ion and Heller, Dagmar (eds), Ecumenical Pilgrims (Geneva, 1995).
Briggs, J., Odoyoye, M. A. and Tsetsis, G. (eds), *A History of the Ecumenical Movement, Volume III, 1968–2000* (Geneva, 2004).
Butler, David, *Dying to be One, English Ecumenism: History, Theology and the Future* (London, 1996).
Carden, John (ed.), *With All God's People: The Ecumenical Prayer Cycle* (Geneva, 1990).
Cashmore, Gwen and Puls, Joan, *Every Bush is Burning* (Geneva, 1985).
Castro, Emilio, *Sent Free* (Geneva, 1985).
Castro, Emilio, *A Passion for Unity* (Geneva, 1992).
*Catechism of the Catholic Church* (London, 1994).
Chadwick, Owen, *Michael Ramsey: A Life* (Oxford, 1990).
*Contemporary Wales: An Annual Review of Economic and Social Research, Volumes I – II* (Cardiff, 1987–9).
Conway, Martin, *Unity – Why not yet?* (London, 1980).
Crow, Paul A., Jnr and Gassman, Günther, *Lausanne 1927 to Santiago de Compostela 1993* (Geneva, 1993).
David, Kenith A., *Sacrament and Struggle* (Geneva, 1994).
Davies, John, *A History of Wales* (London, 1990).
Davies, Noel A., *Wales: Language, Nation, Faith and Witness* (Geneva, 1996).
Davies, Noel A., *Un er Mwyn y Byd* (Swansea, 1998).
Davies, Rupert E., *Methodists and Unity* (London, 1962).
Davies, Rupert E., *Unity Begins at Home, A Report of the First Conference on Faith and Order, Nottingham 1964* (London, 1964).
de Gruchy, John W., *Bonhoeffer and South Africa: Theology in dialogue* (Grand Rapids, 1984).
de Gruchy, John W., *The Church Struggle in South Africa* (London, 1979).
Dunn, James D. G., *Unity and Diversity in the New Testament*, 2nd edn (London, 1990).
Edwards, David L., *The British Churches Turn to the Future* (London, 1973).
Ellingsen, Mark, *How Churches Speak on Social Issues* (Geneva, 1993).
Ellis, Christopher J., *Together on the Way: A Theology of Ecumenism* (London, 1990).
Evans, G. R., *The Church and the Churches* (Cambridge, 1994).
Evans, G. R., *Method in Ecumenical Theology* (Cambridge, 1996).
Evans, Owen E. (ed.), *Gwarchod y Gair* (Denbigh, 1993).
Fey, Harold E. (ed.), *A History of the Ecumenical Movement, Volume II, 1948–1968*, 2nd edn (Geneva, 1986).
Flesseman-van Leer, Ellen (ed.), *The Bible: Its Authority and Interpretation in the Ecumenical Movement*, Paper on Faith and Order No. 99 (Geneva, 1983).

## SELECTED BIBLIOGRAPHY

Forrester, Duncan, *The True Church and Morality* (Geneva, 1996).
Fung, Raymond, *The Isaiah Vision* (Geneva, 1992).
Gassman, Günther (ed.), *Documentary History of Faith and Order 1963–1993* (Geneva, 1993).
Gill, David (ed.), *Gathered for Life, The Official Report of the Sixth Assembly of the World Council of Churches, Vancouver, 1983* (Geneva, 1983).
Gill, Robin, *A Textbook of Christian Ethics* (Edinburgh, 1995).
Goodall, Norman, *The Ecumenical Movement* (Oxford, 1961).
Goosen, Gideon, *Bringing Churches Together: An Introduction to Ecumenism* (Newtown, Australia, 1993).
Habgood, John, *Confessions of a Conservative Liberal* (London, 1988).
Harling, Per (ed.), *Worshipping Ecumenically* (London, 1995).
Hastings, Adrian, *A History of English Christianity, 1920–1985* (London, 1987).
Hastings, Adrian, *Robert Runcie* (London, 1991).
Healey, Denis, *The Time of My Life* (London, 1990).
Hopkins, C. Howard, *John R. Mott, 1865–1955* (London, 1979).
Howells, Ron, *A Tale of Two Grandmothers: Memoirs of an Ecumenist* (Swansea, 1994).
Hughes, Trystan O., *Winds of Change: The Roman Catholic Church and Society in Wales, 1916–62* (Cardiff, 1999).
International Commission of Jurists (ed.), *The Trial of Beyers Naudé* (London, 1975).
Jenkins, David, *God, Politics and the Future* (London, 1988).
Jones, Erastus, *Croesi Ffiniau: Gyda'r Eglwys yn y Byd* (Swansea, 2000).
Jones, R. Tudur, *Teyrnas Crist a'r Tywyllwch yng Nghymru* (The Kingdom of Christ and the Darkness in Wales) (Swansea, 1994).
Jones, R. Tudur, *Faith and the Crisis of a Nation* (ed. Robert Pope) (Cardiff, 2004).
Kinnamon, Michael, *Truth and Community* (Geneva, 1988).
Kinnamon, Michael (ed.), *Signs of the Spirit, The Official Report of the Seventh Assembly of the WCC, Canberra 1991* (Geneva, 1991).
Kinnamon, Michael and Best, Thomas E. (eds), *Called to be One in Christ: United Churches and the Ecumenical Movement* (Geneva, 1985).
Kinnamon, Michael and Cope, Brian (ed.), *The Ecumenical Movement* (Geneva, 1996).
Leeming, Bernard, *The Vatican Council and Christian Unity* (London, 1966).
Linn, Gerhard (ed.), *Hear What the Spirit Says to the Churches* (Geneva, 1994).
Lossky, N., Bonino, M., Pobee, J., Stransky, T., Wainwright G., and Webb, P. (eds), *Dictionary of the Ecumenical Movement* (Geneva, 1991; 2nd edn 2002).
Matthews, John, *The Unity Scene* (London, 1986).
Morgan, D. Densil (ed.), *Torri'r Seiliau Cedyrn* (Llandysul, 1993).
Morgan, D. Densil, *The Span of the Cross: Christian Religion and Society in Wales, 1914–2000* (Cardiff, 1999).

## SELECTED BIBLIOGRAPHY

Morgan, Kenneth O., *Rebirth of a Nation: Wales 1880–1980*, vol. V in Glanmor Williams (ed.), *A History of Wales* (Cardiff, 1981).
Morgan, W. J. (ed.), *The Welsh Dilemma* (Llandybïe, 1973).
Müller-Fahrenholz, Geiko, *God's Spirit* (Geneva, 1995).
Naudé, C. F. Beyers and Sölle, Dorothee, *Hope for Faith* (Geneva, 1986).
Newbigin, Lesslie, *The Gospel in a Pluralist Society* (Geneva/London, 1989).
Newbigin, Lesslie, *The Other Side of 1984* (Geneva, 1990).
Nicholls, Vincent (ed.), *Reflections* (London, 1986).
Paton, David, M. (ed.), *Breaking Barriers, The Official Report of the Fifth Assembly of the WCC, Nairobi 1975* (Geneva, 1976).
Payne, Ernest A., *Thirty Years of the British Council of Churches, 1942–72* (London, 1972).
Phillips, Alan Butt, *The Welsh Question: Nationalism in Welsh Politics, 1945–70* (Cardiff, 1975).
Phillips, G. O., *Yr Eglwys ac Ynni Niwclear* (Penarth, 1978).
*Pope Teaches, The, Addresses and Homilies of Pope John Paul II* (London, 1982).
Potter, Philip, *What is the World Council of Churches?* (Geneva, 1979).
Preston, Ronald H., *Religion and the Persistence of Capitalism*, The Maurice Lectures for 1977 (London, 1979).
Raiser, Konrad, *Ecumenism in Transition* (Geneva, 1989).
Raiser, Konrad, *To Be the Church* (Geneva, 1997).
Rasmussen, Larry L., *Earth Community, Earth Ethics* (Geneva, 1996).
Rouse, R., and Neill, S. (eds), *A History of the Ecumenical Movement, Volume I, 1517–1948*, 3rd edn (Geneva, 1986).
Slack, Kenneth, *Report of the Nairobi Assembly of the WCC* (London, 1976).
Stendahl, Krister, *Energy for Life* (Geneva, 1990).
Taylor, Michael, *Not Angels but Agencies* (Geneva/London, 1995).
Templeton, Elizabeth, *God's February: A Life of Archie Craig, 1888–1985* (London, 1991).
Thurian, Max (ed.), *Ecumenical Perspectives on Baptism, Eucharist and Ministry* (Geneva, 1983).
Thurian, Max (ed.), *Churches Respond to BEM, Volumes I–VII* (Geneva, 1986–8).
Torrance, T. F., *Conflict and Agreement in the Churches, Volume I: Order and Disorder* (London, 1936).
van Beek, Huibert, *Sharing Life* (Geneva, 1989).
van der Bent, Ans J., *Voice of Unity, Essays in Honour of W. A. Visser 't Hooft* (Geneva, 1981).
van der Bent, Ans J., *From Generation to Generation* (Geneva, 1986).
van der Bent, Ans J., *Commitment to God's World: A Concise Critical Survey of Ecumenical Social Thought* (Geneva, 1995).
VanElderen, Marlin, *Introducing the World Council of Churches* (Geneva, 1992; revised Martin Conway, 2002).

SELECTED BIBLIOGRAPHY

Villa-Vicencio, Charles and de Gruchy, John W. (eds), *Resistance and Hope: South African Essays in Honour of Beyers Naudé* (Grand Rapids, 1985).
Visser 't Hooft, W. A., *The First Assembly of the World Council of Churches, The Official Report* (London, 1949).
Visser 't Hooft, W. A., *Memoirs*, Second Edition (Geneva, 1987).
Visser 't Hooft, W. A., *The Genesis and History of the World Council of Churches* (Geneva, 1987).
Webb, Pauline, *She Flies Beyond* (Geneva, 1993).
Webb, Pauline (ed.), *A Long Struggle* (Geneva, 1994).
Williams, Jeff, *Nes Unionir y Cam* (Swansea, 1988).
Williams, R. and Davies, N. A. (eds) *Wales: A Moral Society?* (Llandysul, 1996).

## 2. Minutes, documents and reports

### A. Council of Churches for Wales

Annual Reports of the Council, from 1960 onwards, but which were not published annually throughout the period.
Baptism, Eucharist and Ministry, Report of a Consultation (Swansea, 1985).
Cleddyfau yn Sychau (Swansea, 1983).
Discussion pack, The Family of God, 1985.
General letters of the Council of Churches for Wales, 1956–1990.
Message to the Churches, Conference on Faith and Order, Carmarthen, 1963.
Minutes and papers of the Working Party jointly between The Council of Churches for Wales and the Roman Catholic Church in Wales, 1980–1983.
Minutes and papers of the Youth Committee, Council of Churches for Wales, 1965–1980.
Minutes and reports of the Department of Ecumenical Action, The Council of Churches for Wales, 1965–1980.
Minutes and reports of the National and International Committee, The Council of Churches for Wales, 1982–1990.
Minutes of the Council of Churches for Wales, 1959–1990.
Minutes of the Department of Church and Society, Council of Churches for Wales, 1972–1982.
Minutes of the Industry Committee, Council of Churches for Wales, 1965 onwards.
Minutes of the Working Committee of the Council of Churches for Wales, 1961–1990.
People Next Door, The Council of Churches for Wales, 1967.
Preliminary Report of the Review Working Party, Council of Churches for Wales, 1988.

SELECTED BIBLIOGRAPHY

Publications of the Inter-Church Process (London, 1986): *Views from the Pews, Reflections* (ed. Vincent Nicholls), *Observations* (ed. Colin Davey).
Report of the Commission on Mid-Wales, The Council of Churches for Wales, 1960.
Report of the Conference on the Churches and Society, The Council of Churches for Wales, Carmarthen, 1970.
Report of the Forum on Nuclear Energy, Wrexham, The Council of Churches for Wales, 1977.
Report of the Forum on Nuclear Waste, Wrexham, The Council of Churches for Wales, 1981.
Report of the Peace Council, The Council of Churches for Wales, 1987.
Report of the Working Party on Baptism, Eucharist and Ministry, The Council of Churches for Wales, 1984.
Report on the Report of the Kilbrandon Commission, The Council of Churches for Wales, 1974.
Reports of the conferences of the Industry Committee, The Council of Churches for Wales, 1967 onwards.
Reports of the Joint Committee on Covenanting: The Call to Covenant (1965), Covenanting in Wales (1968), Covenanting for Unity in Wales, Parts I and II (1971), Why Covenant? (1972).
Statement on Unemployment, The Council of Churches for Wales, St David's Day, 1987.
The Family of God at Worship, The Council of Churches for Wales, 1986.
The Theology of Experiment, Report of the Advisory Theological Group, The Council of Churches for Wales, 1971.
The Unity We Desire, The Council of Churches for Wales, 1964.
Uppsala and Wales, The Council of Churches for Wales, 1968.
Thine is the Glory, Liturgical Study Group, The Council of Churches for Wales, 1971.

NB The above are deposited in The Council of Churches for Wales Collection at The National Library of Wales, Aberystwyth.

*B. Other reports*

*Baptism, Eucharist and Ministry*, Paper on Faith and Order No. 111 (Geneva, 1982).
*Baptism, Eucharist and Ministry 1982–1990, Report on the Process and Responses*, Paper on Faith and Order No. 149 (Geneva, 1990).
*British and Irish Churches Respond to BEM* (London, 1988).
*Church and World: The Unity of the Church and the Renewal of Human Community*, Paper on Faith and Order No. 151 (Geneva, 1990).
*Churches Together in Pilgrimage* (London 1989).
*Conversations between the Church of England and the Methodist Church*, A Report (London, 1963).
*Devolution and the British Churches*, report to the Assembly of the BCC for their Assembly in Bangor, Spring 1977 (London, 1977).

## SELECTED BIBLIOGRAPHY

*Four Nations, One Church?*, paper by the BCC, Department of Ecumenical Affairs (London, 1982).
*God's Reign and Our Unity: Report of the International Commission of Anglican and Reformed Churches* (St Andrews/London, 1984).
*In Each Place: Towards a Fellowship of Churches Truly United* (Geneva, 1977).
*Not Strangers but Pilgrims*, papers for national conferences of the Inter-church Process (London, 1987).
*One Baptism, One Eucharist and a Mutually Recognized Ministry*, Paper on Faith and Order No. 73 (Geneva, 1975).
*Principles of Visible Unity in Wales* (Bangor, 1980).
*Prospects for Wales*, Peter Brierley and Byron Evans (London, 1983).
Sixth Report of the Joint Working Group between the Roman Catholic Church and the World Council of Churches (Geneva, 1990).
*The Easter People*, Message of the Catholic Bishops of England and Wales in the light of the National Pastoral Association (London, 1980).
*Towards Union* (Tuag at Undeb), Joint Committee of the Four Denominations, 1963.
*Ut Unum Sint*, Encyclical of Pope John Paul II on Commitment to Ecumenism (London, 1995).
*Whose Rubicon?* Report on the visit to South Africa by representatives of the churches of Britain (London, 1986).
*Your Kingdom Come*, Report of the World Conference on Mission and Evangelizing, Melbourne, 1980 (Geneva, 1980).
*Your Will Be Done* (ed. Frederick R. Wilson), Report of the World Conference on Mission and Evangelism, San Antonio (Geneva, 1990).

## 3. Journals

*Dysgedydd, Y.*
*Ecumenical Review, The.*
*Efrydydd, Yr.*
*Eurgrawn, Yr.*
*Haul, Yr.*
*International Review of Mission, The.*
*One World.*
*Porfeydd.*
*Tyst, Y.*

# Index

Aberystwyth meeting 1973
   issues discussed 37–8
Abraham-Williams, Gethin
   General Secretary of Enfys 26–7
Abrecht, Paul
   Geneva Conference, on 75
   World Council of Churches, on 76
agricultural industry 4
Anti-Apartheid Year (1978) 142
ap Gwynfor, Sian
   pacifist standpoint 165
apartheid 137–58
   arms trade, and 137
   condemnation of 149–50
   lack of thorough theological study 156–7
   policy of Council 157
   theological beginnings 137
   theological themes 156–7
   ways of engaging Christian witness against 157–8
Archbishop of Canterbury
   Malvinas war, on 185
*Areas of Ecumenical Experiment* 36

Ballard, Paul
   industrial society, on 117–18
baptism
   order for 27
bilingualism
   promotion within ecumenical family 46
   worship material 29
Bonino, Professor Jose Miguez
   Malvinas, on 188
Bowen, Professor E. G.
   land use in Wales, on 69–70
British Council of Churches
   report on South Africa 1979 145
British Faith and Order
   Conference (1964) 12, 14
   evangelicals, and 15
   Lund Dictum 17
   observers from Roman Catholic Church 15–16
   response of Welsh delegates 17
   response to resolution of 19
broadcasting 70–2
   Advisory Committee 71–2
   Brown, Jo 50
   Pilkington Committee 71
   sacred aspect 74

*Call to Covenant, The* 21–2
Campaign for a Nuclear Freeze 170
Carter, Harold
   industrial society, on 115–16
Christian Institute of South Africa
   concern about future of 140–1
   declaration of illegality of 141–2
Church and Industry
   conference (1962) 102–3
*Church for All Men* 34–5
Churches and society 67–82
   beginnings 67–82
   foundations 67–82
Clark, Bishop Alan
   ecumenism, on 57

# INDEX

Clwyd County Council
  nuclear disarmament, and 173–4
CND Wales
  formation of 162
coal and steel industries
  transformation of 4
coal-mining industry dispute 121–36
  approach and perspective of Industrial Committee 135–6
  Christian witness, and 131–3
  churches, and 121–36
  churches as mediators 130
  Council of Churches for Wales resolution (1984) 121–2
  discussion between NCB and NUM 124
  letter to Prime Minister 126
  nature of economic decisions within society, and 132–3
  Neil Kinnock on 126–7
  new partnership, creation of 133–4
  Nicholas Edwards, on 123
  pastoral work in mining communities 127–8
  Peter Walker on 125
  political aspect 128
  proposal for review body 131
  proposals of Welsh churches 128–9
  responsible stewardship of resources of creation 131–2
  statement of 1987 134–5
  unemployment statistics 134
Commission of the Covenanted Churches 38
  formation 26
Commission on Land in Mid-Wales 68–70

Consultative Council of Churches of Argentina 182–3
Conway, Martin
  effectiveness of steps towards unity, on 30
Council of Churches for Wales 1
  archives 3
  *Baptism, Eucharist and Ministry*, and 201, 202
  basis of formation 6
  British Council of Churches, and 205
  building the ecumenical house 208
  challenges around identity and unity 207
  challenging and radical movement, as 197
  Christian unity, and 198–200
  churches, and 194–7
  communication with churches 196
  *Companions for a Change* 199
  conference (1990) recommendation 154
  Covenant for Visible Unity in Wales. See Covenant towards Union in Wales
  definition of 'responsible society' 67–8
  disillusionment, and 4
  dynamic instrument, as 8
  ecclesiastical institution, as 197
  facilitator of natural understanding and cooperation 195–6
  financial difficulties 196–7
  future payments 206–8
  identity and unity, challenges around 207
  inaugural meeting 5–6
  inauguration 1
  influence of 203–4

240

# INDEX

inter-church climate, and 199
international affairs 193
international delegation 206
message from first meeting 10
National Assembly, and 206–7
need for wider vision of Christian unity 200
need to redefine ecumenism in global and pluralist environment 207
new initiatives since 1990 198–9
New Welsh Bible 203
officers 210–13
origins 1
pioneer, as 195
promotion of discussion of theological issues 202
public life, and 200–1
publications 198
racism, and 201
re-affirmation of ecumenical task 206–7
re-evaluation of search for Christian unity 206
request for financial support 197
resources 196
responsibility of denominational representatives 195
restructuring (1981) 7
Roman Catholic Church, and 199–200
social developments, and 5
South Africa, and 201
statement on Zimbabwe 143
status of denominational representatives 195
successes of 45
*Swords into Ploughshares* 202
tension between institutional and individual Christianity 200–1

Theological Consultative Group 202
theological engagement, and 201–2
*Towards a Contemporary Theology of Work* 201–2
vision of early pioneers 203
WCC Faith and Order programme 207
Welsh language, and 203–4
witness in industry 203
World Council of Churches, and 204
worldwide conferences, and 204
worldwide ecumenical movement, and 204–6
Covenant towards Union in Wales
articles 22–3
bilingualism, and 29
Church in Wales, and 25
covenanting, implications 24
denominations agreeing to enter into 25
goal of union 29
implications 24
local division, and 28–9
ministry, article on 23
origins 19, 21–30
reasons for 24
significance 28
theology in Wales, and 28
threefold pattern of early centuries 23–4
uncertainty of ministry in different traditions 29–30
Crowther Commission 88–9
adoption of report 90
report 89
response to report 89–90
terms of reference 88
Cytûn
Malvinas war, on 186

# INDEX

Network of Industrial and
  Economic Issues 107
role of 208
self-government in Wales, and
  94–7

Daniel, Professor J. E.
  self-government, on 85
Davies, E. Curig
  British Faith and Order
    Conference 1964, on 18
Davies, Noel
  Rhodesia, on 144
  self-government in Wales, on
    92–3
  visit to South Africa 151–2
  Wales and Argentina, and
    188–9
Decree on Ecumenism 48–9
  Christian unity, on 49
  influence of 49
Department of Church and Society
  apartheid, and 138–9, 140
Department of Ecumenical Action
  conference for local councils of
    churches and local
    congregations 39
  ecumenical centres 33
  effect of Covenant towards
    Union 36
  evaluation of Welsh
    experiments 36–7
  local supervision, on 37
  regional groups 33
  regions 33
  setting up of 32
  work of 33
Department of Social
  Responsibility (See also
  Department of Church and
  Society)
  areas of work 81
  setting up of 80–1

Ellingsen, Mark
  nuclear disarmament, on 162–3
Elliott, Charles
  *Wales in the World* 115
Eloff Commission 148–9
Enfys 26–7

Faith and Order Working Group
  32
Four Denominations Committee
  11
Fox, Bishop Langton 50–1
Friends of the Council of
  Churches for Wales 32–3

Geneva conference (1966) 74–6
Gill, Robin
  just war, on 166
Gleneagles agreement (1977) 147
Glynllifon conference (1967) 35
God's Family Festival 43–4
  cost 44
  purpose 44
Griffith, Huw Wynne 9, 12, 13,
    19, 22, 25, 31, 51, 93,
    161, 178, 179, 211
  British Faith and Order
    Conference 1964, on 19
*gweinidogaethau bro* 39

Habgood, John
  prophecy and policy, on 164
Holdsworth John
  Strategic Defence Initiative, on
    170–1
*Holy Communion, The* 27
Howells, Ron 56, 57
Hughes, John Poole
  death of David Wilkie, on 125
Hume, Cardinal
  Malvinas war, on 184–5

industrial chaplaincies 104
  continuing failure 108–9

# INDEX

difficulties 106
importance of 114–15
Industrial Committee 104
   privatization, on 119–20
   publications 114, 115
   regional consultations 114
   relationship with other industrial institutions 111
   report to Council 1980
   Thatcherite era, and 113
industrial society 101–20
   Christian witness, in 101–20
   national conference (1967) 105–7
   'presence' 103
   Rhoose conference 105–7
   theology of work 116–18
   *Towards a Contemporary Theology of Work* 117
Inter-church Aid and Refugee Service 3
Islwyn Lake, M.
   British Faith and Order Conference (1964), on 17–18

Jenkins, Clive
   work, on 112
Jenkins, Daniel
   Welsh nationalism, on 84–5
Joint Committee 2
Joint Covenanting Committee 21
   final report 22
   representatives 22
   *The Call to Covenant* 21–2
Jones, Erastus 9, 10, 19, 33, 47, 50, 51, 52, 110, 113, 123, 146, 211, 212, 229
Jones, R. Tudur
   *This Land and People* 83–4
Jones, Iorwerth
   British Faith and Order Conference 1964, on 18
Jones, O. P. 43–4

Kairos Document 150
Kilbrandon Commission
   report 89

land use in Wales 68–70
   churches, role of 69
   social and religious crisis in rural Wales 68
Lee, David
   industrial society, on 105–6
Lewis, Saunders
   Welsh language, on 87
Liturgical Study Group 214–15
   formation 214
   general principles of worship 214
   special studies on sacraments 214–15
   summary of work of 214–15
   tasks on behalf of Council 215
local councils of churches
   effectiveness 41
   growth in number of 41
   Roman Catholic church, and 41–2
   significance of 43
   special ceremony 43–4
local covenanting 42
   significance of 42
Local Ecumenical Projects 38–9
   buildings, burden of 40
   common characteristics 40
   establishment of 39
   importance of 40–1
   shared ministry 40
local ecumenism 31–46
   fostering 31–46
Longley, Clifford
   Malvinas war, on 183–4
Lund Dictum 17
   areas of ecumenical experiment 17

Malvinas war 177–93

# INDEX

British Council of Churches, and 178
colonial sovereignty 179
Council of Churches for Wales, and 179–80
Cytûn on 186
Fellowship of Reconciliation in Wales, and 181
Foreign Office, and 181–2
greetings to Consultative Council of Churches of Argentina 182
Huw Wynne Griffith on 178
interference in politics 183–4
international challenges 187
morality of 184–6
opposition to use of military force 180
pacifist standpoint, and 186
perils of rejoicing in victory 190–1
Pope John Paul II, and 183
pragmatic response to 191
questions to Christians 183–91
response to British churches 177–8
service in St Paul's Cathedral 190
Wales and Argentina 187–9
World Council of Churches, and 178
Mandela, Nelson
election as President 154–5
freeing of 154
Message to the Churches of Wales 12–13
*Ministry in an Uniting Church* 27
morality of war 159–76
*Missionary Structure of the Congregation, The* 34
Morgan, Kenneth O.
changes during twentieth century, on 5
Morris, Edwin

timetable for work of Holy Spirit, on 16
Mullins, bishop
ecumenism, on 57–8

National Assembly
inauguration 98
National Conference on Social Responsibility 76
attendance at 79
decision-making in economic and political issues 78
effectiveness 79
influence of 80
key tasks, identification of 79–80
Nationality and the Unity of Mankind 78
participating in decision-making and in community 78–9
recommendations 79
specialist papers 77–8
technological, economic and social change 77–8
New Welsh Bible 3
North East Wales Industrial Mission 107–8
Nottingham motion on Areas of Ecumenical Experiment
Welsh response to 45–6
nuclear disarmament 159–76
analysing 167–72
deterrence, on 169
development, relationship with 169
divine purpose, and 163
Eastern Europe, and 175
effects of nuclear weapons 167–8
expertise of Council 172
guidance to churches 174–5
implications for churches 175
interpreting 167–72
just war, and 165

# INDEX

medical effects of nuclear weapons 168
messages to government 172–4
moral requirements of just war, and 167
national and international debate 161
nuclear threat 168–9
political changes, and 175–6
resolutions on 161
*Shalom*, and 165
*Swords into Ploughshares* 161, 163, 164–5, 171
theological foundations 162–7
vengeance of God, and 163–4

Parry, Trefor
  British Faith and Order Conference (1964), on 18
*People Next Door* 33–4
  nature of 34
Phillips, Alan Butt
  nationalist movements, on 86
Phillips, Mervyn
  nuclear disarmament, on 173
Pilkington Committee 71
pit closures
  resolution on 101–2
Pope John Paul II
  Malvinas war, and 183
  visit to Wales 60–1
*Porfeydd* 10
Potter, Philip
  *oikos* and *oikoumene*, on 208
*Principles of Visible Unity in Wales, The* 27
Pritchard Survey 76–7
Programme to Combat Racism
  Special Fund 142
  support for activity 157
public houses
  Sunday opening 72–3
    Kenneth O. Morgan on 73
    referendum 72–3

Racism in southern Africa 137–58
  consistency of engagement of Council 155
  economic sanctions 146
  Gleneagles agreement (1977) 147
  Kairos Document 150
  sport 147–8
  Uppsala Assembly 138
Renowden, Raymond
  deterrence, on 170
  just war, on 166–7
responsible society
  definition 67–8
Rhoose conference 1967 35
Roman Catholic Church 47–66
  avoidance of difficult questions 63
  Baptists, and 64–5
  BCC membership, and 55
  bilateral dialogues 63
  change in attitudes of other denominations to 62–3
  church building schemes 62
  consultant observer, as 50
  cooperation with 51
  Council of Churches for Wales, and 199–200
  Cytûn, and 59–60
  Decree on Ecumenism 48–9
  delegate observers 52
  difficulty of dealing with 47–8
  divisive aspects of doctrine 64
  educational process, need for 53
  importance of Scripture, and 63
  inter-denominational statements on moral and social issues, and 65
  involvement in ecumenical pilgrimage 65–6
  Irish immigrants, and 61
  Joint Working Group 52, 56
    first meeting 1981 56–7

# INDEX

membership of local councils of churches 62
moral and social questions 65
National Pastoral Congress 53–4
New Welsh Bible, and 48
relationship with 47–66
representatives 51
retreats, meetings at 59
situation in England, and 54–5
statistics 61
*The Easter People* 54–5
trans-substantiation 64
Welsh bishops 58–9

Sansbury, Bishop Kenneth
address of November 1967 74
search for Christian unity in Wales 9–20
Second Vatican Council 48–9
self-government in Wales 83–100
churches, role of 100
Consultative Paper 97–8
Cytûn, and 94–7
divide between two 'Christian' attitudes 84–6
Free Church Council for Wales, and 96
referendum 98
relationship between Christianity and Welsh nationhood 83–100
resolution on devolution 91–2
Steering Group 96–7
theological foundation of different viewpoints on 95
theological perspectives on 97
Welsh language, and 87, 94
Service of Thanksgiving for the Covenant 25–6
Sharing of Church Buildings Act (1969) 35–6
Simon, Glyn
industry, on 103

South African Council of Churches
Eloff Commission, and 148–9
Student Christian Movement in Wales 2
Sunday opening 72–3
*Swords into Ploughshares* 192

television broadcasting
Welsh-language 70–1
Temple, William
ecumenism, and 1
Theological Advisory Group
report on theology of experiment 57
Thomas, Brinley
*The Industrial Scene in Wales* 102
trans-substantiation
doctrine of 64
*Tuag at Uno* 10, 11
Tutu, Desmond 44
Eloff Commission, and 148–9
visit to Wales 152–3

unemployment
approaches to 109–10
resolution on 101
Welsh Office, and 111
*Unity we Seek, The* 13
*Uppsala and Wales* 35
Uppsala Assembly 75–6
racism, and 138
*Urdd y Deyrnas* 2

*Views from the Pews* 42–3
statistics 42–3
Visser't Hooft, W. A.
ecumenical movement, on 14–15

*Wales: A Moral Society* 96–7
Wales and Argentina 187–9
Welsh colony in Patagonia 188

# INDEX

Wales for Christ 3
war and peace 159–76, 177–93
  partnership with ecumenical
    bodies 193
  reasons for lack of attention to
    160–1
  study of 192
  theological foundation 191
  theological unanimity, whether
    192
War on Terror 176
Welsh Ecumenical Society 2
  aims 31
  conference (1963) 12
  disbanding 32
  formation of 31
  membership 31–2
Welsh Language Society 4
*Why Covenant?* 24
*Why Work?*
  national conference (1979) 112
Wilkie, David
  death of 125

Williams, G. O. 16, 21, 22, 25, 52,
    84, 90, 140, 144, 206,
    210, 211, 229
  Welsh nationalism, on 84
Williams, J. E.
  appeals to government 173
  deterrence, on 169
Williamson, Roger
  Malvinas war, on 185–6
World Council of Churches
  Amsterdam Assembly 9
  anti-apartheid activity 155–6
  Harare conference (1985) 151
  New Delhi Assembly 11
  Programme to Combat Racism
    139–41

*Y Dysgedydd*
  debate on ecumenical
    movement 9–10

Zimbabwe
  Patriotic Front 142–3